Conversations with Bharati Mukherjee

Literary Conversations Series
Peggy Whitman Prenshaw
General Editor

Conversations with Bharati Mukherjee

Edited by
Bradley C. Edwards

University Press of Mississippi
Jackson

www.upress.state.ms.us

The University Press of Mississippi is a member of the Association of American University Presses.

Copyright © 2009 by University Press of Mississippi
All rights reserved
Manufactured in the United States of America

First printing 2009
∞
Library of Congress Cataloging-in-Publication Data

Mukherjee, Bharati.
    Conversations with Bharati Mukherjee / edited by Bradley C. Edwards.
        p. cm. — (Literary conversations series)
    Includes index.
    ISBN 978-1-60473-226-9 (cloth : alk. paper) — ISBN 978-1-60473-227-6 (pbk. : alk. paper) 1. Mukherjee, Bharati—Interviews. 2. East Indians in literature. 3. India—In literature. I. Edwards, Bradley C., 1969– II. Title.

    PR9499.3.M77Z46 2009
    813'.54—dc22

                                                                        2008047011

British Library Cataloging-in-Publication Data available

Books by Bharati Mukherjee

The Tiger's Daughter. Boston: Houghton Mifflin, 1971; Markham, Ontario: Penguin, 1971;
London: Chatto and Windus, 1973.

Wife. Boston: Houghton Mifflin, 1975; New Delhi: Sterling, 1976.

Days and Nights in Calcutta. With Clark Blaise. Garden City, N.Y.: Doubleday, 1977;
Markham, Ontario: Penguin, 1977.

Darkness. New York: Penguin, 1985; Markham, Ontario: Penguin, 1985; London: Virago,
1985; New Delhi: Penguin, 1990.

The Sorrow and the Terror: The Haunting Legacy of the Air India Tragedy. With Clark
Blaise. Markham, Ontario: Viking, 1987.

The Middleman and Other Stories. New York: Grove Press, 1988; Markham, Ontario:
Viking, 1988; London: Virago, 1988; New Delhi: Penguin, 1988.

Jasmine. New York: Grove Press, 1988; Markham, Ontario: Viking, 1989; London: Virago,
1989.

The Holder of the World. New York: Alfred A. Knopf, 1993; Toronto: HarperCollins, 1993;
London: Chatto & Windus, 1993; New Delhi: Viking, 1993.

Leave It to Me. New York: Alfred A. Knopf, 1997; Toronto: HarperCollins, 1997; London:
Chatto & Windus, 1996.

Desirable Daughters. New York: Theia, 2002; Toronto: HarperPerennial Canada, 2002.

The Tree Bride. New York: Theia, 2004; Toronto: HarperCollins, 2004.

Contents

Introduction

"I see myself as an American writer in the tradition of other American writers whose parents or grandparents had passed through Ellis Island," writes Bharati Mukherjee in the introduction to *Darkness*. With these words, she pledges allegiance to her adopted country. Born into a rigid hierarchy as a Bengali Brahmin and raised in the elite of Calcutta society, "top family, top school, top caste, top city," she joined the American masses by choice after a decade and a half in Canada.[1] This journey from a privileged yet circumscribed life to one of free will and risk supplied the experiences she has turned into literature. The sacrifices and rewards of her transformation are detailed in the following interviews spanning three and a half decades.

Mukherjee experienced a claustrophobic early childhood in a traditional, extended-family household of about four dozen relatives, which ended at age eight when her family moved for three years to England and Switzerland. Upon returning to Calcutta, her immediate family resided in a mansion within the walled compound of her father's pharmaceutical manufacturing plant. She attended exclusive Loreto House, a British convent school run by Irish nuns, where, she tells Angela Elam, elocution was the most important subject, followed by table manners. Though she was sheltered, the infamous squalor of Calcutta was within view, and she has so often described being driven to school amidst a caravan of bodyguards that the image is iconic of her youth. After taking master's degrees in ancient Indian culture and English at the University of Baroda, Mukherjee fulfilled her childhood horoscope by crossing "the black waters" to the United States.

Her first revolution was to wed Clark Blaise, fellow student at the Iowa Writers' Workshop. Defying her father by ignoring the arranged marriage he had planned for her with a nuclear physicist in India, she informed her parents that by the time they read her telegram, she would already be married. She tells Sybil Steinberg, "I've really grown up with Clark. We have a special kind of literary marriage, because we're both writers and academics." This union, now in its fifth decade, has produced two sons and two co-authored books. Mukherjee earned an M.F.A. at the Iowa Writers' Workshop and a Ph.D. in English and comparative literature, crafting a dissertation on Indian mythology in E. M. Forster's *A Passage to India* and Hermann Hesse's *Siddhartha*.

While still a Ph.D. candidate, she began teaching at McGill University, where she quickly rose to full professor. Bilingual and cosmopolitan, Montreal at first seemed an ideal setting for the pair of young professors to raise their sons, but recurrent personal humiliations and racially motivated attacks against South Asians, which she viewed as tacitly condoned by the official Canadian governmental policy of multiculturalism, led her to break with her adopted country and relocate to the United States. In 1980, she bid Canada an angry farewell in an invective titled "An Invisible Woman."

America offered constitutionally guaranteed rights and the chance to blend into the crowd in public, and she became a citizen. In the *New York Times Book Review*, she cast her naturalization in matrimonial language: "I'm one of you now. It's a civil ceremony, a municipal marriage without a fancy wedding."[2] Like her nuptials with Clark, also a civil ceremony in a lawyer's office, Mukherjee's relationship with America is best described as a "love match," the Indian English term for couples who eschew an arranged marriage. She went so far as literally to drape herself in the stars and stripes in an Iowa cornfield for the lead photo for her essay "American Dreamer" in *Mother Jones* in 1997. Her project to show not only how America changes immigrants but how immigrants change America has made her one of the country's premier writers on immigration, and her fiction consistently celebrates American ideals and constitutional values even while depicting the violence and exploitation that mar American life.

"A consummated romance with the American language" is how Jonathan Raban describes *The Middleman and Other Stories*.[3] She convincingly re-creates minute details of pronunciation and usage, from immigrant Vietnamese and Trinidadians to Southern rednecks to Silicon Valley software engineers. Perhaps this is not surprising considering that she learned English as a second language. As she tells Geoff Hancock, "I am alert to the potency of, and possibilities in, language. English is a language that I have appropriated." That she has taken possession of English is made evident by her ever-growing oeuvre.

Best known for her novels and short stories, Mukherjee is an accomplished writer in many genres, including investigative journalism, travel writing, the personal essay, the memoir, and the book review. Her artistic skill has garnered her a National Book Critics Circle Award, fellowships from both the Guggenheim Foundation and the National Endowment for the Arts, and membership in the American Academy of Arts and Sciences. She is sought after as a lecturer and represents the United States abroad in this capacity for the State Department. In 2006, she chaired the committee that chose the National Book Award for Fiction. That she finds time to undertake such endeavors while teaching full time as a distinguished professor at the University of California, Berkeley, and writing intensely researched novels is testimony to her tremendous energy and love of her vocation.

Mukherjee's varied interests come out in these interviews. The conversation with S. X. Goudie and Tina Chen reveals her professorial acumen as she responds deftly to postcolonialist critics who have challenged her intellectual positions. She considered running for office in Canada, and Fred Bonnie's questions elicit strong political opinions. With Shefali Desai and Tony Barnstone, Mukherjee demonstrates an in-depth knowledge of Indian writers. In my interview, I noted the many times she laughed aloud because I wanted to give readers a sense of her quick humor and vitality. No matter what the topic, she remains a perfect guest or hostess, her convent-school manners and urbane cosmopolitanism revealing themselves in an easy grace and ready wit that come through even in print.

She has been called the *grande dame* of diasporic Indian literature, and her relationships with the others in the group are at times complex. Two men in particular engage her attention. She wrote in 1989, "our collective experience is mirrored in the works of two magnificent writers: V. S. Naipaul and Salman Rushdie. Either—following Naipaul—we are less than fully human, pathetic trained monkeys, mimic men; or we are miraculous translations, Lamarckian mutations, single lives that have acquired new characteristics and recapitulated the entire cultural history of our genotype."[4] Naipaul was an early model for Mukherjee, but her attitude toward him changed after she and Robert Boyers interviewed him in 1979. She spoke at length to me about the evolution of her relationship with Naipaul and his work. She continues to teach certain of his novels even while rejecting his worldview and politics. Salman Rushdie, on the other hand, is a writer whom she has greatly admired, going so far as to publish an homage to him titled "Prophet and Loss: Salman Rushdie's Migration of Souls" in the *Village Voice Literary Supplement* in March 1989, the month after the Ayatollah Khomeini of Iran announced the edict calling for Rushdie's assassination. She and Clark Blaise followed this with an investigative article a year later in *Mother Jones* titled "After the Fatwa," which delved into the politics of immigrant Pakistanis in England as a lens through which to view Rushdie's situation. Mukherjee and Rushdie remain cordial, and she presented him with the award for Lifetime Achievement at the India Abroad awards in 2007.

Many interviewers ask Mukherjee to name her literary influences, and the

scores of authors she mentions reveal an odyssey of the mind. As a child, she re-
treated under beds to live in the world of the great Russians available in Bengali
translation: Chekhov, Babel, Tolstoy, and Dostoyevsky. Her education at Loreto
House provided a solid foundation in the Bible, and though her master's degree
work in India focused on the British canon and ancient Indian culture, she discovered Faulkner in the library at Baroda. In Iowa she expanded her knowledge
of American literature even while writing a dissertation on Herman Hesse and
E. M. Forster. The global range of her reading is revealed in comments on Salman
Rushdie, whom she has called a "Bombay Augie March" and compared to Thomas
Pynchon, Günter Grass, and Gabriel García Márquez. Her collection *Darkness*
is dedicated to Bernard Malamud, a close family friend whose *Selected Stories*
inspired her to write the fiction that would make her name, and for good measure, she draws from the ancient Hindu tales of the *Puranasa* and the epics of the
Ramayana and the *Mahabharata*. Her interviews give the impression of a constant reader, revealing numerous authors, both famous and obscure, whose work
has engaged her.

Feminism is a major theme throughout Mukherjee's fiction, from Dimple,
the protagonist of her second novel who murders her husband, to Tara, the main
character of her most recent two novels who divorces and takes a lover. In her
essay "A Four-Hundred-Year-Old Woman," Mukherjee reflects on her inherited position: "I was born into a religion that placed me, a Brahmin, at the top
of its hierarchy while condemning me, as a woman, to a role of subservience."[5]
Mukherjee's notions of feminism are rooted in her upbringing and the example
set by her mother. Berated for bearing three daughters in a culture that traditionally prized sons, her mother battled relatives to provide an education for
her girls, making Bharati determined to live up to her mother's defiant retort,
"My daughters will prove better than your sons." Her deep-rooted cultural perspective becomes apparent as Mukherjee describes how American feminist critics have interpreted scenes differently than she intended. For example, she tells
Connell, Grearson, and Grimes that the title character of the story "Jasmine" was
not meant to be seen as exploited but rather as a woman exercising the power of
her own sexuality when she seduces the married man whose house she cleans.
Mukherjee reflects, "But no one got that, you see. It was meant to be a very political ending." Women and power are constants in her fiction, and her unique
perspective has led her to create scenes that have delighted or disconcerted critics
throughout her career.

The Tiger's Daughter is about a young Bengali woman, married to a North
American writer, who returns to Calcutta after seven years and finds a city in tur-

moil. Though Mukherjee denies that the novel is autobiographical, the external similarities between protagonist Tara Banerjee Cartwright and Bharati Mukherjee Blaise show that she based much of the book on her own experiences. Unlike Mukherjee's memories of tuning out the squalor of Calcutta while riding as a teenager to and from school in a caravan of bodyguards, Tara cannot ignore the violent mob pressing against her car as the novel ends. The city and culture in dissolution are emblematic of the narrator's psychic upheaval, and the novel ultimately paints a portrait of a young woman painfully realizing that she is an expatriate who cannot go home again. Mukherjee later uses the work as a point of reference to show how her writing changed as she became an American. She explains the difference to Alison B. Carb: "My first novel, *The Tiger's Daughter*, has a rather Britishy feel to it. I used the omniscient point of view and plenty of irony. This was because my concept of language and notions of how a novel was constructed were based on British models." Just as the novel depicts a young woman estranged from her past, so the novel has come to represent a narrative perspective and subject that the mature Mukherjee has abandoned.

Published in 1975, *Wife* is Mukherjee's second novel, written in response to a question asked her while she was spending the academic year of 1973–1974 in India. She tells Geoff Hancock, "Clark and I were having breakfast at a long dining-table one morning when a Columbia professor next to me asked, 'What do you Bengali girls do between the ages of fifteen and twenty-five?' So I wrote a novel to explain to him what we did." The novel features Dimple, a young Bengali woman who marries an engineer and moves to New York City. Other characters model a range of assimilation for Dimple, but she is unable to effect change in herself. *Wife* provides a counterpoint to *The Tiger's Daughter*. Dimple's lack of self-awareness and inability to break away from the Bengali culture in which she feels trapped even as she moves to New York City contrast with Tara's perceptive realization that she cannot reenter her home culture. Both feel the pain of their situations, but Dimple cannot envision an escape. From her lashing out to bludgeon first a mouse then cockroaches to stabbing her husband at the novel's end, her violence reveals the psychological trauma of a young woman banging against an invisible cage. Mukherjee explains the ending to Hancock: "Dimple's decision to murder her husband is her misguided act of self-assertion. If she had remained a housewife living with her extended family in India, she would probably not have asked herself questions such as, am I unhappy, do I deserve to be unhappy. And if by chance she had asked herself these questions, she might have settled her problems by committing suicide. So turning to violence outward rather than inward is part of her slow and misguided Americanization." A sad story of an immigrant who fails to achieve a new life, *Wife* nevertheless is important as the first of Mukherjee's major works to explore what it means to become an American.

Published in 1977, *Days and Nights in Calcutta* is a memoir jointly written by Mukherjee and her husband about their sabbatical year in India. Each contributed a section, resulting in a two-part book that reveals as much about the authors as the city. The title alludes to the film *Days and Nights in the Forest* by internationally acclaimed director Satyajit Ray, with whom the couple became close during their sojourn, even enjoying private screenings as his guest. Mukherjee's half of the book is an insider's view of upper-class Calcutta that intimately portrays the lives of her extended family and former schoolmates while retaining the objectivity gained during fourteen years in North America. Her section is a wealth of biographical information about her family, for instance that her sons were named after writers John Bart Gerald and Bernard Malamud. She tells Geoff Hancock, "While writing that book, I realized that I had moved from thinking of myself as an emotionally committed Canadian citizen. The book turns on this self-discovery." This is perhaps seen early in her account when she writes, "It is, of course, America that I love." Interestingly, she wrote these words roughly half a decade before leaving Canada for the United States.

Darkness grew out of emotionally somber times, and the trauma of those years takes shape in the imagery of Mukherjee's first published collection of short stories. In the fall of 1972, Idi Amin expelled ethnic Indians from Uganda. Thousands sought refuge in Canada, leading to a backlash of racism against South Asians throughout the country. Mukherjee experienced recurrent derision and humiliations, including being accused of prostitution and being roughed up by thugs. She spent the rest of the decade struggling against Canada's official policy of multiculturalism, which she saw as inherently sanctioning bigotry, leading her to move her family to the United States in 1980. Mukherjee explains in the introduction that she was transformed by the move, "from the aloofness of expatriation, to the exuberance of immigration." But as Fakrul Alam argues in *Bharati Mukherjee*, exuberance appears more clearly in her next collection, *The Middleman and Other Stories*.[6] In *Darkness*, Mukherjee appears to be exorcizing the ghosts of resentment over being forced to see herself as "part of an unwanted 'visible minority'" during her last years in Canada, as she tells Hancock. Inspired by Bernard Malamud, to whom she dedicated the volume, *Darkness* marks Mukherjee's recovery of her artistic voice.

The Sorrow and the Terror was the second book published collaboratively by Bharati Mukherjee and Clark Blaise. She tells me it was "the most important" and "most life-changing book" that they had written because of what they discovered about terrorism and the "human capacity for hate, greed, hope, and yes, love." This exposé explores the psychology of the Sikhs who claimed to have bombed Air-India flight 182 on June 23, 1985, in an effort to draw attention to their goal of a separate Sikh state, Khalistan. More gripping than the terrorists are the portraits of the affected. The Irish are the heroes of the narrative, and their empathy is deep as they set up protocols to help the grieving to identify bodies ravaged by the violence of the fall and the sea. Most heart-wrenching are the words of surviving family members, mostly immigrant husbands and fathers who remained in Canada to work while their wives and children went to India during summer vacation. Mukherjee tells me that their request that she and Clark tell the world their stories was what kept her going even as she would break down listening to them. The publication of the book led to Mukherjee and Blaise being denounced in Sikh temples in Canada and put on a death list, serious threats that forced them to use false names while flying and to stay on specially secured floors of hotels for a time.

Winner of the National Book Critics Circle Award for 1988, *The Middleman and Other Stories* elevated Mukherjee among the elite of American writers. She tells Alison Carb that the theme of the stories was "the new, changing America," and says of the characters, "as they change citizenship, they are reborn." Immigration as reincarnation becomes a major theme in Mukherjee's fiction in this collection, a conceit she elaborates to great effect in her subsequent novel, *Jasmine*. With a dramatic expansion of scope, her entire experience and imagination seem distilled into the range of her characters. Alfie Judah, the middleman of the titular story, seems equal parts hustling Baghdadi Jew (a background very similar, surely not coincidentally, to that of her father's erstwhile business partner) and charming Don Juan (perhaps inspired by Michael Cain's character in the 1966 film *Alfie*). In the Steinberg interview, Mukherjee explains that the story "came about because I happened to be in Costa Rica at a time when American and Central American history was being made." "The Management of Grief," based on the Air India bombing and one of her most-anthologized stories, demonstrates the emotional difficulty of consoling oneself and others as Shaila Bhave, who has also lost her family in the crash, attempts to assist Canadian social workers as they visit the bereaved. Other memorable characters include Jeb Marshall of "Loose Ends," a Vietnam vet turned hit man whose fascination with snakes betrays his own cold-blooded approach to life, and Jasmine of the short story "Jasmine," a Trinidadian girl who may be read as Mukherjee's rebuttal of Naipaul's claim that to be born on his native island was to be doomed. She summarizes the collection for Alison Carb: "The immigrants in my stories go through extreme transformations in

America and at the same time they alter the country's appearance and psychological make-up."

Mukherjee explains the genesis of the novel *Jasmine* to Connell, Grearson, and
Grimes: "I didn't know when I finished the story that it would become a novel.
It was just that this was a character that I fell in love with. This was a character
I would have liked to have been." Though the character is based loosely on her
own life, for example both Jasmine and Mukherjee had horoscopes that foretold
their exile and both bear scars in the middle of their foreheads where Hinduism
places the mystic third eye, nevertheless Jasmine's circumstances are much more
restricted than those of the author. Mukherjee explains her intent to Connell,
Grearson, and Grimes: "She became a deeper, more complicated character in my
head, over the months, so I had to give her a society that was so repressive, traditional, so caste-bound, class-bound, genderist, that she could discard it in ways
that a fluid American society could not." In contrast to the author's privileged
childhood, Jasmine's low beginnings in a village without running water or electricity highlight the extent of her odyssey to America, which takes her to many
of the places Mukherjee called home in the 1980s, including New York City, Iowa,
and California. In fact, Mukherjee had no conscious plans to move to California
from New York when she finished the novel with the protagonist on her way to
Stanford. Perhaps it was fate.

Jasmine repeatedly employs the image of a jarred record needle skipping into
a different groove as an analogy for personal reincarnation, commemorating the
last days of the analog era. *The Holder of the World* documents the exploding possibilities of the digital age and marks the flourishing of Mukherjee's fascination
with information technology. When I emailed her that I had obtained a copy of
her earliest interview, she replied, "How amazing that the 1973 *Desh* interview has
surfaced! Nothing is not retrievable in today's universe." Her reaction brought
to mind the notion of approximated time travel through virtual reality that in-
forms this lengthy historical novel. The genesis of this work is as complex as the
plot. Mukherjee tells Francisco Collado Rodríguez that she "started the novel
mainly because of two germs. One was Hawthorne's *The Scarlet Letter*." The
other was a Mughal miniature painting titled *An European Woman in Emperor
Aurangzeb's Court* that she saw at Sotheby's in New York. Strands from *The Scarlet
Letter* woven intertextually into her own novel show overtly how she is expanding
American literature. Continuing her program to show how America has not only
changed immigrants but been changed by them, Mukherjee deliberately chose a
precolonial setting when the wealth of India drew European immigrants and adventurers. But the novel is much more than a revisionist version of *The Scarlet*

Letter. After she "became bored creating a straight historical novel," Mukherjee added another layer of complexity with contemporary asset hunter Beigh Masters, with whom Mukherjee shares initials, as she told Collado Rodríguez. While doing historical research to locate a legendary diamond known as "the Emperor's Tear," Masters becomes obsessed with Hannah Easton, the blond "Salem Bibi" in a Mughal miniature painting, who had become the consort of an Indian raja after leaving Salem, Massachusetts. With the help of boyfriend Venn Iyer, who is working on a virtual-reality project at MIT, Masters is able to take the data she has gathered and approximate time travel for an encounter with Hannah Easton. Thus the aesthetics of the Mughal miniature painting and cutting-edge computer programming combine with colonial American history and *The Scarlet Letter* to produce Mukherjee's most complex work to date.

The Haight-Ashbury neighborhood of San Francisco, emblematic of sixties counterculture, is a short walk from Mukherjee's home in Cole Valley. She moved to the city in 1989, a generation after the summer of love, and *Leave It to Me* is, as the title suggests, about the legacy of the sixties. Adoptee Debby DiMartino renames herself Devi Dee and searches for her birth parents, an American hippie known as Clear Water Iris-Daughter and a man identified at first only as an Asian national. With such parentage, she clearly represents the love-child resulting from the affair sixties counterculture had with India. When Devi finds her father, he turns out to be a sex-guru serial murderer named Romeo Haq. Mukherjee is always careful with names, and "Haq" is a variant spelling of the Hindi root word that became "thug." Like the original thugs, professional robbers who historically plagued India's roads, he strangles his victims. Daughter Devi also casually inflicts violence, but she is not meant to be evil. Mukherjee intended to show that Devi was "part of a larger design in which some higher power uses her to restore some kind of balance and purge evil out of our California." She tells Ron Hogan that Devi was meant to represent divine justice in the Indian Hindu tradition: "I realized that in order to make my concept of divine justice, which sometimes involves great violence, understandable to the reader, I'd have to dig into and share the Hindu mythology of the goddess Devi worshipped in Bengal, who was created by the Cosmic Spirit to do battle with the baddest bad ass of all the demons, the Buffalo Demon, and is therefore quite violent." Significant for its setting, experimentation with slang, and incorporation of myth, *Leave It to Me* also marks a trend in Mukherjee's fiction, for Devi Dee's quest personalizes the historical research of *Holder of the World* into the American-style roots search that drives successors *Desirable Daughters* and *The Tree Bride.*

Desirable Daughters grew out of an autobiographical project Mukherjee meant to do with her sisters, which took on a life of its own as fiction. When the novel begins, protagonist Tara Chatterjee is involved with a Hungarian-born, ex-biker, Buddhist carpenter and has divorced her Indian husband, Bish Chatterjee, in an attempt to develop her own individuality. Describing him as the Bill Gates of the South Asian community, Mukherjee tells Michael Krasny that Bish was the bridegroom she imagined her parents would have chosen for her. When a young man claiming to be the illegitimate son of her sister approaches Tara, she begins to probe her family's past, leading her deeper into historical mysteries that have created the foundation of her identity. Mukherjee tells Krasny: "I am coming to terms, as is Tara the narrator, who though is much younger than I am, with what my Indian heritage has left me as residue and what America I have discovered, and discovered as empowerment, and knitting the two together so that I know who I am in ways that I didn't want to know when I was writing my earlier novels." Tara's roots search leads her to the story of her namesake, Tara Lata the tree bride, who was betrothed to a tree and became a leader in the Bengali resistance against the British. As she learns more about her heritage, Tara experiences historical convergences as past events begin to impact her personal life. Surely reflecting on her own experience of death threats, Mukherjee tells Krasny that she wanted to show that "we can lead our innocent lives of self-absorption when suddenly a larger plot is going to enmesh us in its nightmarish vision." Once again mapping the fine line between personal agency and cosmic destiny, *Desirable Daughters* demonstrates Mukherjee's cultural fluency as she seamlessly weaves the narrative across the black waters of time and space from the present preoccupations of California to the historical incidents of India.

    The Tree Bride is the second novel in a planned trilogy, and in it Tara Chatterjee's quest into the past leads her not only to an American-style roots search into her own genealogy, a lá Devi in *Leave It to Me*, but also to an investigation of such epic subjects of history as the British colonization of India and its legacy. As Mukherjee tells Angela Elam, "For us, colonial forces—the encounter between the imperialistic white man, good and bad, and the language imposed, the sense of right and wrong, democracy or feudalism imposed—has gone into the very shaping of what language I write in." The resulting novel shows Tara diving ever deeper into the history of British involvement in India, from the precolonial days Mukherjee explored in *Holder of the World* to the colonial period and through the Indian Independence movement right up to her life in San Francisco at the start of the twenty-first century, a mix that seems at first chaotic but gradually yields a kind of dynamic order. Mukherjee tells Elam, "Chaos theory is close to the Hindu explanation of how the world works. Quantum physics is really what our creation, destruction, re-creation is all about." The reverberations of one's actions can resound across the centuries, as Tara learns, showing that the "butterfly effect" of chaos theory mentioned in *Jasmine* (whereby a butterfly's wings can start a chain of events triggering a hurricane) may be amplified over time as well as distance. In the end, Tara seems to find resolution and peace in Hindu ceremony, but with the third novel to come, there are sure to be surprises in store for both her and the reader.

This brief description of Bharati Mukherjee's life and work attempts to provide insights into her intentions for each book as well as to give an overview of the subjects she has found compelling during her career. As her characters undergo reincarnations of identity, so her own life demonstrates the metamorphic possibilities of immigration. Through ups and downs, from battling racism to receiving awards, even as she has changed citizenship, learned to negotiate in new languages, and gone from thinking of herself as an expatriate to an immigrant to an American, she has remained true to the realization at age three that she was a writer and has continued to create fine literature inspired by her unique experiences.

The guiding principles of selection have been to provide scholars and fans with original material and an array of the best in-depth interviews representative of Bharati Mukherjee's books, biography, and ideas. Her earliest interview, given in her native Bengali to the renowned Kolkata journal *Desh*, makes its English premiere in a first-rate translation by Somdatta Mandal. Michael Krasny's radio interview makes its print debut. My original interview is the most extensive to date. Longer interviews tend to delve more deeply into important topics so are here privileged over briefer ones. With scholarship in mind, the interviews included here have been arranged chronologically and are deliberately unedited. Interviewers' introductory comments have been omitted to allow the inclusion of more primary material. As with any such collection, there is an unavoidable repetition of certain questions; but her answers to these form the foundation of Mukherjee's self-presentation. For example, her oft-cited courtship of two weeks and five-minute civil ceremony to wed Clark Blaise was not just an impulsive act but, in the context of details she gives about her childhood, an extraordinary revolt against her traditional upbringing. The most difficult part of editing this collection has been excluding much very good work. Excellent interviews by Runar Vignisson, Dave Weich, Russell Schoch, Bill Moyers, and one in the Ballantine Reader's Circle edition of *Leave It to Me* may be accessed online so are not included. I regret that there is not enough space to include superb interviews by Ameena Meer, Sandip Roy-Chowdury, Suzanne Ruta, Christine McQuade, Patricia Holt, Naomi Epel, and Beverly Byers-Pevitts, among others.

This collection has been made possible by the assistance and good will of many people. First thanks go to Bharati Mukherjee, who graciously invited me to her home and spent an entire Saturday answering questions with élan. I will always be grateful to two key members of the University Press of Mississippi: Seetha Srinivasan gave me the opportunity to edit this collection, and I have had the privilege of working with Walter Biggins, a true professional who answered inquiries with alacrity. Jim Nagel has been a model scholar and has generously provided insightful counsel for many years. I am appreciative of David Dudley, chair of the Department of Literature and Philosophy at Georgia Southern University, for his interest in my work and support of my travel. Gautam Kundu gave much-needed help with Bengali words. Somdatta Mandal provided an excellent translation of the *Desh* interview. Ryan Pickrell lent his transcribing skill and attention to detail. Thanks also to the interviewers and editors whose work comprises the bulk of this book and without whose permission this collection would not be possible; it has been my pleasure to correspond with many of those featured here.

BCE

Notes

1. Bharati Mukherjee, "Immigrant Writing: Give Us Your Maximalists!" *New York Times Book Review*, 28 August 1988: 28.
2. Mukherjee, "Immigrant Writing," 1.
3. Jonathan Raban, "Savage Boulevards, Easy Streets," *New York Times*, 19 June 1988: 1.
4. Bharati Mukherjee, "Prophet and Loss: Salman Rushdie's Migration of Souls," *Village Voice Literary Supplement* 72, March 1989, 12.
5. Bharati Mukherjee, "A Four-Hundred-Year-Old Woman," in *Critical Fictions: The Politics of Imaginative Writing*, ed. Philomena Mariani (Seattle: Bay Press, 1991), 24.
6. Fakrul Alam, *Bharati Mukherjee* (New York: Twayne), 50–51, 78–79.

Chronology

1940   Born on July 27, 1940, in Calcutta, India, to noted chemist Sudhir Lal Mukherjee and Bina (Banerjee) Mukherjee.

1947–51   Attends school in London, England, and Basel, Switzerland, while her father conducts research.

1951   Attends Loreto House in Calcutta, India, through high school.

1959   Receives a B.A. with honors in English from the University of Calcutta.

1961   Receives an M.A. in English and ancient Indian culture from the University of Baroda; attends the Iowa Writers' Workshop at the University of Iowa as an International Peace Scholar of the P.E.O. Sisterhood.

1963   Marries Clark Blaise on the first day of the school year; receives an M.F.A., producing a creative thesis titled "The Shattered Mirror," and is admitted into the Ph.D. program of the University of Iowa.

1966   Moves to Montreal and begins teaching at McGill University.

1969   Receives a Ph.D. in English and comparative literature from the University of Iowa, producing a dissertation titled "The Use of Indian Mythology in E. M. Forster's *A Passage to India* and Hermann Hesse's *Siddhartha*."

1971   Publishes *The Tiger's Daughter*.

1973   Awarded a Canada Arts Council grant.

1973–74   She and Clark go to India for a sabbatical year, an experience they chronicle in *Days and Nights in Calcutta*.

1975   Publishes *Wife*.

1977   Publishes *Days and Nights in Calcutta* with Clark Blaise; awarded a Canada Arts Council grant.

1978   Awarded a Guggenheim Fellowship.

1980   Leaves Canada to settle permanently in the U.S.A. and begins teaching in and around New York City.

1985   Publishes *Darkness*.

1986   Receives a creative writing fellowship from the National Endowment for the Arts.

1987   Publishes *The Sorrow and the Terror: The Haunting Legacy of the Air India Tragedy* with Clark Blaise.

1988   Publishes *The Middleman and Other Stories*, which wins the 1988 National Book Critics Circle Award; becomes a naturalized American citizen.

1989   Publishes *Jasmine*; moves to San Francisco and begins teaching as a distinguished professor at the University of California, Berkeley.

1993   Publishes *The Holder of the World*; becomes a member of the American Academy of Arts and Sciences.

1996   Publishes *Leave It to Me*.

2002   Publishes *Desirable Daughters*; begins to lecture abroad for the U.S. State Department.

2004   Publishes *The Tree Bride*.

2006   Chairs the committee that selects the National Book Award for Fiction, choosing *The Echo Maker* by Richard Powers.

Conversations with Bharati Mukherjee

Person and Personality

Parimal Bhattacharya / 1973

From *Desh* (September 1, 1973). © 1973 by *Desh*. Reprinted by permission of the publisher. Translated by Somdatta Mandal.

The location is the International Guest House of the Ramakrishna Mission Institute of Culture. Pressing button number two of the elevator, we landed on the second floor. As soon as I knocked on the door of room number sixteen, a smiling Bharati Mukherjee welcomed me in.

Calcutta's daughter Bharati has made a name for herself in the United States of America by writing *The Tiger's Daughter*. This novel has been highly praised in journals like *Newsweek*, the *New York Times*, the *Washington Post*, and *New Statesman*. *Time* magazine has also published a review of the book along with her photograph. According to the *Wall Street Journal*, *The Tiger's Daughter* is the best piece of fiction published in 1972. Plenty of copies have been sold. A British edition of this novel has also been released from London in June this year. It has also been discussed in *Desh* magazine. It has made her famous because she has depicted the change in Calcutta society where the traditional values and morals of a Brahmin family have been shattered forever. According to Bharati, it is a kind of social revolution. All old values, beliefs, customs, class differences are just washed away. Traditionally, the Brahmins were considered to be the tigers of Bengal, but that is no longer so. After returning from America, this daughter of a Brahmin finds that her family is on the path of decadence and is suffering internally. She has lived for a long time in America and even married an American. But still she is not free from the pain and suffering.

In her personal life, Bharati no longer carries the title of Mukherjee. After marrying Clark Blaise, who is settled in Canada, she is now Mrs. Bharati Blaise. They teach literature at two different Canadian universities and both are creative writers. Bharati teaches English at McGill University and is the director of the graduate studies program. Clark is professor of English creative writing at Sir George Williams University, Montreal. They have two sons. The elder one is nine years old and is named Bart Anand. The younger one, Bernard Sudhir, is five. Bharati and Clark have jointly named them by mixing English and Bengali

3

names. Bharati had met Clark as a fellow student in 1962 when she attended the Writers' Workshop at the University of Iowa. They married in 1963.

Since I had earlier informed them of my visit, both husband and wife were waiting for me. I had learnt of their arrival in Calcutta from a writer friend of mine. They stayed here till the end of August and then went to Delhi. They have been residing in Calcutta for a long time in order to collaborate on their project called "The Bengal Journals"—an informative work written in diary form and focusing on the lifestyle of the people in West Bengal. They will come back again around January or February.

This is Clark's first visit to Calcutta, and Bharati returned to the city after fourteen years. Out of these fourteen years, twelve years had been spent abroad. In spite of living abroad for such a long time in a different society and a different environment, her love for the city has not waned. "I love Calcutta. I feel at home here. The people, the streets, the foliage seem all my own. Except for some high-rise buildings, the city is still the same. Only it's a bit more crowded," she stated.

Fourteen years ago, Bharati had left the city to accompany her father to Baroda. She had studied in an English medium school here—the Loreto Convent—and so spoke and behaved like the English without any scope for learning Bengali or Hindi. Bharati got her Master's degree from the University of Baroda in English and ancient Indian civilization and left for the United States. There at the University of Iowa she did her MFA in creative writing and went on to pursue her PhD degree. In the meantime, she enrolled in the Iowa Writers' Workshop which had three specializations—fiction, poetry, and translation. Bharati joined the fiction group and, along with other creative writers and poets, received a scholarship to pursue this course. It was during this time that Clark came from Canada and enrolled in the same course.

Clark belongs to Canada. There are no restrictions of movement between the United States and Canada, and there are no significant differences between the moods and habits of people in these two countries. English is spoken in both places, and there are different interrelated customs and cultures that they share. Both are nations of immigrants and are, therefore, multicultural. But some people in Canada are too much involved with the French language. We tend to believe that the attitude, behavior, and lifestyle of the Americans are always very dazzling. They are somewhat aggressive and full of the zeal and fervor of life. Moreover, since we live far away, we do not look at America and Canada as separate entities.

One does not find such western traits in Clark. He is not extravagantly dressed and is a simple, easygoing person engaged in his studies and work. Speaking for a couple of minutes makes you feel close to him. Equally interested in knowing and disseminating knowledge, he has made quite a name for himself with his story "I'm Dreaming of Rocket Richard." He is now busy writing two books, *A North American Education* and *Tribal Justice*. He is also co-authoring "The Bengal Journals" with Bharati. During his stay in Calcutta he has attended plenty of lunches and dinners, visited different libraries, and attempted to learn Bengali, his wife's mother tongue. Just before meeting us, he was busy practicing the script in large fonts. Bharati showed us his Bengali handwriting notebook and said that he was having trouble with compound words.

Clark was very happy with the warm treatment he received in Calcutta as a son-in-law. He has been graciously received in the homes of Indian families and friends. In fact, sometimes he felt uncomfortable with all the attention given to him. As a shy person, he felt quite embarrassed at times and, on informing Bharati about this, he was told that this was how sons-in-law were treated in Bengal—plenty of attention along with plenty of food. When he sat down to eat, all the members of the family would surround him. He felt uneasy with the food that tasted different and also because strangers were crowding around him all the time. Yet within a few days he got used to this, and now the sincerity of these people has overwhelmed him.

Though she has resided in the west for a long time, gained a reputation there, and has married a foreigner, Bharati has not changed much. Her manners and her use of the Bengali language are still quite native. She does not dress gaudily. She was wearing a light colored printed sari, with jeweled earrings and a thin necklace. A light red dot adorned her forehead, and her eyes wore a distant nostalgic look. All this combined to make her quite a pleasing personality.

I sought her permission to ask a few more personal questions. Bharati smiled and replied that I could ask whatever I wanted to, but answering them or not depended entirely upon her. I asked her when and where she met Clark.

"In 1962 at the Iowa Writers' Workshop. The next year we got married." Replying to the question as if she had repeated it several times earlier, she looked at Clark and he smiled back. I liked the shy smile and asked Bharati, "Won't you add anything more?"

"What more is there to say? We met, got acquainted, fell in love, and then married. Now we are happy with our two sons."

On asked how she felt marrying a foreigner and settling down in a new environment, Bharati replied, "Actually the relationship between a husband and a wife is based on mutual understanding. Both have to sacrifice something at some point. What we call 'adjustment' remains true of all relationships, no matter whether your husband is a foreigner or a local person."

On talking about the new environment Bharati added, "I am from Calcutta. I have married in Canada. These countries are polar opposites in social and economic terms. However progressive Indian husbands might be, they still want to retain their patriarchal control over their wives. In matters of controlling the kitchen and home expenses, the wife is important. But beyond that there is nothing. In all other matters the husband has the last word. And the wife has to abide by it. Here the husband's behavior is dictatorial. But the situation is not similar in Canada or America. Though not always, but in most cases the role of the wife there is that of an equal partner. In literal terms, one is not subservient to the other."

Tea was served from downstairs. Clark started preparing it and asked in Bengali, "Milk?"

I said, "Yes."

"How much sugar?"

"One and a half."

Aloke Mitra, my colleague and photographer asked Bharati, "How long has he been learning Bengali?"

"Ever since he came to Calcutta. Previously he never showed any interest when he was in Canada, but after arriving here and mixing with different people, he is going head over heels in learning the language. After all, it is his in-laws' place. So I have to teach him Bengali day and night. I sometimes cannot keep pace with his tremendous enthusiasm."

Bharati then looked at me and tried to conclude her opinion on the new environment she lived in: "You see, like any other girl I could have been married here. If my parents wished, they could have done that, as there were no impediments. If they did so, I would have had to adjust to the local environment here. Maybe time would gradually condition me in such a way that I would not even feel bad about it. But since that did not happen, I do not like to think about it anymore. Living in Canada in a different environment has enhanced my individualism to a great extent." She further added, "Wives in that country usually work part-time as there is a difference in the opportunity men and women receive in getting good job offers. Compared to many other places, women in Canada have fewer opportunities for promotions and their 'grades,' meaning their positions, are lower. But women are gradually becoming vocal against this discrimination. The difference in pay has also created different reactions in family relationships as well." Sipping her cup of tea Bharati explained her own situation, "We do not have such problems. Both of us enjoy the same position and respect in the workplace. We are both professors. Moreover, both of us are writers."

There is a rule in the North American academia that after serving for seven years, one gets leave for a year with full pay. Both of them are now here on such a sabbatical leave with the intention of traveling, as well as gathering resources for their creative work. Bharati will write a book on Indian writers in English, and the Canada Arts Council has sanctioned a small grant for it. I asked Bharati, "Do you write regularly within a strict routine?"

"Not at all. Where is the opportunity to write regularly? I have to look after the children and the household and then go to work. Managing these three things, it is very difficult to write with any regularity. I write during holidays. Our summer break is from June to August. There is again a month's holiday during Christmas time. The novel I am writing at present has a female protagonist from Calcutta. She grew up here and also got married here. After that she goes to America. In the new environment of New York her outlook of life changes radically. There is a lot of difference between the lifestyle of Calcutta and New York. The society in which she grew up in Calcutta is diametrically opposite to that of New York. She adjusts herself to the new life. The rapid change from the coy bride of Calcutta to this new woman brings with it many conflicts and trouble, the result of which will be tragic. My second novel will therefore end in tragic circumstances."

On being asked whether she felt Calcutta to be a new place after fourteen years, Bharati replied, "No, not really new. Except for some new houses and high-rise buildings, the city is still the same. Of course, it has become more crowded, and many people are forced to live in the streets. There is garbage lying all over the place. But I cannot call Calcutta a dirty city. Actually, Calcutta is not so dirty a city as it is publicized to be." A little later she added, "I love Calcutta. I love it more than Bombay or Delhi. I feel the pleasure of reunion here. People are very friendly. When I lived here, I did not realize it. Coming back after living a long time in the west, I can realize it better now. I like Calcutta even more now—the streets, the foliage, the people, all seem related to me."

I asked Bharati what she thought about the problems in Calcutta. She replied, "The middle class here have different kinds of problems. There is a constant rise in the cost of living. Electricity is rationed. There is no surety when there will be electricity or not. There is no guarantee that students will be able to take their examinations on time. Even after the exams are over, the results are delayed for months on end. Educated young people do not get jobs, and so they are gradually getting more and more frustrated. In our country there is a huge problem of getting suitable jobs. So the problems of the middle-class people are endless."

The protagonist of her first novel, *The Tiger's Daughter*, was the daughter of a Brahmin in Calcutta. The story unfolds how she sees a changed Calcutta after returning to it after a long stay in the United States. The decadent middle-class society that she witnesses all around her raises many questions in her mind. What should have been done and what is being done complicate her thoughts further. So Bharati has successfully projected the problems of society in her first novel. In spite of writing it from the point of view of a social scientist, she has not compromised its artistic values at all. This is where her true achievement lies. She has chosen the same kind of social conflict for her second novel also. She has personal experience of living both in Calcutta and in America and has relied on that for writing this novel. It is not always necessary to have personal experience to write a novel. Writers often fill up the gaps from their imagination. This is where their strength lies. But the things that Bharati has written about require personal experience to elucidate her ideas. Even if one did not have personal experience, one needs the probing eye of a social scientist to do so.

Bharati was born in a middle-class family with no brothers but two sisters. Her parents have tried to bring them up well. Bharati studied in Loreto House in Calcutta. From Calcutta she went to Baroda and from there to the United States for further education. She married and settled in Canada. She did not get the opportunity to learn from the ordinary citizens of Calcutta. Even on this trip she has not had such an opportunity. The people with whom she interacted, the people with whom she enjoyed social gatherings can in no way be called ordinary middle-class citizens in the Indian context. All of them are more or less established in life.

In her novel, Bharati wanted to focus on the waning of the middle class in Calcutta. But along with this decline, her writing fails to identify the new social structures that were simultaneously being created. She lived far away from Calcutta when she wrote *The Tiger's Daughter*. Living out of Calcutta for a long period of fourteen years, she missed the nuances of change that the city had undergone in the meantime. Due to various economic and political changes, the nature of Calcutta's social life has also undergone a radical transformation. Along with that, the nature of different class structures also underwent change. There is nothing called a single social entity in Calcutta anymore. It is comprised of different kinds of worldviews, lifestyles, and tribulations, and all these add together to form the unified social image of the city. The decadent middle class is just one of the components of this larger structure.

Before completing her second novel, Bharati completes her visit to Calcutta. Fourteen years ago, introducing a foreigner as a husband to all her friends and relatives would have evoked mixed reactions. Some would welcome them whole-heartedly, some not. Now there are no such problems. The warm reception that Clark has received in different households proves that. We hope in her second novel Bharati will be able to portray the real nature of a changed Calcutta. If she cannot do that, then her visit to Calcutta will be in vain. She knows that. So she will come back again around January or February to complete that task.

An Interview with Bharati Mukherjee

Geoff Hancock / 1987

From *Canadian Fiction Magazine*, 59 (May 1987), 30–44. © 1987 by *Canadian Fiction Magazine*. Reprinted with the permission of the publisher.

Hancock: Let's start at the beginning. Where did you grow up, and did that affect your later outlook as you expressed it in your fiction?

Mukherjee: I was born in Calcutta. Yes, I am positive that Calcutta shaped me. Calcutta is a very special city—it's a world-city, but at the same time it's a small town capable of exciting parochial passions and fiercely chauvinist loyalties. I am what I am because I was born into an upper-middle-class Bengali family in a city where to be Bengali was to be part of the mainstream. I didn't grow up in a multi-racial society in which to be Indian was to be a patronized or hated minority, as did V. S. Naipaul. North Americans don't always understand that an Indian growing up in India as part of the confident mainstream has a very different sense of self than an Indian growing up in a multiracial country.

India became an independent country in August 1947, and not long after, my parents, two sisters, and I made our first trip outside the country. My sister and I went to school in Britain and Switzerland for a few years, so we learned as fairly young children that there was a great big world *out there* that knew little about our native city.

My very early childhood was lived in British-ruled Calcutta. I have only one "colonial" memory, but it's a memory that over the years has become important to me. I can still see myself, feet hooked into the grille-work of the wrought-iron gate of our house—I must have been about four at the time—watching the funeral procession of a teenage freedom-fighter whom the British, very unfairly I now realize, called an "anarchist." Everybody had come outdoors to honour the funeral party. Mothers, grandmothers, boy scouts, servants, everybody. It's a heady memory, because what I remember, or *think* I remember, is the mix of fear, that trouble may break out between neighbourhood mourners and the police, and the confidence that very soon India would be free. I feel lucky that I was born just before Independence—I know firsthand how precious liberty is.

New York is my home now, and you know, in many ways it isn't too different from Calcutta. Like Calcutta, New York has a delightfully arrogant sense of itself as the literary and intellectual centre of the universe. And, of course, both cities have sizeable communities of homeless people living on sidewalks. Maybe it's the gradual Calcuttaization of New York that makes me feel so at home here.

Hancock: Could you tell me something about your family?
Mukherjee: Even more than Calcutta, I've been shaped by my family. I come from a very traditional Bengali Brahmin family. We are an extremely close-knit family. My father, who passed away in 1985, was an absolutely extraordinary man. He was a self-made man. From a one-room laboratory, he built a very successful pharmaceutical firm. He was very much the benevolent patriarch. He was the protector and lavish provider. At the same time, he was a visionary and a great risk-taker. Though he insisted on an almost anachronistically sheltered adolescence for us, he was able to send us three sisters abroad, out of his reach, for schooling. He wanted the best for his daughters. And to him, the "best" meant intellectually fulfilling lives.

Clark's written very affectionately about him in *Days and Nights in Calcutta*. And he is the model for The Tiger in my first novel, *The Tiger's Daughter*.

My mother is one of those exceptional Third World women who "burned" all her life for an education, which was denied to well-brought-up women of her generation. She made sure that my sisters and I never suffered the same wants.

Hancock: Are we getting a distorted view of India through such things as David Lean's film of *A Passage to India*, Kaye's *The Far Pavilions*, and the TV adaptation of Scott's *The Jewel in the Crown*?
Mukherjee: Well, we're getting a disproportionate focus on the British Raj in India. The Raj and the machinery of imperialism seem to sell well in North America, but the real India—the India of the Indians—is perceived as being boring or inaccessibly alien.

But I'm pleased that India is finally getting serious media attention. I thought *The Jewel in the Crown* was a remarkably affecting TV series and that it provided a stern, uncompromising picture of British imperialism.

Hancock: You've guest-edited recently a special issue of the *Literary Review* called "Writers of the Indian Commonwealth." In your introduction you wrote that "India's children in the new world are a mystery to me that you are eager to discover." Could you elaborate on that?
Mukherjee: I am an immigrant, living in a continent of immigrants. I am fascinated by what Clark calls the processes of "unhousement" and "rehousement"

in *Resident Alien*. I read voraciously the literature of deracination and assimilation. So it seemed to me natural when the *Literary Review* asked me to guest-edit an issue on Indian literature that I think of Indian literature as being rooted not so much in the geographical entity, India, as in a habit of mind that might be labelled Indian. Until this issue, no editor or critic had thought of Indian literature as a literature of a dispersed people. The summer 1986 *TLR* contains stories and poems by second- and third-generation Caribbeans, Fijians, Africans, and first-generation North Americans of Indian origin as well as the work of well-established India-based Indian writers.

Hancock: Are you also interested in authors like George Woodcock as a journalist and Janette Turner Hospital, who write about India as well, but as non-Indians?
Mukherjee: I'm interested in good writing no matter what the author's national origin.

Hancock: Who do you see as your contemporaries?
Mukherjee: A Third World writer isn't limited as a First World writer is in choosing her contemporaries. Having been born in a city that prided itself as the second city of the British Empire, and having been brought up on British literature, especially on Victorian and Edwardian literature, I feel as close to Jane Austen, Galsworthy, Wilde, and Coward as to Bernard Malamud, Alice Munro, Mavis Gallant, Ann Beattie, and Raymond Carver.

If you are asking me, do I see myself as another V. S. Naipaul, the answer is: no. The generational gap between us manifests itself more dramatically than the generational gap between, let's say, me and Mavis Gallant. Naipaul seems to have made himself the spokesman for the permanent, and one's tempted to say, the professional, expatriate from the Third World. His characters savour their marginality. I write about New Americans and New Canadians, about belated homesteaders from nontraditional countries. My characters grow and change with the change in citizenships.

Hancock: As a professor of creative writing, currently at Columbia, and on various other campuses with creative-writing programs in Canada and America, do you try to keep up to date? What do you talk to your students about?
Mukherjee: Every writer has a "given." I try to help the apprentice writers in my workshops discover that given material and find their "voice." More specifically, in a workshop situation we try to zero in on useful questions about narrative strategies. We try to explore the narrative options.

Hancock: You said that *Darkness* was written in a quick period of time, within three months, plus a few earlier stories. Do you feel that working in the hothouse confines of a creative-writing department which has students and instructors dealing with matters of form, technique, content, style, details, images, dramatic confrontation, and so on, helped to accumulate all that information for you until it suddenly found an explosive outlet?

Mukherjee: No. I like to write, I have always liked to write. I am not one of those writers who dread the typewriter. I wrote *Darkness* as soon as I'd freed myself from the feelings of anger and powerlessness brought on by the racism I experienced in Canada. Right now, my main problem is finding enough time to write. I teach five courses per semester. That's a very heavy teaching load by any standard. If I could afford to live just on my writing, I expect I'd be rather prolific.

But I *do* like to run fiction workshops. Workshops give me a chance to hone my theories about writing.

Hancock: Do you talk about things like finding a metaphor for the book, as the painting operates in *Darkness?*

Mukherjee: The best discussions are freewheeling. But I hope that I get across to my students my own concern with precision in language and with finding controlling metaphors for stories.

By the way, I don't teach only writing courses. I have a PhD in English and Comparative Literature, and most of the courses I teach in any given semester are straight, academic courses at the graduate or undergraduate level.

As a teacher of writing, though, I want my students not only to write well but to become canny readers of their own writing. So, sometimes, I bring in fiction—it may be just a few paragraphs—by writers I admire, for instance, Cheever or Updike or Munro or Gallant or Blaise—to see how they have solved technical problems.

I have to confess that when I sit down at my Kaypro, I have little idea what'll emerge on the screen.

Hancock: You keep a strong dramatic sense, though. Details, gestures work forcefully together in your characterizations. Do you see the characters?

Mukherjee: It depends on the work. Yes, definitively, with the two novels. I was mesmerized by the main characters, Tara and Dimple, in those novels. They became companions; I felt that they had lives almost independent of me. Most North American writers start with short fiction, then go on to novels. I started with novels.

Short stories don't always occur to me as being about a character. Sometimes a line or a possible title will set me going. "The Lady from Lucknow," for instance, began with the title. In stories, the hard thing is to find the right "voice," by which I mean locating a centre. Once I find the "voice," I don't seem to need to revise drastically. When I wrote novels, I found myself doing three drafts—the first to find out what the novel was *really* about; the second to sharpen the narrative; the third to catch any infelicities. But nowadays the short stories usually come to me at one sitting. I believe in revision, though. Or rather, I believe that good writing consists of decisions and calculations. One must know why one chooses this word instead of that. I share Isaac Babel's belief that the well-placed comma can stab the heart. I try to make my writing students sensitive to how a word looks and sounds.

Hancock: You mentioned encouraging your students to experiment with the page. Do you ever get involved in that big debate that was central in American letters a few years ago, the morality of fiction versus the experiments of fiction?
Mukherjee: If by "ever get involved" you mean do I sit on panels that discuss moral fiction as defined by the late John Gardner, the answer is: no. I don't engage in academic debates on this subject. But my own writing always locates a moral centre. The characters themselves may be immoral or amoral, but they operate in a deeply moral world. Some readers have written to tell me that they find my stories scary or unsettling because of this "moral centre."

Hancock: Do you find there's a difference between the Canadian and the American story?
Mukherjee: Yes. I think there's a measurable difference between contemporary Canadian and American fiction. I believe that culture, national mythologies, literary traditions shape both the "inside" and the "outside" of a work. One can detect in choice of syntax, for instance, some cultural assumptions. In the eighties writers from traditional societies, for example India-based Indian novelists writing in English about India, are more likely to feel comfortable using an omniscient point of view than are American writers.

By the way, in my world literature course at Montclair State College in New Jersey, I always use a novel by a Canadian author. Timothy Findley's *The Wars* works very well in the course. My students certainly feel that in *The Wars* they are encountering a society and a mode of processing that are very different from theirs. They realize that the First World War is central to the English Canadians in a way that it isn't to Americans.

Hancock: You said somewhere that Canada "fired up your rage."
Mukherjee: Yes. My experience with racism in Canada unleashed an anger that eventually led to potent fiction. But initially I expended my energies addressing civil-rights problems. Writing "An Invisible Woman"—the essay for *Saturday Night*—was very painful.

Hancock: Do you see that your work is equally concerned with form and language as it is with the particular issues of your content?
Mukherjee: I'm a careful writer. I am alert to the potency of, and possibilities in, language. English is a language that I have appropriated. At age three, I was sent to an English-medium school in Calcutta. Perhaps we who appropriate English are more aware of the language's powers than are native-speakers. Language gives me my identity. I am the writer I am because I write in North American English about immigrants in the New World.

Hancock: Have you found where you belong now? You travel widely enough. At the drop of a hat, you cross the continent and the world. That gives you energy.
Mukherjee: I like New York City. It's the Calcutta of the Americas. But I can make myself feel that I "belong" almost anywhere—I was happy in Iowa City, and I was very prepared to be happy in Toronto and Montreal. Perhaps, it's because as a Bengali woman I was brought up to be adaptable.

Newness excites me. When I move into a new city, I want to get to know it quickly, and make it my own. I want to "possess" it through my fiction. My characters don't see themselves as lost, marginal people in an unfamiliar city. On the contrary, my characters present an unexpected "insider's" view.

Clark and I have moved around because we must go where there are jobs for us. Yo-yoing through continents isn't my goal; settling-in as quickly as possible is.

Hancock: Here's a what-if question. What if you had stayed in Calcutta? Would you have written about something different? The liberation of Goa, the Lucknow uprising?
Mukherjee: Who knows! I'd have been a very different person, and therefore a very different writer, if I had stayed back in Calcutta. I still have some close friends in Calcutta, women I went to grade school with. They lead lives of grace, ease, privilege. When I visit them, I realize that outwardly my life in Calcutta would have been much like theirs. But the point is I didn't stay back. My writing has changed over the years. Since *The Tiger's Daughter* . . .

Hancock: I was going to say *The Tiger's Daughter* seemed a British book to me, while *Wife* seemed an American book, and *Darkness*, in part at least, seemed a Canadian book.

Mukherjee: My first novel does have, as you remarked, a Britishy feel to it. *The Tiger's Daughter* was written between classes at McGill; actually most of the manuscript was finished during two Christmas breaks and a summer vacation. As a child I was brought up on the novels of Jane Austen, Dickens, Forster, and when I came to write my first novel, the writers I'd read, especially Forster, became models to both mimic and subvert. I couldn't write another *The Tiger's Daughter* even if I wanted to; when I was writing it, the world seemed to me whole and examinable. I was far enough removed from India to look at upbringings like mine with affection and humour, but I wasn't yet integrated enough into Canada to appropriate Canadian issues. What's Britishy about that novel is its authoritativeness—it's hard for me now to write in an omniscient point of view.

By the time I started writing *Wife*, I'd become more North Americanized and that change comes through in the writing. I am not at all an autobiographical writer, but my obsessions reveal themselves in metaphor and language. When I was writing *Wife*, a limited third-person point of view seemed more natural and comfortable than an omniscient one. I was totally engrossed in Dimple. I knew I wanted to stay close to Dimple—an immigrant wife who starts to question her traditional values—and show the immigrants' world through her. And since I was telling the story of the traumatic changes—cultural, psychological—through Dimple, the language, too, was Dimple's; it was more intense, less authoritative and stately, than in *The Tiger's Daughter*.

Days and Nights in Calcutta, which Clark Blaise and I co-authored, was a very hard book for me to write. In my half of the book, I was supposed to write of a sabbatical year we spent in Calcutta in the seventies; I was supposed to write of the upper-middle-class life around me. What I ended up writing, however, was an accidental autobiography. While writing that book, I realized that I had moved from thinking of myself as an emotionally committed Canadian citizen. The book turns on this self-discovery.

Hancock: You worked closely with Clark on *Days and Nights in Calcutta* and your forthcoming account of the Air India disaster, *The Sorrow and the Terror*. Is the collaborative process a great stimulus?

Mukherjee: I don't know about the collaborative process itself, but collaborating with Clark is always exciting. We've collaborated in very different ways in the two nonfiction books. With *Days and Nights*, we were essentially writing two separate accounts about overlapping experiences. What turned the distinct accounts into a cohesive "book" was the unplanned converging and diverging of our two points of view.

Our collaboration in the new book, *The Sorrow and the Terror*, is a more concerted one. There isn't a single segment that hasn't been worked on by both of us.

Hancock: Do you ever show each other fiction-in-progress? That strikes me as a daunting experience, with two professors of creative writing commenting on each other's work.

Mukherjee: Clark's a good sport; he's always eager to see my work, and he makes very helpful suggestions. I should be a better sport.

Hancock: Your work has similarities. You both deal with alienation, victims, outsiders, though Clark's is more autobiographical, slightly removed.

Mukherjee: I don't think about my fiction as being about alienation. On the contrary, I mean for it to be about assimilation. My stories centre on a new breed and generation of North American pioneers. I am fascinated by people who have enough gumption, energy, ambition, to pull up their roots. My stories are irreverent, and, I like to think, funny. *(Laughs.)* My stories are about conquests, and not about loss.

Hancock: In your interview with V. S. Naipaul in *Salmagundi*, you said you admired him for "articulating a postcolonial consciousness without making it appear exotic." You added that you shared that sense of "being cut off from a supporting world," of "reaching across and bringing an unfamiliar society to a different audience." Does that relate to what you just said about pioneering?

Mukherjee: No, I don't think so. I admire V. S. Naipaul's early fiction, I especially like *A House for Mr. Biswas*. When I first read him, as a student in Iowa, I thought, here's another writer who isn't British or American and who is writing with feeling about a world that'd be considered "off-centre" by mainstream English readers. But Naipaul and I have had radically different experiences of dislocation, and therefore treat dislocation very differently in fiction. We intersect the Americas at very different points. My characters are not the descendants of indentured laborers. They've been spared, to use Naipaul's phrase, "the overcrowded barracoon" experience. My characters *choose* to uproot themselves from their native countries. For my characters, breaking away is part of maturing.

What interests me about Naipaul now is his appropriation of another people's culture, manners, traditions. In that context—the context of appropriation—I find Conrad, too, totally fascinating.

Hancock: Do you see "English" as a foreign language?

Mukherjee: That's an interesting question. The process of appropriating—and reinventing—language became real to me as I was guest-editing the special issue of the *Literary Review* (Summer 1986). As I was putting that issue together, I realized how strongly culture influenced not only the writer's use of English, but the shape of her/his fiction.

Of course English is a foreign language for me. My mother-tongue is still Bengali. Let's just say that I think of North American English as my step-mother-tongue!

Hancock: Could you elaborate on the parody of Forster that appears in *The Tiger's Daughter?*

Mukherjee: I talked about the "parodying" of Forster on a panel at McGill University during an E. M. Forster Festival, and since that talk is already in print, I don't see much point in going over it here. Briefly, in my novel I was trying to subvert the Anglo-Indian literary conventions. For instance, in my novel I shrank Forster's Mau Tank to a poorly filtered swimming pool. Parody and subversion have energy; mimicry doesn't.

Hancock: Do your characters speak for you?

Mukherjee: If you are asking, do my characters faithfully articulate my personal views, the answer is: no. My characters, as you know, come from many different social classes and support many different political positions. But if the question is, do my characters speak *to* me, then the answer is: yes. I hear them speak. My head's bursting with stories. The trouble, as always, is to find the time to write them.

Hancock: Time is the problem. Like Clark, do you manage to get to retreats or writers' colonies?

Mukherjee: I don't have time to go to writers' colonies! I teach summer school.

Hancock: Are the voices of your characters bits and pieces of information that you've accumulated through osmosis or clippings or pass along stories or fabrication based on the nuances of the experiences as you understand them?

MUKHARJEE: I write about what obsesses me—the rehousement of individuals and of whole peoples.

Hancock: You have used those terms before: rehousement and unhousement. Could you explain them?

Mukherjee: Unhousement is the breaking away from the culture into which one was born, and in which one's place in society was assured. Rehousement is the rerooting of oneself in a new culture. This requires transformations of the self.

Hancock: Are obsessions important for a writer?
Mukherjee: Obsession is essential.

Hancock: Do you have a sense of audience? Or various audiences? Or do you worry about audiences?
Mukherjee: I am my ideal audience. I don't have a specific or targeted audience in mind, but I think that as long as a writer isn't writing in her/his diary, she/he assumes the existence of an ideal, maybe phantom, audience.

Hancock: Would it be an audience that either recognizes or shares the experience of the fiction?
Mukherjee: I know what you're getting at. But I intend to evade the question. Oh well, all right, let me try to meet your question head-on. When I sit at my Kaypro I don't think of audience. I write because a story has become urgent inside my head. But one is always divided between the person punching the keyboard, and the person reading the screen. That's what I meant when I said that I was my ideal audience. Clark and my editor occupy the next two rows of ideal audiences.

Then when I find out that there is an audience, however small, *out there*, I am wonderstruck. I got quite a bit of mail on *Wife*. There were some really moving letters; I especially remember one from a British war-bride in a New Jersey suburb and another from a German woman in the Maritimes. To know that one's fiction has reached even one person is staggering; it's humbling. I believe in the word. The word creates or locates its own audience. My father, who was a very successful scientist and businessman, too, believed in the power of the word. He was very pleased with my essay, "An Invisible Woman." I had kept that essay from him because I hadn't wanted him to know how pained I was by my racial experiences in Canada. But just before he passed away, someone snuck him a copy of the essay. I am glad now that he saw it.

Hancock: Is obsession enough? Or does a writer need ego as well? By that I mean the courage necessary to get the work done, as Norman Mailer once said.
Mukherjee: If ego means stamina, I suppose, yes. A writer needs the ability to carry on in spite of rejection.

Hancock: Could you tell me a bit about your friendship with Bernard Malamud?
Mukherjee: Bernard Malamud was like a second father to us, especially to Clark,
I knew him for over twenty years, Clark knew him longer. In fact, I met him
through Clark; he was very much a part of the family.

At the same time he was a writer who brought out the best in us as writers. In
a way, reading Bern's *Selected Stories* made me want to write *Darkness*. That's why
Darkness is dedicated to him. There are many dazzling-enough writers, but few
works have the compassion and wisdom that Bern's do.

Hancock: There's been many changes in the Canadian publishing community as
well. Do you see yourself as a Canadian writer, or a North American, or an international writer? Do you see that there's been changes in the Canadian publishing
community as well? A new generation of publishers, editors, readers is more receptive to your work now than when it was first published.
Mukherjee: I remember some years ago reading about Cynthia Goode, the senior
editor at Penguin Books, in *Quill and Quire*. The article quoted her as saying—I
am paraphrasing what I remember after all these years—that she was looking for
Canadian writers who were also international. I remember thinking to myself
with relief that finally, thanks to editors like her, Canadian literature has come
of age, that it has moved away from the fiercely parochial nationalism of the late
1960s and of the 1970s, that it can now accommodate writers who write of the
"other" Canada.

Clark and I came to live in Montreal in 1966, as you know. I taught fiction-
writing at McGill and, for a longish time, directed McGill's Creative Writing program, and my first novel, which was published in the States in 1972, did rather
well.

What I'm saying is that I got started as a writer—in 1972 I was a Canadian novelist with an "international" reputation—at a time when nationalist Canadian
writers were defining Canadian literature by exclusion rather than by inclusion.

Hancock: Do you admire writers like Salman Rushdie and others who are bringing a new energy to the writing of India?
Mukherjee: I admire Salman Rushdie enormously. Before *Midnight's Children*,
writers of Indian origin writing in English were encouraged by convention to
write of their world with detachment and irony. Their method was reductive.
They treated their characters as though they were uncomplicated. With *Midnight's Children*, Rushdie breaks down those conventions. He aggrandizes, and
that's marvellously healthy. The sections on Bombay have a superb excess of energy. Many of the writers before him tried, very unfortunately, to "tame" India for

foreign readers. The other interesting thing about Salman Rushdie is that he discards British models. His fiction is closer to that of Günter Grass and Márquez than to Forster.

Hancock: That also happened in Canadian writing, as you know, with what I'll broadly call "fiction of the marvellous." Does that particular mode of perception appeal to you as a writer?

Mukherjee: In Hindu story-telling—I am talking about the ancient tales from the *Puranasa* and the two epics of the *Ramayana* and the *Mahabharata*—the magical is the norm. All Hindu children, especially children in villages, are told the ancient stories again and again. Shape-changes are common in these tales. Birds talk. Animals practise ethics. It was colonialism that derailed Indian writers from continuing that convention of "magic." I am not eager to use the term "magic realism" because it doesn't precisely convey what I mean about this Hindu oral literature. Colonialism forced generations of Indian writers to value British models and to look down on the native. The British managed to convince Indians that British literature was rational, realistic, and superior, and that Indian literature with its magical qualities was childish. Do I write magic realism? I include "the marvellous" in my fiction, especially in my first novel. My fiction clearly inhabits a space in which there are extra-rational presences.

Hancock: Do you find the critics and reviewers sensitive to your work?

Mukherjee: Sensitive to my work? I think so. A few *choose* to misread, because they have agendas of their own.

Hancock: Could you tell me about the origins of *The Tiger's Daughter*? Was that your MFA thesis in Iowa?

Mukherjee: No, I wrote a collection of stories for my MFA thesis. My doctoral dissertation was on a purely academic topic. Let me tell you how I came to write my first novel. When I was a student in Iowa, I wrote a story called "Debate on a Rainy Afternoon" for one of my fiction workshops. The workshop seemed to really like that story. Well, Clark sent off a copy to the *Massachusetts Review,* and my story was published. The story then won an Honorable Mention in the *Best American Stories* for that year. About the same time, editors from three major American publishing houses wrote me, asking to see a novel. The editor from Houghton Mifflin was the most persistent, so I wrote her back that I was terribly busy finishing my PhD dissertation—and teaching full-time, and raising two kids—but that as soon as I had a summer break, I'd get to work on a novel. And that's what I did.

Hancock: How did *Wife* begin?

Mukherjee: Clark and I were in Calcutta on a sabbatical one winter. We were staying at a place called the Ramkrishna Mission, it's a place where foreign scholars generally stay. The idea is that the scholars will work in reasonably priced, comfortable enough, hotel-style rooms during the day, and engage in exciting intellectual conversations at meal times. Clark and I were having breakfast at a long dining table one morning when a Columbia professor next to me asked, "What do you Bengali girls do between the ages of fifteen and twenty-five?" So I wrote a novel to explain to him what we did.

Hancock: You said that *Darkness* came about as a result of your second trip to the United States to live.

Mukherjee: Moving out of Canada gave me back my voice. The last seven years or so in Canada I felt I was constantly being forced to see myself as part of an unwanted "visible minority." All I say about the move and its effects on my fiction I have said in the Introduction to that book.

Hancock: Ironically, in Canada, you won a National Magazine Award for your honest invective.

Mukherjee: In my acceptance speech I said that only in Canada would someone win a prize for indicting the society. I couldn't have written "An Invisible Woman" if I hadn't left Canada, though.

Hancock: Are names the metaphor for characters? Dimple seems like such a perfect name, "a small surface depression" as you noted in the epigraph.

Mukherjee: Names are very important to me. Dimple, by the way, was a very popular—very chic, if you like—name for Indian girls in the early seventies. But I was also trying to suggest "slight disturbances" through that name.

Hancock: Do you see a character like Tara Bannerjee? Or do you slowly create her to fit the demands of the fiction?

Mukherjee: Tara wasn't based on any real person. And the novel wasn't autobiographical. But I *was* writing about a small class of people, a passing way of life, that I knew very well. The novel demanded that the narrator figure be passive. So, to some extent, I'd have to say yes to your second question—Tara's passivity was dictated by her dramatic function in the novel. She had to be porous and passive in order to record the slightest tremors in her culture. She had to react rather than to act. The novel centred on the violent passing of an era—and the characters were intended to be fleshed out abstractions. As I was writing, they took on surprising lives of their own. I suppose that because I have a comic vision, most of the characters, even when they are caught in ghastly situations, acquit themselves in amusing ways.

Hancock: Do you find that being an academic and a professor of creative writing gets in the way when you work? Do you have to forget all that? When I asked Clark that, he said it was as if none of it existed.

Mukherjee: I was going to say the same thing. When I sit in front of the screen, the story takes over. In the first draft, I have no idea where the story's going, what characters will do or say.

Reader-effect is important to me, though. I do know, while I am working—maybe not till the second draft—what I want a reader to feel in any given scene. By reader I don't mean a real person, but the imaginary "other" inside me that we were discussing earlier this afternoon.

Hancock: Do you tell your students things about work habits? About doing the work that is necessary to get the job done? Or so many hours a day? About getting a discipline?

Mukherjee: I always tell them that writing requires self- discipline. Yes, I warn them about hard work. I tell them that many good writers I know keep notebooks and write every day. But then I tell them that I don't keep notebooks, and I don't have time to write every day.

Hancock: One of the things that appealed to me about both your novels was that the prose was so heavily textured. *Wife* had ads, letters, scenarios, various dialogues, the four electric cows. The prose itself was a surprise from page to page. Did you do that on the second draft?

Mukherjee: If you are asking me, did I inject "texture" in a deliberate way into the second draft, the answer would have to be: no. Both novels occurred to me in terms of a character—Tara, Dimple—caught in a crisis situation, and to me a character is who she is because of the language she thinks and feels in. My characters are often in the process of forgetting one language and inventing another. The texture of the novel comes from the language used by the focal characters— in that sense, the texture is part of the first draft.

Hancock: Does the television act as an ironic mirror to this unhappy story?

Mukherjee: Dimple is an isolated woman because she doesn't speak much English. She tells herself that she is learning American English and getting to know Americans by watching T.V.

Hancock: Dramatically, you establish the direction of *Wife* fairly quickly. You set up the idea of murder in New York, of violence and chaos, and variations on that motif, blood, pin pricks, punctures, and other hurtful things of various kinds. Did you plan that part of your narrative strategy from the beginning?

Mukherjee: Most of it, yes. I think of plot as an arrangement or a design. The juxtaposition of images, the composition and the framing: all these are important to me. But I hope the ending comes as a surprise. How Dimple settles her problem should shock or at least surprise the reader.

Hancock: Is infidelity and murder the only solution?

Mukherjee: Dimple thinks so. The ending, I guess, is discomfiting.

Dimple's decision to murder her husband is her misguided act of self-assertion. If she had remained a housewife living with her extended family in India, she would probably not have asked herself questions such as, am I unhappy, do I deserve to be unhappy. And if by chance she had asked herself these questions, she might have settled her problems by committing suicide. So turning to violence outward rather than inward is part of her slow and misguided Americanization. *Wife* is a novel that is very dear to me.

Hancock: The antagonists your characters face are not evil characters, are they?

Mukherjee: My fiction locates very clearly, I think, what's morally right and what's not. But I don't have guys in white hats slugging guys in black hats. There's villainy growing out of misunderstandings and malice, but there's no Devil.

Hancock: Your protagonists in *Darkness* are a wide range of characters: illegals, rich, poor, a psychiatrist, a restaurant worker . . .

Mukherjee: There are a hundred thousand voices in my head waiting to be heard.

Hancock: One reviewer said your characters "bring false ideas of what to expect in the new world, and in defence, create false memories of what they leave behind. As a result, both the old and the new don't exist, and the creators of these worlds become more and more unreal themselves."

Mukherjee: I guess I missed that review. I don't know what the reviewer means because I don't have the context. But I do want my characters to be seen as inventing their own Americas and Canadas. The breaking away from rigidly predictable lives frees them to invent more satisfying pasts, and gives them a chance to make their futures in ways that they could not have in the Old World. We're talking, then, about relocation as a positive act. In immigrating, my characters become creators. By creating, they become more real to themselves, instead of unreal.

An Interview with Bharati Mukherjee

Alison B. Carb / 1987

Reprinted by permission from the *Massachusetts Review*, vol. 29, no. 4 (Winter 1988).

Bharati Mukherjee: The stories were done in two intense flurries, although I had been thinking about the book for a long time. As soon as *Darkness* was published in 1985, I started working on stories for *The Middleman.* One cycle of stories was written over an eight-month period during a semester off from teaching and on an NEA grant. Then my work was interrupted while I was teaching and writing the book on the Air India crash, *The Sorrow and the Terror,* with my husband. Once that book was over, I wrote another cycle of stories for *The Middleman* over the summer of 1987. So it took me about a year and a half to write this book if one includes the break in between.

Carb: Where did you get the idea for the book?

Mukherjee: It grew out of an incomplete novel about a man who served in the Army in Vietnam, and who, after the war, becomes a professional soldier and hires himself out in Afghanistan and Central America. While I was working on that novel, a character with a minor role, a Jew who has relocated from Baghdad to Bombay to Brooklyn, took control and wrote his own story. He attracted me because he was a cynical person and a hustler, as many immigrant survivors have to be.

So Alfie Judah, the protagonist in *The Middleman,* travels around the world, providing people with what they need—guns, narcotics, automobiles. The story takes place in an unnamed country in Central America where he becomes involved in a guerilla war.

Incidentally, the Vietnam veteran, Jeb Marshall who comes from Miami, is featured in his own story in this collection, called "Loose Ends." A large number of these stories are told by native-born Americans, but even when I write about them I tell how their lives are affected by newly arrived or first-generation Americans.

For example, one of my stories, "Fighting for the Rebound," is narrated by an Atlanta stockbroker who falls in love with a former millionaire's daughter from the Philippines, who supports Marcos. As a writer, my voice is supple and I can enter diverse characters' lives and let each of them speak for themselves.

The new, changing America is the theme of the stories in *The Middleman.* For me, immigration from the Third World to this country is a metaphor for the process of uprooting and rerooting, or what my husband Clark Blaise in his book *Resident Alien* calls "unhousement" and "rehousement." The immigrants in my stories go through extreme transformations in America and at the same time they alter the country's appearance and psychological make-up. In some ways, they are like European immigrants of earlier eras. But they have different gods. And they come for different reasons.

Carb: What is special about this collection?

Mukherjee: I write about well-known American establishments, such as the family, in unique ways. In my stories, the families are not the American families which we are accustomed to reading about in fiction. The American family has become very different, not just because of social influences and new sexual standards, but because of the interaction between mainstream Americans and new immigrants.

For example, there's a story in *The Middleman* entitled "Fathering," in which the secure life of a yuppie living with his girlfriend in a small town in upstate New York is disrupted when the half-Vietnamese child he had fathered in Saigon comes to visit.

In another story, "Orbiting," a New Jersey woman of Italian origin invites her parents and her Afghan boyfriend for Thanksgiving dinner at her home and a crisis occurs over who should carve the turkey, her father or the boyfriend. My stories are discomfiting because they challenge accepted codes of behavior in this country and show the changes taking place here.

Carb: Do you see changes in your writing style in *The Middleman?*

Mukherjee: My style has changed because I am becoming more Americanized with each passing year. American fiction has a kind of energy that fiction from other cultures seems to lack right now. The stories in *The Middleman,* I like to think, have this energy and passion as well. Each character and story suggests a different style.

When I sit down in my study to write, I don't immediately say, "I have to write an experimental story." The story idea itself dictates the appropriate voice for it and how lean or fleshy a paragraph might be. I write some stories from a very authoritative third person point of view. With others I use an intimate, textured style and a first person point of view.

My first novel, *The Tiger's Daughter*, has a rather British feel to it. I used the omniscient point of view and plenty of irony. This was because my concept of language and notions of how a novel was constructed were based on British models. I had gone to school in London as a young child and later to a British convent school for elite young women in postcolonial India, where we read English writers like Jane Austen and E. M. Forster.

By the time I wrote *Darkness* I had adopted American English as my language. I moved away from using irony and was no longer comfortable using an authoritative point of view. In addition, I started to write short stories instead of novels. The short story form requires us to express our thoughts concisely and not waste a single sentence or detail.

Carb: How does your writing contrast with that of other India-born writers?
Mukherjee: There is a large difference between myself and these authors. Unlike writers such as Anita Desai and R. K. Narayan, I do not write in Indian English about Indians living in India. My role models, view of the world, and experiences are unlike theirs. These writers live in a world in which there are still certainties and rules. They are part of their society's mainstream. Wonderful writers as they are, I am unable to identify with them because they describe characters who fit into their community in different ways than my naturalized Americans fit into communities in Queens or Atlanta.

On the other hand, I don't write from the vantage point of an Indian expatriate like V. S. Naipaul. Naipaul, who was born in Trinidad because his relatives left India involuntarily to settle there, has different attitudes about himself. He writes about living in perpetual exile and about the impossibility of ever having a home. Like Naipaul, I am a writer from the Third World but unlike him I left India by choice to settle in the U.S. I have adopted this country as my home. I view myself as an American author in the tradition of other American authors whose ancestors arrived at Ellis Island.

Carb: Which authors do you think your writing most closely resembles?
Mukherjee: (Emphatically) I see a strong likeness between my writing and Bernard Malamud's, in spite of the fact that he describes the lives of East European Jewish immigrants and I talk about the lives of newcomers from the Third World. Like Malamud, I write about a minority community which escapes the ghetto and adapts itself to the patterns of the dominant American culture. Like Malamud's, my work seems to find quite naturally a moral center. Isaac Babel is

another author who is a literary ancestor for me. I also feel a kinship with Joseph Conrad and Anton Chekhov. But Malamud most of all speaks to me as a writer and I admire his work a great deal. Immersing myself in his work gave me the self-confidence to write about my own community.

Carb: How does your writing differ from Malamud's?

Mukherjee: When you are from the Third World, when you have dark skin and religious beliefs that do not conform to those of Judaism or Christianity, mainstream America responds to you in ways you can't foresee. My fiction has to consider race, politics, religion, as well as certain nastinesses that other generations of white immigrant American writers may not have had to take into account.

I was born into a Hindu Bengali Brahmin family which means that I have a different sense of self, of existence, and of mortality than do writers like Malamud. I believe that our souls can be reborn in another body, so the perspective I have about a single character's life is different from that of an American writer who believes that he only has one life.

As a Hindu, I was brought up on oral tradition and epic literature in which animals can talk, birds can debate ethical questions, and monsters can change shapes. I believe in the existence of alternate realities, and this belief makes itself evident in my fiction.

Carb: Do you think American readers and editors have been receptive to your work?

Mukherjee: Yes. Americans have a healthy curiosity about new writers and new ideas. American publishing houses have been far more ready to receive my writing than have houses in Canada, where the attitude in the sixties and seventies was that if one hadn't played in snow and grown up eating oatmeal one didn't have anything relevant to say to Canadian readers.

I was touched when one of my "immigrant" stories, "The Tenant," which was printed in a small literary quarterly, the *Literary Review,* was read by people and eventually made it into *The Best American Short Stories 1987.*

Writing short stories helped too. As soon as I started writing them, my work became more available to American readers than my novels had been. The novels were not easily obtainable because initially there were no paperback editions. This past year they were reissued by Penguin Books.

Unfortunately, one of the difficulties that writers like myself face are editors of large-circulation magazines who are unwilling to risk publishing writers whose fictional worlds are not intensely familiar or overtly sellable. They say my work is "too strong" for their readers.

Carb: What other difficulties have you experienced as a writer?

Mukherjee: (In a low, strained voice) I had a very bad time during the 1970s when my husband and I lived and taught in Canada. I had gone there with him because his family lived there. The seventies were horrendous years for Indians in Canada. There was a lot of bigotry against Canadian citizens of Indian origin, especially in Toronto, and it upset me terribly when I encountered this or saw other people experiencing it.

There was a pattern of discrimination. I was refused service in stores. I would have to board a bus last when I had been the first person on line. I was followed by detectives in department stores who assumed I was a shoplifter or treated like a prostitute in hotels. I was even physically roughed up in a Toronto subway station.

I found myself constantly fighting battles against racial prejudice. Toronto made me into a civil rights activist. I wrote essays about the devastating personal effects of racism. For many years I didn't find the strength to turn my back on Canada and do what I really wanted to do: write fiction.

But in 1980 I did leave. We were living in Montreal at the time. I resigned my full professorship at McGill University and came to the United States with my family. I felt guilty about pulling my husband and sons away from what was home, but it was a question of my own self-preservation. It was the only way I could think of removing myself from the persistent hurt.

Being in the U.S. was a tremendous relief after Canada. I suddenly felt freed to write the thousands of stories inside my head. In the U.S. I wasn't continuously forced to deal with my physical appearance. I could wear Western clothes and blend in with people on a New York City street. America, with its melting pot theory of immigration, has a healthier attitude toward Indian immigrants than Canada. Although this country has its share of racial problems there are human rights laws and ways to obtain legal redress in the courts.

Carb: Do you find it easy or difficult to write?

Mukherjee: I *like* to write but finding the time isn't easy. It would be ideal if I could write from nine to three or four every day. But I have so many jobs to do, teaching, lecturing, writing articles and reviews, taking care of my family, that I can't write as much as I would like. When I do sit down at the word processor in my study, I'm ready to go and the writing just flows. Especially where short stories are concerned. I hear a voice inside my head and start typing. Not everything I write appears in a book though, I'm a great reviser.

My husband, Clark, also helps me with my fiction. He is an American-Canadian author. Like me, he teaches in the English Department at Columbia

University. We work well on joint writing projects such as the nonfiction books we did, *Days and Nights in Calcutta*, about our year-long stay with my family in India in 1977, and *The Sorrow and the Terror*.

We have an intensely literary marriage. We talk about writing and Clark is a very good audience for my work. He reads it and comments on it just as he did when we were students in the Writers' Workshop at the University of Iowa, where we first met.

Carb: Were you interested in writing before graduate school?

Mukherjee: Yes. I always knew I was going to be a writer. I had wanted to write since I was a child. The world of fiction seemed more real to me than the world around me. I started my first novel when I was about nine or ten. It came to seventy or eighty pages. It was about English children and was set in England.

But it wasn't until I was in high school in Calcutta that I started writing short stories for school magazines. I don't remember what these stories were about and I want to forget them (laughs), but I recall writing one from Napoleon's point of view. My imagination was stimulated by reading about European history and Western civilization. By the time I was at college I decided that I wasn't going to be a chemist like my father. I enjoyed writing far too much.

Carb: You have come from a complex background and world. Is it hard for you as a South Asian immigrant writer to convey the immigrant experience to native-born American audiences?

Mukherjee: No, no, no. My task as an author is to make my intricate and unknown world comprehensible to mainstream American readers. This is what good novels and stories do. If my fiction is effective, unexplained and cultural aspects about the Indian community in Queens or the Korean community in New York will become accessible.

We immigrants have fascinating tales to relate. Many of us have lived in newly independent or emerging countries which are plagued by civil and religious conflicts. We have experienced rapid changes in the history of the nations in which we lived. When we uproot ourselves from those countries and come here, either by choice or out of necessity, we suddenly must absorb two hundred years of American history and learn to adapt to American society. Our lives are remarkable, often heroic.

I attempt to illustrate this in my novels and short stories. My characters want to make it in the new world; they are filled with a hustlerish kind of energy, like Alfie Judah in *The Middleman*. Although they are often hurt or depressed by setbacks in their new lives and occupations, they do not give up. They take risks they wouldn't have taken in their old, comfortable worlds to solve their problems. As they change citizenship, they are reborn.

My aim is to expose Americans to the energetic voices of new settlers in this country, not only through my own writing but by editing and reviewing the fiction of writers from nontraditional nations, including India, Sri Lanka, Egypt, and South Africa. By doing this I hope to make editors aware of how these writers are changing the scope and structure of American fiction.

Bharati Mukherjee

Sybil Steinberg / 1989

From *Publishers Weekly* (August 25, 1989), 46–47. © 1996 by *Publishers Weekly*. Reprinted with the permission of the publisher.

Like the eponymous narrator of her new novel, *Jasmine*, Bharati Mukherjee has changed citizenships and cultures with disorienting rapidity. She has written about her several lives in two previous novels, a nonfiction work, and two collections of short stories—*The Middleman* collection won the 1988 NBCC award for fiction. In *Jasmine*, out from Grove next month, Mukherjee encapsulates many aspects of the immigrant experience in America, in the process revealing the ways in which newcomers from the Third World are being absorbed by, and at the same time are transforming, our society.

Just back from a visit to her family in India, Mukherjee meets *PW* in the Grove offices in lower Manhattan. Intense, elegant, and articulate, she is eager to talk about the changes wrought in her life by the NBCC award and her nascent celebrity. "The prize has made an enormous difference, not only in getting my current books into bookstores but also in reviving interest in my earlier work. I've been writing since 1972, and I'd always had a wonderful critical reception. But although my first two books were BOMC alternates, they never went into paperback. Now for the first time there's a tremendous interest here, in Europe, and in India. This has vindicated what I always tell my students: Concentrate on putting out a good word. A good word will not die. Someday it will find an audience."

In Mukherjee's case, the path to her audience was circuitous. Raised in an upper-class Bengali family of Brahmin caste, one of three daughters of a research chemist, she attended private schools in India, London, and Switzerland—before a business disaster wiped out the family's fortune. In 1961, she got a scholarship to the University of Iowa Writers' Workshop, where she met writer Clark Blaise and married him two years later. The couple lived first in Canada with their two young sons, supporting themselves through a grueling schedule of teaching and other jobs, and writing in the small hours of the morning and weekends. Then a series of near tragic accidents sent them to Calcutta for a year to recuperate both physically and emotionally. In *Days and Nights in Calcutta* (Doubleday; Penguin paper), the book they wrote about this experience, Mukherjee says, "To be a Third World woman writer in North America is to confine oneself to a narrow, airless, tightly roofed arena."

Financially, too, the outlook was bleak. "I was brought up spectacularly rich—in the Third World sense—and have been spectacularly poor almost all my adult life," Mukherjee says. "At one time, I had to calculate whether I had enough money to buy orange juice as well as milk for breakfast. There was a time when I thought, should I be looking into a job as a chambermaid. But then I remembered I didn't know how to drive, and couldn't get to a motel," she laughs.

"For more than twenty years Clark and I have held three and four jobs per year in order to make ends meet. Now for the first time I'm able to take a semester off from teaching to work on my own novel," Mukherjee continues. "But the momentum of a work-in-progress has always carried me. There's not a single moment when I'm not thinking stories in my head. Sometimes endings will come to me in dreams."

Because she and her husband have shared a peripatetic lifestyle—"I've lived everywhere; that's what happens when you take teaching jobs anyplace that will have you"—Mukherjee has found herself "thrust into adventures. Once I left the very protective, overly nurturing society [of India], my life intersected history. The title story in *The Middleman* came about because I happened to be in Costa Rica at a time when American and Central American history was being made."

Mukherjee's characters have always reflected her own circumstances and personal concerns, and one is able to trace her growth in self-confidence and her slowly developing identity as an American through her fiction. When she wrote *The Tiger's Daughter* (Houghton Mifflin, 1972), Mukherjee was living in Canada, where she was conscious of being "a brown woman in a white society." Commenting on that first book, she says, "It is the wisest of my novels in the sense that I was between both worlds. I was detached enough from India so that I could look back with affection and irony, but I didn't know America enough to feel any conflict. I was like a bridge, poised between two worlds."

Wife, published three years later, "was very much an immigrant book. The wife was going through feminist and immigrant crises. The style was distinctly American in that omniscience was no longer natural to me. I was closer to my character and the material was more passionate. I had sacrificed irony for passion."

The characters in her short story collection titled *Darkness* (Penguin, 1985) were still South Asian immigrants who were trying out new lives. Only three years later, with *The Middleman*, she was confident enough to include a wide range of characters from various countries and strata of society. "With that book I realized that I can enter any gender and any culture, if the character and story excite me," she says.

One of the distinctions of Mukherjee's recent books is her adroit adaptation of the American vernacular. Her characters have urgent, riveting voices; they speak in the contemporary idiom as immigrants handle it, each richly reflecting the cadences of their original language on which they have grafted a new, distinctively regional Americanese. Mukherjee credits her flawless ventriloquism to a very good ear that unconsciously picks up nuances of language and has her talking like a native of whatever region she is in at the moment. "More importantly, it's having married an American writer who has opened up for me an America that is normally closed to immigrants," she says.

Her compact but fluid style is similarly a matter of gradual evolution. "I have lived through so many worlds and have been put in so many odd, momentous situations, accidentally, that all those worlds somehow creep into a single sentence. Mine is not minimalism, which strips away, but compression, which reflects many layers of meaning."

Her newest heroine, Jasmine, starts life as Jyoti in a tiny village in India, is called Jasmine by her husband, comes to America after she is tragically widowed, and becomes Jane Ripplemeyer in Iowa. Jasmine seesaws between her aspirations to make something of her life in America and her belief in an implacable fate. Though Mukherjee says that "Jasmine contains the shape of my life and my desires, but no incident is at all autobiographical," she admits that, like her heroine, she too coexists between two opposed philosophies. "I do believe in personal striving. Like Jasmine I want to reposition the stars. At the same time I'm aware of a larger design. My way of solving this is to say that every single moment has a purpose. I want to discover that purpose."

The original Jasmine, in the story of that name in *The Middleman*, was a Trinidadian illegal working in a seedy hotel in Detroit. "The character wouldn't die," Mukherjee confesses. "I am intrigued by that particular kind of survival."

In her second incarnation, Jasmine has a star-shaped scar on her forehead, a mark she has come to think of as her third eye, though in India it is a blemish that reduces her bridal value. The author, too, has a faint scar on her forehead, scarcely noticeable except to one who recognizes the resemblance to her fictional character. At age three, she slipped and smashed her head into a metal ring door knocker. The wound was never sutured, an omission that she now finds "odd, in India, where for a Bengali girl to have a physical imperfection is to be unmarriageable."

While Mukherjee was a student in Iowa, however, her father wrote to say that he had, in fact, found the perfect groom for her, "a nuclear physicist, Bengali, right caste, right background, right education." Plans for marriage were set in motion, but in the meantime, Mukherjee met Clark Blaise. "If I had married this man— who is now very important in the Indian nuclear industry—I would have been a very different kind of person and a different kind of writer," Mukherjee says. "If I had stayed in India, I would have written elegant, ironic, wise stories which would be marked by detachment. But I never could have stayed in India. It was not so much restlessness, but enthusiasm and eagerness that has always made me curious about the rest of the world.

"I knew from the moment I got here that I wanted to stay," she continues. "I preferred unpredictability to a privileged but predictable life." But when the couple moved to Canada they experienced a society less open to immigrants than the U.S. "Canada and the U.S have very different ways of treating newcomers, very different responses to the threat of de-Europeanization. Here diversity is accepted; the melting pot helps the newcomer to feel more welcome." Mukherjee "put the matter of racial discrimination on the public agenda," with an essay called "An Invisible Woman," which appeared in 1981 in Canada's *Saturday Night* magazine. "Bags of mail," much of it hostile, came in response. One reader suggested she change her unpronounceable name. "One said, 'If you didn't play in snow as a child you have no right to regard yourself as a Canadian,'" Mukherjee recalls. Yet the net result of that experience was positive, she feels.

The courage to speak out against prejudice brought Mukherjee to the defense of Salman Rushdie: during the first heated months of the controversy, she sported a large Rushdie button, and she and her husband appeared on Lewis Lapham's TV program *Bookmark* in Rushdie's defense. They too had experienced terrorist pressure in what she calls "a very modest way" after the publication of their 1985 book *The Sorrow and the Terror*, which described the terrorist-directed crash of Air India Flight #182. For months afterwards the couple received death threats.

The support of other authors has been crucial in Mukherjee's life. Bernard Malamud, who was Blaise's teacher at Harvard, was "a second father to Clark, and he became a second father to me, too," she says fondly. "He was a man of great moral force, and he showered his life on us—sometimes in practical ways, like money, so that we wouldn't starve—other times as role model."

Margaret Atwood also played a pivotal role in Mukherjee's career. It was she who "insisted that we get a good agent and introduced Elaine Markson to us," Mukherjee says. "And Elaine got my material to the right editor"—Walter Bode at Grove. The couple's first agent was the "wonderfully eccentric" Diarmuid Russell.

Then there was a long spell of "unfortunate representation," she says. She found herself stereotyped—"I was boxed as a certain kind of elegant woman writer, appealing only to India hands."

During those bad years, her husband's faith buoyed her confidence. "I've really grown up with Clark. We have a special kind of literary marriage, because we're both writers and academics. There's not a moment when we're not talking literature. If I'd married a nuclear physicist, in some way I'd be a lonelier person. This sameness of focus helped us get through extraordinary cultural and religious differences."

Best of all, her marriage has helped her feel American. "Mine is a clear-eyed but definite love of America. I'm aware of the brutalities, the violences here, but in the long run my characters are survivors; they've been helped, as I have, by good strong people of conviction. Like Jasmine, I feel there are people born to be Americans. By American I mean an intensity of spirit and a quality of desire. I feel American in a very fundamental way, whether Americans see me that way or not."

An Interview with Bharati Mukherjee and Clark Blaise

Michael Connell, Jessie Grearson, and Tom Grimes / 1990

With the assistance of David Hamilton, general editor. From the *Iowa Review*, 20 (Fall 1990), 7–32. © 1990 by Michael Connell, Jessie Grearson, and Tom Grimes. Reprinted with the permission of the authors.

TIR: You said at one point, "There are no harmless, compassionate ways to remake one's self ... we murder who we were so we can rebirth ourselves in the images of our dreams." Do you see violence as necessary to a transformation of character?

BM: Yes. And I can see that in my own life it's been psychic violence. In my character Jasmine's case it's been physical violence because she's from a poor farming family. Plus terrorism is a virus of the eighties, so there is the initial violence of the village, where her husband dies in a fire bombing. Because she is an undocumented, poor alien, she necessarily goes through a kind of physical harassment that someone like me was exempt from. But just growing up in my Calcutta, the daughter of a very rich factory owner in a time when West Bengal, and especially Calcutta, was becoming Communist, I had to personally experience a great deal of labor violence and unrest. There were many times when I went to school with what we used to call "flying squads." Military policemen in vans in front, special policemen in vans in back, our car, with chauffeur and bodyguard in between so we could, the three sisters, take part as pretty maidens in gondoliers. Gilbert and Sullivan light operas, etc. I'm coming out of a nineteenth-century world, and have witnessed a lot of violence for myself which didn't physically scar me—I mean, no one threw acid on my face as was feared. But Jasmine actually encountered it, because it's not a realistic novel. It's meant to be a fable.

TIR: Can we talk about your upbringing for a bit?
BM: Certainly.

TIR: Is Bengali your native language?
BM: Yes.

TIR: You spoke it before you spoke English?

BM: Yes. I was unilingually Bengali for the first three years of my life. This was before Independence in 1947, the tail end of the British Raj, when the Raj already knew it was crumbling and there were a lot of nationalistic struggles in and around Calcutta.

I went at age three to a school run by Protestant missionaries and that was a sort of bilingual school for elementary schoolchildren. The courses were taught in Bengali, but they introduced English. That's how I knew mat, bat, cat—more complicated sentences, actually—by the time I went to school in England at age eight. And that was the three years in England and Switzerland when I felt I was totally bilingual. I could operate in both languages equally well. And I could speak English like a Cockney when necessary, or establishment English because it was a fancy Sloane Square school that I was sent to. When I came back to India, to Calcutta, to a very special girls' school called Loreto House run by Irish nuns in independent Calcutta, I became less Bengali-speaking.

TIR: Your English had taken over?

BM: Yes.

TIR: Was this a matter of choice, or had you just lost the Bengali by then?

BM: I hadn't lost it, but there was an instilling of value systems, cultural value systems, which now strikes me as so ironic. The nuns were Irish to begin with, but in the outpost, they became more British than the British. And during the schooldays we were taught to devalue—I was going to say sneer at, but that's putting it a little too strongly—Bengali plays, Bengali literature, Bengali music, Bengali anything. And then we went home—I came from a very orthodox, very traditional family—so we had to negotiate in both languages. But, as I'm sure happens with minority children who are being channeled into fancy prep schools and all, it created complications within the Hindi community, within the Indian upper-class community of my generation. It wasn't until I became a graduate student at Baroda (where, if I wanted to get a master's degree in English, I also had to take either a regional master's in a regional Indian language, or in ancient Indian culture) that I really came to know the marvels of Hinduism. No, I knew Bengali, but the culture itself I hadn't really studied formally until then. I just imbibed it by osmosis.

TIR: How did you happen to come to the Iowa Writers' Workshop?

BM: Well, this is the story I've told a lot of newspaper people. My father was a very expansive sort of man, very sociable, and so every foreigner who came through our town—European, American—was always invited to dinner at our house. And in 1960, there was a group from UCLA (Project India or something like that) and there was a young drama professor who was probably the first black man my father had even seen. He came with a couple of his students and my father said to him, "I want this daughter to be a writer. Where do I send her?" And the guy, out of the blue—I mean, he was from California, what did he know?—said, send her to Paul Engle in Ames, Iowa. And my father sent off this letter, just Paul Engle, Ames, Iowa, and the letter did reach Paul, and he said come and I came. The PEOs arranged the scholarship. There was a PEO lady who was in town because her husband was a Fulbright scholar of history, and so she said—she was Paul Engle's neighbor I think—let me write you a letter of recommendation, and so I think that helped me get the scholarship, as well. And then twenty-five years later, in Seattle last month, Clark and I were giving a reading in a bookstore called Elliot Bay, and there in the audience was the lady who wrote the letter of recommendation. Isn't that wonderful?

TIR: How early did you meet each other and become readers for each other? Was that soon after you got here?
CB: I entered in February of '62, she entered in September '61, so I was behind her by a semester. And we married in September '63. We've been married twenty-seven years. So we really had that summer of '63—
BM: —that we didn't show each other our writing.
CB: No. We really didn't read each other's work. I mean, I'd read—
BM: —but only as someone, you know worksheets . . .
CB: Yes, it wasn't really during the workshop years that we read for each other. But immediately afterward, yes.

TIR: So you do read each other's work first now? Are you each other's first readers?
BM: Clark is my first reader. I delay a lot.
CB: There's a lot she hasn't read.
BM: No, the early stories I find so painful, and I know they're autobiographical, so it took me a long time to deal with that. A couple of years ago Clark and I gave a reading in Gainesville, Florida, and he took me to see many of the houses and the areas where he had grown up and where the stories are set. I said, "This doesn't seem so bad, so nightmarish."

TIR: Clark, in *Resident Alien*, you said that your move to Canada in the mid-sixties was "your imperialism, totally." Bharati was against it?

CB: She would never have gone.

BM: I would never have gone. I cried as I was crossing the border.

CB: The tears of Windsor.

BM: Right. America represented a kind of glitziness—as in *Jasmine*—a chance for romantic reincarnation, whereas moving to Canada was like going to England, a step backward to an old world, a hierarchical society.

CB: Whereas Canada for me, is, in some ways, a solution to my identity crisis. America was the place where I knew vast suffering, and vast turmoil and chaos. But in Canada I had a certain place, in a certain world, with a certain identity. I belonged. And I knew I belonged.

BM: That's interesting, because I wanted to get away from that sense of belonging. I didn't want anyone to know where I fit in, so I could be whoever I wanted to be, anywhere, and I could keep moving.

CB: Whereas with my name, Blaise, a French-Canadian name, I can only be French-Canadian. She can only be Bengali Brahmin with her name, but here nobody knows that. And to her, it's something to flee. It gives me the only identity I have.

TIR: So that time in Montreal, then, you said it gave you a sense of identity? Did that catalyze your imagination? Because that's when you started writing a lot of fiction.

CB: Oh, yes. It empowered me. And leaving that world has had a great negative effect.

TIR: And with Bharati it's the opposite effect?

BM: Well, I wouldn't say opposite. In the beginning of our stay in Canada, I wrote *The Tiger's Daughter*, *Wife*, and *Days and Nights in Calcutta*. It was in the mid-seventies, 1973, that we started to see the visible effects of racism. Five thousand Ugandan Asians, with British passports, were allowed into Canada as a favor. The Canadians' favor to the British government. Immediately, there was a backlash against what they called the "visible minority." Even though these people were not on welfare, were in fact professionals and businesspeople, their presence created an atmosphere of hostility into which the person on the street was drawn. I started to notice on a daily basis little incidents in my corner Woolworth's in Montreal, or in hotel lobbies, on buses, things just not being quite right. Then it ballooned into very vicious physical harassment by 1977, 1978.

CB: Especially when we moved to Toronto, where it was centered. Not Montreal.

BM: Where people were being thrown on subway tracks, and things. We had endless—everyone from that era has endless—personal litanies of discrimination.

TIR: You call them "crippling assumptions," somewhere in your work.

BM: About my being taken for a smelly, dark, alien other. Yes. You never got the benefit of the doubt, if you were a Canadian citizen of Indian or South Asian origin.

TIR: Did that eventually catch up and paralyze your work? There's that ten-year gap between *Wife* and *Darkness*.

BM: I think it must have. I was writing a lot of scholarly essays, and I was doing administrative work—director of graduate studies, McGill. Human rights work. But I was so angry all the time, and getting more and more shrill. And becoming almost paranoid, so that any incident of disdain wasn't simply rudeness, casual rudeness of a shop salesperson. It had to be race.

TIR: How about the logistics of doing *The Sorrow and the Terror*?

CB: That was a real schlep. We were living in Astoria, Queens, and we were teaching. Bharati was teaching in Montclair, New Jersey, and I was teaching at Columbia. I would finish on Thursday and immediately get in the car and drive up to Toronto, a twelve-hour drive, and start interviewing various family members, or policemen, or whoever wanted to talk. And each of the families would suggest I talk to Mr. So and So, so that I was generally taping these people—

BM: —and sometimes we would have two and three interviews with the same people. You do so many more interviews than you can really use.

CB: Yes. By then we had eighteen or nineteen various cassettes, and we were, of course, having to read, and in some cases liberate, some secret documents from government files. Fortunately, we had friends well placed in the police, and the International Air Transport branch. So we had all of the standard texts. Enormous stacks of material. And personal memories of the people.

BM: We also went to Vancouver to talk to the alleged extremists.

CB: See, the whole thing started in Vancouver. That's where the Khalistanis are.

BM: And they were very forthcoming. It's like a network, so that once someone has approved of you as journalists, then people who were reluctant to talk in the beginning are all fighting among themselves for access to you.

CB: On the weekends when we didn't get to Canada we stayed in New York. The World Sikh Organization, before they got kicked out, had its major offices in New York. Sikhs were inviting us to dinner parties. So we were going into the wealthy areas of New York and Westchester. And in Brooklyn there was a major trial, the Birk trial, which starts the book off. We were at that trial for almost three months on a daily basis. Then we had to transcribe all those tapes, and then go to Vancouver to talk to all those people, and then go to Ireland to be there for the

tripartite—Irish, Indian, Canadian—unveiling of the memorial. And then talking
to all the Irish, and the hospital people, and the diplomats . . .

BM: The morgue.

CB: Right, the funeral homes, the coroner, Mr. Reardon.

BM: Who was wonderful. The coroner was wonderful.

CB: He would raid the coroner's reports on the bodies. He also gave us the seating
plan on the plane which was how we were able to say who was sitting where.

BM: It was an extraordinary amount of work. And because we were not newspaper journalists, we didn't have an editor saying, "This is not a sexy story. Move
on to Beirut, or something else." So we gave ourselves all the time we needed to
follow our hunches and leads. We discovered a great deal more than the Toronto
Globe and Mail, and the local Canadian papers. Or maybe they didn't want to
discover.

CB: Then we went down to Atlanta, where I was teaching at Emory, and we wrote
that month.

BM: But the logistics. Clark had done some of the interviews, I had done some
myself, and we had done some together. We had an enormous amount of material which we then parcelled off into different parts to do the first draft. Then we
edited. I edited his, he edited mine. Every single word was somehow approved by
both writers. And there were so many legal pressures. Every word had to be gone
over by the Penguin lawyers, and we had to change certain things in order to
make sure we couldn't be sued. There were sources who turned out to be very left
wing, or Communist, who also gave us very good leads in the hope, we realized at
the last minute, of dissemination of Communist—

CB: —because you know, these are all Sikhs. The real bloody battlefield in Punjab is between the left-wing and the right-wing Sikhs. The Khalistanis were
very right-wing, and the first people they went out and killed were Congress
and Communist Sikhs, so you have a lot of Sikhs in Canada who are anti-
Khalistani. They are good, liberal, humane civil libertarians, for the most part,
but they also have their own agenda. They want to destroy Khalistanis, because
of long-standing ideologies. So they were giving us information which all turned
out to be very good. Real inside information. They had it on file.

BM: Even though they were unemployed machinists, and so on, they had
telexes—

CB: —Fax machines in the bedroom, wonderful stuff. You're talkin' real high intrigue here. These are all guys who have been set upon by other Sikhs; they have
skull fractures; they're veterans of being set upon by field hockey sticks.

BM: And so once the book came out, and they discovered we were against terrorism, we were denounced from the pulpit of Sikh temples. It was really very frightening for a whole year. We also detected among the same liberal, middle-class white Canadians a kind of racism against the successful Hindus. So that suddenly the terrorists became the salt-of-the-earth, farmers—

CB: —because the terrorists are illiterate, don't speak English, are dirt poor—

BM: They are not really dirt poor.

CB: They have no graces, they have no sophistication. Whereas the people who were killed were all these suburban PhDs, money managers, who were sort of Tory voters, too. So suddenly the liberals are saying, we are defending all of these upper-middle-class—

BM: —Uppity Wogs!

CB: Uppity Wogs with their half-million dollar homes, and their children who are all getting 98s on their test scores. So we were considered elitists, elitist Hindus, and Americans, supporting those victims against those salt-of-the-earth, poor, ignorant, hardworking, good guys. I mean that is exactly what Sikhs are. They are loyal, hardworking, good guys in a particularly rough way.

TIR: What about writing *Days and Nights in Calcutta*? Did you write each section separately and then exchange them?

BM: No.

CB: Just separately, period.

BM: The contract, in fact, with Doubleday was that we would not discuss our experiences with one another, we wouldn't exchange notes. It was to be kept very separate.

TIR: You had the contract first, then, before you wrote it?

BM: Yes. At the end of the year, after we had our manuscripts, we had to sit with an editor in New York and decide whether to do alternating chapters, how to put it together. And the idea was that it would be alternating chapters.

CB: Originally.

BM: In the original contract, it was called *The Bengal Journals*. It was meant to be simply the record of a day-to-day account of two people going to India— Clark for the first time, me having to reconnect with the family. Then when we started writing, I realized that it wasn't just the account of one year I wanted to talk about, but that the urgency was my life, the life of a particular class at a particular time in Calcutta's history. In many ways I was very much like all my school friends in Loreto House, and in some very basic ways I was different. It was while writing *Days and Nights* (a traumatic book for me to write) that I realized for all the trouble I was going through in Canada, it was still the new world that I wanted to live in, and that the old world was dead for me. Emotionally, and inspirationally. There were just so many aspects of India that I disliked by then. So a lot of my stories since are really about transformation—psychological transformation—especially among women. As opposed to economic transformation.

CB: Which would be more an Asian man's situation. He comes for economic transformation, and he brings a wife who winds up being psychologically changed. This is one of the tragedies you see being played out in all the New Jersey shopping malls these days. The Indian women walking around in the malls with nothing to do all day, while the men are out busily making money. The men have a sense of accomplishment. They have no idea of staying here. The idea is saving money and going. But they don't realize the women have been transformed.

TIR: It comes up in the stories. The men have a sense of "nostalgia."

BM: Yes. It's reactionary. Their image of India is frozen in the year they left the old country. In 1989 they're still thinking of the society being in the late sixties or early seventies. This is causing a lot of conflict within the South Asian immigrant families, especially for the children. In their minds they are Americans. But the parents want them to do well in school, then come back and be culturally perfect Indians.

TIR: How did you structure the screenplay for *Days and Nights*? Did you have the Syd Field "page 23 plot twist" sort of thing?

BM: No, not at all. We came into the screenwriting unprepared, ignorant and innocent. It was meant to be a feature film, so the first thing we learned, in the initial writing of treatment, was that we must not think of these characters as us. So the moment that we gave them separate names, Lela and Colin—it came to me in the middle of the night. I said, "Hey—

CB: —Colin, wake up."

TIR: You gave yourself a lover?

CB: "I know what we need."

BM: Right. I said "what we need" because then I realized that would then be a way of discarding India. By discarding the lover, Lela would be discarding India. The moment we got separate names we could look at the characters and their stories in a certain way. We realized, through trial and error, that in film you have to forget the text, forget the book and start afresh. You have to grind down the characters so that they can come up again. We learned phrases like "the arc," and "payoff," and so on. Every scene had to have some dramatic purpose so it was a very slow process for us. As novelists, we can work very subtly and build in lots of variations, but the director, who really held our hands through the whole process, made us see that you have to prove whatever you want to prove about the characters or situation in one scene. Instead of having it like a novel, with many little scenes and foreshadowings.

Clark often says, "Work in threes." Has he said that in workshop? Here we learned to forget the building up of plot devices and do it in one shot. And we learned how to use minor characters differently. For example, I had a very nice friend, out of many nice friends in *Days and Nights*, that I picked as a foil. But that friend, who in the novel, the text, is an interesting enough character with roundedness of her own, became too rounded a character in the screenplay and the director made me cut her scenes because there shouldn't be that much competition between Lela and the friend. And also, it turned out that some of the gutsy confrontation scenes that we were going to have between lover and husband just weren't necessary in the final version. So finally it's meant to be an "art" movie.

CB: It has kind of a *Rashomon* structure, like the book. You follow a joint part initially, then there's my twenty-five minutes of India through my eyes, and then you turn back to the beginning through her eyes, with a very different texture and feeling, of course, trying to avoid any sort of ennui that can set in when you make transitions. Very quickly, as soon as Lela's part starts off, we had to start feeding fresh, new material to the viewer. Colin's stuff ought to have been interesting because it was fresh and new, the first time you saw it. Lela's stuff has to be even more interesting, in a sense.

BM: Because you already know the story line.

CB: Right, you know the story line, that there's going to be tension and that there's going to be a lover. The viewer knows all these things, yet how do you keep it all interesting? In fiction there is a structure where you can actually give away your whole plot in the very first paragraph and still tell a whole novel, like Ford's *The Good Soldier*. But that is hard to do in film.

BM: And in terms of collaboration, the script-writing meant that it wasn't just Blaise and Mukherjee, but there was a story editor, hired briefly, and the director. The story editor was saying to Clark, "We don't want Colin, who is a writer, educated," because that is going to turn off the audience. We need to see him as a truck driver. We had to fight that kind of detail.

TIR: So what does Colin become?

BM: He remains a writer. And an elitist writer to boot.

CB: We put an Expos cap on him. He walks through his scenes in Calcutta with an Expos cap on.

TIR: Bharati, do you believe in reincarnation?

BM: That's a tough question. This is where the English and British training of my postcolonial years has been very damaging. I've always found it hard to cope with what are the very basic tenets of Hinduism. But yes, I suppose, if you were asking me casually, I would say, as a believing Hindu, yes. But it has been a real struggle. My way of dealing with it has been to say, like in my novel *Jasmine*, we are reinventing ourselves a million times. I like to think that Hinduism is a kind of geophysical vision, rather than a religion, in the conventional Western sense. When we talk about reincarnation it might be as simple as saying that once the body dies and is cremated, the charred bits going up in smoke become something else. They are absorbed in water or are absorbed on the land. I don't know.

TIR: That sense of the metaphysical and the literal seems to run through your work. Do you see immigration as an experience of reincarnation?

BM: Absolutely! I have been murdered and reborn at least three times; the very correct young woman I was trained to be, and was very happy being, is very different from the politicized, shrill, civil rights activist I was in Canada, and from the urgent writer that I have become in the last few years in the United States. I can't stop. It's a compulsive act for me. It's a kind of salvation, and the only thing that prevents me from being a Joyce Carol Oates, and I'm not talking about quality, but just that need to create, is schedule.

TIR: You seem to write about similar characters leading different lives. Does this tie into your idea of reincarnation?

BM: I must be interested in certain types of characters (Maya/Angela/Jasmine) and so they keep recurring to me in different ways. Or what she thinks is the right thing to do has changed as I have changed, as a person.

TIR: Did you plan, for instance, to expand the short story "Jasmine" into the novel?

BM: No. I didn't know when I finished the story that it would become a novel. It was just that this was a character that I fell in love with. This was a character I would have liked to have been. She became a deeper, more complicated character in my head, over the months, so I had to give her a society that was so repressive, traditional, so caste-bound, class-bound, genderist, that she could discard it in ways that a fluid American society could not. I had to find the metaphors and symbolic location for her, and then the right series of events to dramatize the ideas. A novel really gives you so much space to fulfill the character's dreams, so I was able to build in three different sets of responses to being in that position of having to clean up after white people. One is an island woman who came from a middle-class family, just like the Jasmine in the story, but who resents the social demotion. Whereas Jasmine, in the novel, doesn't care about social demotion. And Jasmine in the story also sees all this as opportunity, and I guess part of this is autobiographical impulse.

The kinds of women I write about, and I'm not generalizing about women in the South Asian community here, but the kinds of women who attract me, who intrigue me, are those who are adaptable. We've all been trained to please, been trained to be adaptable as wives, and that adaptability is working to the women's advantage when we come over as immigrants. The males function very well as engineers or doctors or whatever, and they earn good money, but they have locked their hearts against mainstream culture. They seem to be afraid of pollution. Their notion of India seems to have frozen in the year in which they left India, and they don't want to change. Change is frightening; they are like mini-Ayatollahs in some way. They don't want to be part of history and flux. Whereas the women are forced to deal with Americans in the small daily business of life. They have to go to the grocery store and actually interact with real Americans, so they have to attend PTA meetings, be in car pools, and so on. For an Indian woman to learn to drive, put on pants, cash checks, is a big leap. They are, as Clark was saying, exhilarated by that change. They are no longer having to do what mothers-in-law tyrannically forced them to do. And they are free to set up businesses, which they are doing throughout the country. And these new Indian wives are apparently heavy duty users of day care centers, so they can run their boutiques and businesses.

TIR: The men always seem to be translating dollars into rupees, and thinking, "Well, I can always go back and buy this condominium and I'll be safe." But the women seem to be going further and further into America. From *Darkness* through *Middleman* and into *Jasmine*, there seems to be this flight into the American experience.
BM: I don't know if all my women characters make that flight into America successfully though. I think of Maya as a very lost, sad character, who really went out and married a white man and is so well attuned to women intellectuals, her colleagues, but at the same time there is that desire for a wholeness, nostalgia, that India and Indian traditions promised. And so, she's the one who is going out and seeking an advertised, perfect Indian groom, and it works out in strange ways

for her. For her, the turn comes when the guy without arms, the lover without arms, calls her May. Suddenly, she snaps. No, I'm not May, I'm Maya, and people from the outside don't understand me. Whereas a Jasmine, in the short story, is someone who wants to make—is hurtling into an unknown America.

TIR: And bringing turmeric with her. You were talking about what they take. Especially in *Jasmine*, cooking for the community. And she has on sneakers.
BM: Yeah. I want that sense of two-way traffic, that she has transformed America, too, in her ways. Sometimes fatally.

TIR: When you were talking about the psychological transformation that occurred in Indian women, we contrasted it with the nostalgia and the unwillingness to change in Indian males. Were your characters in *Wife* manifesting the darker side of psychological transformation? And what of the more positive benefits of psychological transformation?
BM: I think of myself as a very comic writer and that finally, in a bizarre way, my stuff is meant to be optimistic. Dimple, if she had remained in Calcutta, would have gone into depression, and she would have found a very conventional way out for unhappy Bengali wives—suicide. Bengal has, together with Gujarat, the two highest incidences of wife suicide. But in the United States, she suddenly learns to ask herself "self"-oriented questions. Am I happy? Am I unhappy? And that, to me, is progress. So, instead of committing suicide, turning the society-mandated violence inward, she, in a misguided act, kills the enemy. So, of course, I'm not approving of murder.
CB: But it's a positive act.
BM: It's meant to be a positive act. Self-assertive.

TIR: And in *Jasmine* there is the same turning from suicide.
BM: She comes to commit *suttee*, quite literally, "burn the suit"—which is a symbolic body of the husband—and herself, and then because of the way Half-Face assaults her, she says no. She becomes Kali, the goddess of destruction.

TIR: Right, she cuts her tongue.
BM: Because Kali has her red tongue hanging out. All Bengalis, including me, are Kali worshippers. She is the goddess of destruction, but not in a haphazard, random way. She is a destroyer of evil so that the world can be renewed.

TIR: You were talking earlier about different forms of power, acquiring and expressing power, the different forms of power for women, and it struck me that in your work there is power even in the re-straining and pouring of tea.

BM: Well, certainly all my life, I realize now, all my writing life, I've been interested in the ways people acquire power, exercise power, and even more importantly, I realize, relinquish power or are forced to relinquish power. One of the novels that I started but never finished, is about an Idi Amin kind of figure. The title of this unfinished manuscript is *The Father of His Country*. I guess in different ways I am always trying to find a metaphor, the right character to tell the story, or variants of the story of how to acquire power, exercise it and then have it taken away from you, or voluntarily give it up. For some of the women characters in my stories, fasting is a way of exercising that power. When you have nothing really, withholding food can become the only way to exercise power. What is regarded as passivity, or was regarded in *Wife* as passivity, by feminist *Ms.* magazine-type readers in 1975, was meant to be read very differently. My women are utilizing the tools at hand. I did not build, deliberately build into the center of *Wife*, the *Ms.* magazine way as the "right" way with everyone else defective in their ways of fighting domination, whether it is male or class or poverty. I want to think that power is my central obsession.

TIR: Do you mean that as a positive thing, or sometimes positive?
BM: Sometimes positive, sometimes negative. In "Loose Ends," for example, the Vietnam vet, Jeb Marshall, when he realizes that America isn't the way it used to be, and that he is nobody in the eyes of this young woman who helps run the motel, that is when he snaps, seeing himself as the "other." Seeing himself through the young Indian-American's eyes. So some of it is pleasant, some of it is comic, I like to think, and some of it is, for the women characters usually, heady stuff.

TIR: There seems to be a resistance to a Western idea of feminist thought or philosophy in your work.
BM: Yes, I think a resistance does run through my work. For some non-white, Asian women, our ways of negotiating power are different. There is no reason why we should have to appropriate—wholesale and intact—the white, upper-middle-class women's tools and rhetoric. Especially rhetoric. I think that 1975 was a very dogmatic, prescriptive year in American feminism, and they could not stand any deviations or any rebellions. There were a lot of run-ins. I had a lot of run-ins. I'll give you a small example of the kinds of misinterpretations, in terms of feminism, that my stories go through. "Jasmine," the story in *The Middleman*, ends with young Jasmine, this Caribbean-Indian girl, making love to her white boss on a Turkish rug in front of the fire, in a room which she cleans during the day. Reviewers loved that story generally and loved that scene, but they saw Jasmine as an exploited young woman, and the white male, her employer, as

a sleazy boss who is taking advantage of this poor, innocent, put-upon, au-pair girl. Whereas I meant for Jasmine to know exactly what it is she wants and what she is willing to trade off in order to get what she wants. She is in charge of the situation there. The man has succumbed to lust and to her sexuality. Jasmine is a woman who knows the power, is discovering the power of her sexuality. If there is a villain in that story, it is Lara, the wife, whose feminism and professionalism are built on the backs of underemployed Caribbean or Hispanic au-pair girls. But no one got that, you see. It was meant to be a very political ending.

TIR: The political, or feminist, response to *Wife* in 1975, was pretty harsh, wasn't it?

CB: When *Wife* came out, *Ms.* magazine had a review which said, "Some books can be allowed to die, but others have to be killed." That was their attitude toward *Wife*.

BM: They were really angry.

CB: She's always had a problem with American feminists.

BM: They felt that I was impartially nasty. "Miss Mean-mouth" they called me. But I do disapprove of the imperialism of the feminists, American, and perhaps European feminists, but especially the American feminists of the mid-seventies who felt that they could go to Iran and tell the Iranian women what to do. And you know, I get a lot of mail and some of the mail is from immigrant women, Germans as well as Asians. What they identify with in my book is the characters' being between roles. There isn't a role model for the "Jasmines" or the "Dimples." They have to invent the roles, survive and revise as best as they can. They don't have the consolation of the ready-made, approved, "seal of approval" of the feminist rhetoric. The ones that are being offered by the *Ms.* magazines are not at all appropriate; they just don't work in their lives, they don't ring true for their psychologies. Feminist rhetoric and feminist positions have changed in the eighties, so that it is no longer quite as cantankerous. But I think black women will say the same thing about their relationship to white feminists.

TIR: It has become institutionalized at a certain level. It has become a product.

BM: Consumerized. Jasmine says that she would rather die before she tells the sob sisters about her rape by Half-Face. She doesn't want to talk about the things that are so very painful. So, in a way, I'm building a little joke about the continual self-reflexiveness of the American yuppies. But you see, something has happened. I was now aware of the parallels and contrasts between Dimple and Jasmine. *Wife* was written so long ago and that was a very controversial book. It was a very painful book for me.

TIR: Once it was out?

BM: Yes. The *Village Voice* reviewer loved it, *Ms.* magazine hated it. It was very confusing. I hadn't expected such controversy. *The Tiger's Daughter* was loved by everybody. But I had learned between *Wife* and *Jasmine*, and I had grown enough as a writer, to give the less sympathetic characters good lines too. Or to make the bad guys equally sympathetic or nearly equally sympathetic. So that the feminist, the white feminist, in *Wife*, the one who has false teeth and who takes them off as a gesture, was a very brutally drawn character. Perhaps I have learned to make her a sympathetic character in her own right. A vulnerable person in her own way. Do you understand what I'm saying? It was more clear-cut in my mind who the enemy was in the earlier novel. Now I've sacrificed some of that rage and irony for fuller, more sympathetic, more rounded characters on both sides, both good guys and bad guys.

TIR: Dimple seems much less able to make the leap into America than Jasmine does. Why do you think this is?

CB: Dimple, of course, is a prisoner of the ghetto. She never left that Flushing area in Queens.

BM: And she's educated, so that she's not operating on a purely instinctual level, as Jasmine is. She hasn't—just as I hadn't when I was writing that book—clearly found out what it is that she wants, or what it is she should be doing. So she ends in depression, madness, and murder. The murder at the end of the book is a misguided act. It was intended to be a self-assertive act on her part, but it's very ambiguous. Whereas with Jasmine, a village girl who's used to quite literally fighting the enemy—whether it's a mad dog, or bad guys trying to accost her on the village lane as she's gathering firewood—there's a kind of gutsy village quality.

CB: In Indian terms, she's Punjabi. Dimple's Bengali.

BM: Punjabis are less into reflection. They're more action-oriented. Jasmine is a doer. Whereas Dimple, being a Bengali, and a college girl, is more of a thinker. And those complications brought on by too much thinking get to her. I can see now how, book by book—all this was happening without my noticing at the time—but book by book what I thought of as constituting a novel, or a relationship between author, character, and reader, all this has changed over the years. I have become more American, more North American. So it was very natural for me to write in an omniscient point of view about my characters in *The Tiger's Daughter*. I couldn't think of any other way. It was like *A Passage to India*, or Jane Austen. I was parodying books that people who grew up in the postcolonial days—whether it was in Nigeria, or South Africa, or India—had read. We had a

common storehouse of reading—overseas Cambridge reading—that I was building into the bankruptcy of that material in the book—that culture, that postcolonial, imported, British outpost life. Forster's Mau tank promises regenera-
tion, whereas in *The Tiger's Daughter* it has shrunk to a little swimming pool.
That kind of thing. By the time I came to write *Wife*, I couldn't automatically go
back to omniscience; it didn't feel comfortable. I'm talking about 1972 versus 1975.
Already I had changed so much as a writer that I needed to work with a limited
third-person narrator. I feel that there's a lot more emotional intensity in the relationship between author and character with that technique, and also less irony.
What I've learned to do in *Jasmine*, I want to think, is create a kind of novel form
where there's an intimacy required between reader and author. The reader has to
put together many, many little parts. The author isn't making the big moral judgments. Jasmine isn't necessarily a good person. She's a blackmailer, she's forced
into becoming a murderer. She dumps a good, crippled man who loves her, and
leaves with someone else. So the reader is invited, is seduced—I want to think—
into a kind of relationship with not just the character, but with the author.

TIR: That's a wonderful description. I think people feel that discomfort produced
by the intimacy. They are seduced by Jasmine, and yet they resist her, too, because
she isn't an entirely lovable person.
BM: I think she's lovable, but she's not moral in the conventional sense. She's
moral in her own way. She knows what's right and wrong for her. But she ends up
being a tornado who leaves a lot of debris behind.

TIR: She's remorseless, but there's no malice. At certain points in the book, I felt
that the stories of the American characters were taking over. Jasmine seemed to
have an incredible amount of sympathy for them, particularly the Moffitts.
BM: She's a love goddess, you see. Everyone's in love with her. She doesn't know
how beautiful she is, I think, or what it is that's attractive about her. She's a life
force in some way.

TIR: There's all that "wanting."
BM: Wanting. And believing. She believes that if you want, you might get. That
is what's attractive to me about America. I'm coming out of a culture of despair,
or cynicism. The cool thing to be is a cynic. Jasmine is a woman who hopes, and
what America offers her—in spite of all the bad things that happen to her—is the
hope that things will turn out all right. I think that's probably what's attractive
about her to the Americans around her. Also, she wants to please. That's the feminine quality in her that doesn't jibe with American feminist rhetoric. Yet she's the

one who, unlike (we're talking about the novel now), or far more than Wiley, or any other American woman, manages to leave a futile world, make herself over, pick up men, discard men, and make money. She's an uneducated village girl who is bright and has a career going. She can move on and make a life for herself. So she's an activist—or a woman of action—who ends up being far more feminist than the women on Claremont Avenue who talk about feminism.

TIR: Jasmine's caring seems to come from her sense of "wanting." She says, "In America, everything is in motion." But really, Jasmine's the one who is in motion. Bud is stuck. Darryl's stuck. She uproots her lover, splitting up the Moffitt family. She's the one who is the vortex, the one causing all the motion. That sense of love and compassion seems to come from this. She's in love with the country, and, in a way, she's revitalizing it, if it allows itself to be revitalized.
BM: Yeah, I would agree wholeheartedly with that. That "I want, I want." But for a village girl coming from a nothing family, from a nothing place, the audacity to even say "I want" is the biggest rebellion possible. I wanted it not to be simply grabbing, but revolution.

TIR: She says, "To want English was to want more than you had been given at birth. It was to want the world."
BM: Language. You had to learn to negotiate in the language of the country you had adopted. I really do feel that that's very much a part of the acquisition of power. I don't want to get into the language debates going on in the U.S., especially California. I understand why most liberal activists are for multiculturalism, multilingual policies in schools, but if it is at the cost of creating ghettoes, if it is at the cost of keeping Jasmines locked in their own ghettoes within America, then I think that's a sad and wasted effort on the part of the activists.

TIR: The Jasmine character in the novel seems to be more self-aware, and less materialistic, than her predecessors.
BM: It was meant to be a lighter story. Then things happened I didn't expect. But I wanted to write about being Indian, third-generation, in a fluid society of the Americas. Where you may be technically a Brahmin, or you may be technically a Hindu, but you don't know anything about Hinduism. You've lost whatever that heritage was, but you hang on to certain antique words, phrases, and classifications. I wanted that sense of both openness and confusion of the minorities in the Caribbean. I wanted a new world that was totally multicultural. And I very deliberately set the story in V. S. Naipaul's birthplace because it was my "in" joke, challenging, if you like, Naipaul's thesis of tragedy being geographical. Naipaul's

fiction seems to suggest that if you are born far from the center of the universe, you are doomed to an incomplete and worthless little life. You are bound to be, if you're born like a Jasmine, an Indian in the Caribbean, a comic character, you come to nothing. So I wanted to say, "Hey, look at Jasmine. She's smart, and desirous, and ambitious enough to make something of her life."

TIR: There seems to be a move toward an acceptance of the inevitability of violence in your later work. We go from hesitancy in *Wife* to the resolute action in *Jasmine*.

BM: It's a natural part by then. Having written the book on the Air India terrorism, I realized how pervasive violence is in this country. It's just under the skin of real life. It doesn't seem exotic, or external, anymore. I was coy, or decorous, a person of great decorum, when I was writing *The Tiger's Daughter*. Should I allow the main character in the novel to be deflowered, I had to ask myself. I absolutely didn't want that. And Clark said, when I showed him my manuscript, "The novel demands it, and you have to go through with it." And I thought, Oh, my God. Even though it's not autobiographical, people are going to assume that the same thing happened to me. It's that kind of violence that I was reluctant to write of in the early books.

CB: I think it raises an important question about how fiction writers can use their nonfiction to energize their vision, periodically. Writing *Days and Nights* and *The Sorrow and the Terror* have been very important to our fiction.

BM: Yes. "The Management of Grief" comes straight out of that later book. But I've gotten so much flak from some reviewers about the terrorism in *Jasmine*, with Suki turning up in New York.

TIR: You mean the implausibility of them being here?

BM: Yes. That's why I wish American publishers had published *The Sorrow and the Terror*. They would have known then about the network, how many Khalistani cells are operating here.

CB: They're picked up in Queens, they're picked up in New Jersey.

TIR: In *Jasmine*, Bud says, as he and Jasmine pass an abandoned building, "I financed that place when the rate was such and such." And at the same time, Jasmine is thinking that a terrorist cell might be using it for other purposes.

BM: Exactly.

TIR: But nobody will publish *The Sorrow and the Terror* in the United States?

BM: No, because there were no American victims on that flight. I want that in the interview, please. That American publishers have rejected that book because they have asked again and again if there were any American citizens involved.

TIR: With *Darkness* it was the same thing?

BM: It went out of print so fast. I think it's an important book, certainly important for me. The American publishers who were shown it didn't want to publish it. Their response was, who was going to read about immigrants? That was a bad word. The "I" word was a bad word in 1984–85. The book came out in 1985. So only about six hundred copies were imported into the U.S. by the Penguin office in New York, and it did extremely well because it was used in courses. The *New York Times* did a marvelous review, so the book had a secret cult life. But, at the time, people did not want to know about this particular minority. There were fashionable minorities, and unfashionable minorities. So *Darkness* disappeared kind of fast. It's out of print in the States, as are all the earlier books. But they're being reissued.

TIR: There is a sense of great love in your later works, for the characters and for the landscape, the New World.

BM: That happened somewhere between *Darkness* and *The Middleman. Darkness* was a breakthrough book in the sense that I was writing about changes among the immigrants. It was still darkness, after all, and I was coming out of that whole Canadian mess. I want to think that writing that book was invigorating for me. But for many of the characters, things didn't work out when they transplanted themselves into a new culture. But by the time I came to write *The Middleman,* I was exhilarated, my vision was more optimistic. I knew that I was finally where I wanted to be. And though I was moving in degrees of acculturation, the overall authorial vision is, I hope, consistent.

Let me get back to the sense of the novel for a moment. Because my characters have a nineteenth-century density to their lives, my writing has to show the fullness of those lives. But I'm an American writer, writing in the late 1980s. So I had to find a new form, as well as new sentences, to create these very un-American characters, and to fuse them with my own pre-American sense of what constituted a full life. So the novels are structured—or *Jasmine* is structured—in very short takes. I've tried to cram in a sense of the entire world, whether it's a little village in Punjab, or boats coming off the coast of Ecuador—which is a big center for circuitous Indian immigration. New York, the Midwest, California—they're all in the book because that's the way our lives are constantly being shuttled around. I've exchanged so many cultures, so many citizenships in twenty-five

years, but still, this action has to be very compressed because I don't want to
write a Thackerian or Dickensian novel. Then I would be mimicking the British form. I'm interested in finding the right form for me and my characters,
who are the kinds of Americans who haven't been written about before. So the
characters of, say, an Ann Beattie are significantly different from mine because
they've not been dislocated in such severe and traumatic ways. An oceanic or social view rarely creeps into contemporary American fiction. It is simply—well, not
simply, predominantly—fiction about personal relationships. Even someone like
Raymond Carver, whose work I admire very, very much, and whose stories are
obviously meant to be tragic, is talking about small disappointments. Whereas
in talking about Jasmine's life, I'm really talking about the history of current
America too. So a sentence about a man in Osage beating his wife with a spade
and hanging himself later is as important as Jasmine's story. People like me, because we've come from the Third World, have a very different notion of what
constitutes the novel. A social and political vision is an integral part of writing a
novel, of being a novelist. Whereas I think for contemporary American writers,
fiction exists only in a vacuum of personal relationships.

TIR: How does your work begin to happen for you?
BM: When the writing is going well, the characters take over, and they dictate
what is going to happen to them in the scene. In "Buried Lives," for instance, I
thought, when I started out, that the Sri Lankan, Tamil, was going to die off the
coast of Nova Scotia. There had been two boatloads of refugees who had been
put by unscrupulous captains into boats which sank there. They just deserted
them when they saw the Coast Guard coming. So I assumed that this would be
how this man would end in my story. But the guy wouldn't get on the boat. He
found ways of hanging around, staying on in Germany. Then he found a girlfriend and she gave him his necessary visa papers. So I really do hear a voice when
things are going well. Then I read something about athletes being "in the zone."
And I said, "My God, that's really what's happening in the best of my work." I immediately identified with that idea. I find that I throw away the stuff I've written when I have not entered "the zone." I am like a medium. I am both inside and
outside the character. I'm hearing this voice that's writing itself. The scenes work
themselves out, and each project has its own momentum. I am forced to write so
fast, and with such intensity, because it's always during vacations. I'm working
twenty-one-hour days with everything bubbling in my head. So in the middle of
the night these things are working themselves out. Though I may have gotten up
out of my chair.

TIR: During that time you're sensitive to absorbing things, like photographs?
BM: Yes. Everything works its way in. And I don't waste, it seems. Any overheard conversations, any faces seen—I never know when they're going to work their way into my fiction. I don't keep notebooks, but these details just pop up in the work.

TIR: The book becomes like a magnet?
BM: Yes. Maybe that's exactly what I've been saying about how scraps of conversation during certain periods will feed themselves into the book. It all seems appropriate; I know how to use it all. Or every face will suggest a compulsive story.

TIR: Earlier in your career you talked about "voice" being your prime aesthetic.
BM: Finding the right voice, right. That's something that I came to as a result of talking to, or listening to, Clark. The sense of voice being the way one controls fiction. Voice can be the sum total of every artistic trick in your bag. It's how to use texture, how to use metaphor, how to choose the right point of view, the point of view character, and therefore the idioms, the language. Knowing when to withhold information, when to disclose, etc. Now I realize that in addition to that, voice, for me, is the physical, or actual, hearing of the main character speak. The rest happens automatically. It is all happening without my having to think about it.

TIR: What about essay writing? Is "the zone" involved in that kind of writing, too?
BM: No. I know when I'm doing well, and when the ideas are simply not clear. But it's not the same physiological change that happens to me when I'm writing fiction that I'm really satisfied with. Essays seem to me to be coming out of a different part of my brain. It's not that same internal compulsion. I won't take on a subject that doesn't interest me. I will only do it if I feel I have a special angle on it, and the subject matter is sufficiently interesting to me. I don't come in with preconceived notions of what I'm going to find. But it's a very different kind of writing. It's Mukherjee writing, and Mukherjee assessing and analyzing, rather than something else. I don't have that intermediary. I haven't become someone else. I must not become someone else when I'm writing an essay. I think Clark is such a good essay writer. I've learned a lot from reading his essays. And *Resident Alien* seems to me such a new concept for a book. You have the autobiographical essays, and then the inventions of autobiography. I find it very hard to write autobiography. I'm supposed to write a piece for a place that Clark did an autobiographical piece for. And I said yes when they asked me, and I just can't seem to sit down and write about myself. I've done many essays since and I've said yes to

doing an essay on the art of healing, but to write about myself without the disguises . . . I don't know.

TIR: Do you work on a word processor?
BM: Yes. "Angela" was done on an IBM Selectric. "The Middleman" and *Jasmine* were done on the screen. But even when I'm on the typewriter, I don't know how stories are going to turn out. In *Jasmine*, for example, I didn't know she was going to leave Bud at the end of the novel. She just up and went! Because she got bored with the situation. Not bored. She felt it was a regression, like going back to village life, a life of duty and devotion, to stay on caring for this crippled fellow. The frontier was out there, beckoning. She just left. Then I had to beef up Taylor in the second rewrite, in order to justify her leaving. Plus make Karen, who had been hanging around anyway, be there to look after Bud.

TIR: I didn't really look at it that way. I thought she was going after her adopted son.
BM: Yes, that too.
CB: That was part of the replotting, too, to put him out there in California.
BM: What I had wanted was the sense of reconstituting new American families, so that Bud and Jasmine and Yogi make up one kind of family, but it gets wilder and wackier in that last scene where Jasmine is pregnant by Bud, yet she's going off with Taylor, and the adopted Duff, to link up with Yogi and his sister.

TIR: Maxine Hong Kingston has talked about our needing a "global novel." Do you see your fiction going that way?
BM: Maybe fiction is going that way, but I would never start out with an agenda that I must sit down and write a "global novel." A character has to come to me urgently—a scene, a sentence. The fiction itself must seem urgent to me. I don't like to have the social prescription, or the political prescription, that I am then trying to flesh out. I think there's a propaganda novel or thesis novel that can be important, but the concept strikes me as necessarily lacking life. It doesn't come from the guts, the heart, of the writer. And I don't see at all why good fiction has to be global fiction. It's the lot of some writers, who are—because of the accidents of history—forced to be on the move. Then there are the Richard Fords and the Russell Banks who may be writing of small town America, but with great gifts, and great compassion. It's making life important, making a single life important, rather than having to have a prescription for the global ills which afflict us.

Naming Female Multiplicity:
An Interview with Bharati Mukherjee
Francisco Collado Rodríguez / 1994

From *Atlantis*, 17:1–2 (May–November 1995), 293–306. © 1995 by *Atlantis*. Reprinted with the permission of the editor.

Q. Critical readers of your works may perceive that you are very fond of using an underpinning current of symbolism, however the quality of the prose that you frequently use in your creative writing looks very realistic. Do you think that realistic prose, even if we are talking here only of an apparent realism, is still the best way for a writer to denounce the living conditions of a—race or gender— minority and to encourage social advances?

A. Well, I think that I'm divided in my personality. There is a part of me that is the writer who is thinking of finding the most appropriate narrative strategies for that story or that character . . . but then there is also another part of me that is a politicized citizen who cares very much about carrying out a *mission*, about social reform. However, when I am writing novels, while my mission has social and political emphasis, I really make the decisions about sentences, about language, according to what the story means or the way this or that character would think, and the word that I use for this is *voice*. I may be making many beginnings to a story but I know it doesn't feel right, so as a fiction writer I know that while the *message* is right, aesthetically the story is not fixed until I can hear the character speak, until I've entered into the skin of the character, so that those language decisions are being directed not because I want to communicate my social message straight away but because it feels right, because I think: "this is how the character would speak." Now, having said that and coming back to your question, I also do favor directness, clarity to the obfuscation of experimental art for art's sake, and I think this goes back to the core of my colonial damage, to my access into English language and colonialism: I was brought up in independent India; however I was taught to valorize nineteenth-century well-formulated British clauses and phrase making, you know, that artificial British wit and smoothness . . . and this has been a very empowering experience for me. I wanted to get rid of all that and write with energy and simplicity, sometimes even deliberately using all the crudity of American speech. This has been my anti-colonial effort, a way to express decolonization.

Q. I asked you this question because, as you know, there are many contemporary minority writers who are very fond of denouncing the social conditions of their group in realistic terms. However you seem to have moved from this tendency in your latest novel . . .

A. Yes. My first novel, *The Tiger's Daughter* [1972, New York: Fawcett Crest]— that probably isn't available in Spain—is very *English*, because when I wrote it I was still an expatriate, a postcolonial Indian writer living in the United States. So this novel is very *Janeaustenian*, and what I thought to be the natural easy point of view that constitutes the story is again very British, still Edwardian in a sense: the point of view in my novel was omniscient in a moment in which no one else among my writer friends in the United States were using this omniscient point of view in their books. It seemed so European, bourgeois, and crazy. However, I still thought this was the natural thing to be done; the world was still perfectly ordered for me: here are the gods, here are the demons, here are people; good guys and bad guys doing their things. I cannot tell you how terribly mellifluous and ordered my sentences are in this first novel but I can't and don't want to do that anymore.

Q. And I assume that this is the reason why you started to move to more complex technical grounds. In effect, in later books your narrators began to be also the protagonists or participants in the stories they narrated. However, more recently you built up the technical structure of *The Holder of the World* in which a historical personage is virtually re-created in the mind of the narrator while two different historical periods start to inform each other. And, still related to this issue of the technical development in your narrative, can you mention the names of any writers who may have been influential in your own progress as a novelist?

A. First of all, I'll tell you something: Ideologically I despise the idea of having mentors because I'm continuously rebelling against a culture that has encouraged women—and everybody else, but particularly women—to be very pliant to gurus, to mentor/disciple relationships, so my rebellion against this has led me to discourage mentors, but there are people who don't write anything like me who, however, might have exerted some indirect influence on me. I have read them at just the right time and thought then that I have understood something not only about their work but also about how to write mine, and—weirdly enough—I am referring here to very different writers, such as Flannery O'Connor with her dramatizing of morality, where the punishments are very disproportional to the actual crimes. Anton Chekhov was also very important to me at one time, because I

saw in my earlier years the passing of my aristocratic way of life in Calcutta with
the coming in of the Communist Government, as being reflected in Chekhov's
literary presentation of a decadent Russian society. And Bernard Malamud was
like a second father to [my husband] Clark and me: he was Clark's teacher and
when I got married that event also meant our friendship. I loved his writing but
I didn't think it had anything to do with my own literary vision, with my world,
until I had a very low moment in my life, in 1984. I had then very little money left
because of a racist wave in Canada, I was not allowed there any more and legally I
could not even have a job; and I was sitting in the kitchen reading Bernard Malamud's *Selected Stories* [1983, New York: Farrar, Straus & Giroux] that the writer
had sent me himself and suddenly, out of my self-despair, I said, "My God, he
is writing about the Jewish community, about their attempts to accommodate
to and assimilate American culture or about their failing to do so, which is precisely what I want to write about my own community." And that was my inspiration, in a way, for *Darkness* [1985, Markham: Penguin Books], my first collection
of stories.

Q. But has not your writing been also affected by the Writers' Workshop and by
your direct acquaintance with other writers and their opinions about literature?
A. Yes, of course I have the experience of the Writers' Workshop in Iowa and so,
in a sense, I know almost every American writer of my age group because in the
1960s, in the early 1960s especially, the Writers' Workshop was the only place in
the United States where creative writers could keep up, and that meant for us the
best aspect of the Workshop: the creation of a community of writers.

Q. In a sense my next question also deals with your studies at the university level:
often your readers may think that especially your narrators sound very "poststructuralist." Their minds, as reflected in their words, seem to be specifically
oriented towards a poststructuralist understanding of life: to what extent do you
think that your ample university studies have affected Bharati Mukherjee the
Bengali woman who went to America and became a creative writer?
A. I try to keep both my personalities—my writing persona and my academic
persona—very separate, to the extent that as a writer I live in a funky apartment
in San Francisco, but then I also have a rented apartment in Berkeley where I am
a *Professor* [laugh]. When I am writing I am not really thinking of literary theory
at all, but then I'm a scholar and so I also have that love of getting to know the
raw material for my stories, of getting my hands on every bit of data that I can
find on the subject matter when writing; that is a kind of additive pleasure for me
to the extent that I put a huge amount of energy in research, in acquiring all the

information that otherwise I may not even need at all . . . on shipping routes, or the diaries of seventeenth-century European traders and travelers to India. Take the case of Captain Kidd, for instance: he comes in *The Holder of the World* only for two sentences, but I have read almost every book available on him. I could now write one full novel only about Captain Kidd!

Q. It sounds as if it is true what your narrator says in the novel: you, the same as Beigh, have read about five hundred books in order to write this novel . . .
A. O yes, at least! So I would not like to talk in terms of literary theory. I think it can be very damaging for creative writing. Only second-rate fiction is produced by those who write propaganda or thesis novels . . .

Q. Do you also include here the novels of literary theorists such as John Barth or Raymond Federman?
A. No, no, by no means. I am talking about minority groups who meet to, let's say, create model characters and write texts to be taught in different ethnic studies programs. This is what happens with literary theorists like bell hooks, the African-American critic that I have referred to a couple of times in my lecture yesterday. She and other minority critics—like Gayatri Spivak—would say that the role of criticism, or what bell hooks describes as "gestures of defiance," and also all writing by minorities should be used to valorize minority characters and to break down the hegemonic social structure, which means that all white characters—as representative of the dominant culture—*have to* be bad; and when this type of critics are teaching texts, they are looking not at the novelist's novel but only for their own criteria to be met in such academic courses; they are looking for texts to be used in courses where they can make the political and ethnic argumentation. The result is that too many writers are producing propaganda novels just for this kind of readership. That's what I think is very harmful for fiction.

Q. However, social commitment is also quite clear in your books. Connecting this issue with my previous question about the impact of literary criticism in your creative writing: you are also very fond of offering both your protagonists and your readers a web of binary oppositions; your characters frequently have to choose one way or another. This is not exactly what I would qualify as *applied deconstruction*, but perhaps it shows that you already have a worldview that, to a certain extent, coincides with some postulates of poststructuralist discourse . . .
A. Yes, it could very well be so. I'm not thinking consciously about it, though. What I think when I'm writing is that a good story requires a conflict. Take, for

instance, what we may have in the structure of a short-story: you begin on a day
when things seem to be very normal for your character but really, unconsciously
perhaps, there is always a little *vehicle*; the character may not know it but then
suddenly there is a wake-up call from the unconscious and that marks the beginning of the conflict. Then, the character has to choose between temptation
or morality, and either choice will be able to resolve the trial . . . so I'm thinking
like a dramatist: there is no story, really, it's just another day, and then the conflict
appears when you order the banality of daily sequences.

Q. Some of your narrators are also the protagonists in the stories that they nar-
rate but when we come to your latest novel, *The Holder of the World*, readers have
to cope with a different, more innovative technique: here you have chosen a narrator who is external to the story she is telling and who actually tries to build up
or re-create a sort of historical romance that at times may also remind the reader
of Hawthorne's masterpiece *The Scarlet Letter* [1850; Harmondsworth: Penguin,
1978]. Were you aware when writing this novel of the existence of a contemporary
literary trend in which historical information goes hand in hand with the imple-
mentation of metafictional devices that tend to undermine the reader's belief in
historical truth? I am referring here to the type of fiction being written by novelists like Doctorow or even Pynchon, a writer who is also mentioned in your latest book.
A. I have enjoyed all Pynchon's writings very much—I'm not talking about
Vineland [1990, London: Secker & Warburg], however—and I have also admired Doctorow's books, but I think that these works were not in my mind
when I started my research for *The Holder of the World*. I became interested in
seventeenth-century European travelers: Italian, French, English in—for them—
a very alien country, India, where they had to survive this alien condition; and
so I went to these seventeenth-century travel documents, memoirs, and trading journals, because I thought of these travelers as people like me or like characters in, let's say, *The Middleman and Other Stories*, making their living in rather
frightening or perilous surroundings. So it was not that I wanted to write about
history; I was trying to do the reverse. History was my second subject at the university; if I had not got my Ph.D. in English I would have done it in history, but
then I loved the story part of history. When I read travel documents, I was more
interested in the way how travelers see an alien country, how they represent that
country, meaning how they make it familiar by saying things like "O, it looks
like Devon," even if they are somewhere in India or Dubai; or, on the other hand,
there are also those travelers who in their reports turn the natives into headless

men or any sort of monsters . . . so, I became interested in the representation of the other. I started the novel mainly because of two germs. One was Hawthorne's *The Scarlet Letter*, a novel that I had to read for my Ph.D. and also for my teaching classes and that has always been a favorite book of mine. I was always more interested in Pearl, the "legacy of passion," than in Hester but then I also felt that the end of the book had also been subject to a Eurocentered decision on the part of some critics who simply assume that Pearl Prynne has married an European count and has gone to Europe after the events told in the story. They have assumed this because at the end of the book Pearl is sending to her Puritan mother in colonial Massachusetts all these very exotic presents with heraldic crests that could not be decoded.[1] Now, I thought that these heraldic crests should have been decoded if they were European, and then the more documents I read, the more I realized how much trading there was for the importation of objects, ideas, even people—freaks especially—from the Coromandel Coast in India. So Pearl Prynne was one of the inspirations for my book.[2] But then I also saw a painting when I was very much involved in the research for the novel. I saw a miniature painting at Sotheby's in New York that was entitled *An European Woman in Emperor Aurangzeb's Court*, and she was a woman in a splendid court heroine outfit, you know, like a princess. At that moment I felt that I had my character. Originally, however, the novel was just about this character, Hannah Easton, but as somebody writing in the 1990s I soon became bored creating a straight historical novel, and it wasn't until suddenly [narrator] Beigh Masters, who has my initials, popped into my head with her boyfriend from MIT—as would a lot of young American women in the Harvard or Cambridge area [laugh]—that I was able to possess the novel: it became not a historical novel but *my* novel. So what I'm saying is that, as an individual, I don't really see the point in writing a historical novel that is simply a passive retrieval of past data. I need to experience history and have my readers experience history rather than be told historical information. On top of that, I've always been interested in technology and science as a way of interpreting the world, as an access to it, and I think—whether it's chaos theory or Hindu

---

1. "Letters came, with armorial seals upon them, though of bearings unknown to English heraldry. In the cottage there were articles of comfort and luxury, such as Hester never cared to use, but which only wealth could have purchased, and affection have imagined for her" (Hawthorne 1978, 274).

2. The Grand Mughal calls protagonist Hannah "Precious-as-Pearl, the Healer of the World," and by the end of the novel we are informed that, "She wasn't Hannah anymore; she was Mukta, Bhagmati's world for 'pearl.' And she gave Bhagmati a new name: Hester, after the friend she had lost. *The friend that had indirectly brought her to the Coromandel Coast*" (Mukherjee 1993, 271; my emphasis).

beliefs—that the kind of technology I mention in the novel [computerized virtual reality] is complementary to art rather than the enemy of art.

Q. From your own words I also imply that *The Holder of the World* is for you a book that demands a reader who has to be rather perceptive. In the pages of this novel you are frequently offering little clues for the reader to decode your creative building: your initials in the narrator's name, the custom house, Pearl, Chief Factor Prynne . . .

A. Yes, there are little nuggets, many secret cues and clues so that, for instance, scholars of Puritan America—whether we consider here literature or American studies—may find many references to historical figures and skirmishes during the [King Philip's] Indian wars of 1675 and 1676, when the Indian leader Metacomet rebelled against the English colonists. At the time, as a result of these wars a literary trend started to become very popular in America, the "captivity narrative": you may have heard of one of the writings that I mention in my novel, the *Narrative of the Captivity and Restoration of Mrs. Mary Rowlandson* [1682; C. H. Lincoln, ed., New York: Barnes and Noble, 1952], in which this woman recounts what happened to her in that war; her book was something like our bestsellers are now, and I decided to also introduce some elements of this minor genre in my novel, including Hannah being taken captive. But I had to redo all this. I mean, as a woman writing in the 1990s and as a feminist born in India I had to reject the Sita model but then I also had to use it for Hannah's captivity narrative [Mukherjee 1993, 173–76]. All this came out by research; but I also introduced the kidnapping of Bhagmati, something similar to what happened very often in India; girls who, like Bhagmati, were kidnapped could not be taken back by their Hindu families because they had lost caste. In this way, I worked in the narrative of the Puritan American literary tradition, and I worked it together with many other references, such as the fate of pirate William Kidd or the episode of Peter the Great freeing slaves; I put them together into one fabric . . . I remember that I started reading about a Mughal Emperor who lived in the sixteenth-century and who seemed to be quite a nice person, and then I read on and on until I found his descendant, his great-grandson Emperor Aurangzeb who fitted in all I wanted to say in the novel: I was working on religious fundamentalists, starting with the American Puritans on the one hand, and then I continued with Muslim fundamentalists on the other, people such as Aurangzeb who really devastated temples and charged Hindus with heavy taxes. Finally, I also moved to Hindu fundamentalism: that's my Raja character, Jadav Singh, who is modeled a little bit—I mean, "imagined upon"—a guerrilla Hindu leader who was also like a "desert rat," you know, the name the Muslims give the Raja in my book.

Q. We may turn now to some other recurrent elements that at times can also be noticed in your narrative. In *The Middleman*, for instance, your readers may have the impression that the only value that we can find in the contemporary "American dream" is money and the necessity to possess more and more things. Money seems to be the only available replacement for traditional hierarchic societies, such as the Hindu. Is money really the only way to free the emigrants from the traditional bonds of a caste-oriented society?

A. I see, a very interesting question somehow related to the idea of contemporary American imperialism. However, in *The Middleman* I was doing this critique less consciously. I was not yet thinking of the American dream also as temptation and as empowerment but then I came to *The Holder of the World*, having written *Jasmine* [1989, New York: Fawcett Crest] in between, and I was *showing*—because each novel is, in a sense, covered autobiography, or disclosure of my own psychological state—that other America that embodies the will to transform. In Hannah you see the benevolent side; she goes as far as her imagination will take her and she has a tendency to follow her impulses; but then there is the other side as reflected in the white traders who try to imperialize; this dark side of the American will is to transform the *other*, to control the *other*, actually this shows up even in a character like Hannah who thinks that she can stop the centuries-long war between Muslims and Hindus. But, is this already showing in *The Middleman*? I don't know. I think this is where scholars and reviewers are able to detect things that the writer in the process of creating a novel did not think about.

Q. Going on, then, to another of those aspects that we may sometimes perceive in your writings from our outside position, I have the impression that sometimes your female protagonist—let's think of Jasmine, for instance—is able to forsake husband or lover to move on and improve her living conditions. Is it simply a need to defend herself or it is that perhaps you think that human beings are *essentially* selfish creatures?

A. Well, when writing a novel things seem to come "from the guts" although I hope intelligence is integrated somehow in the process [laugh], and when thinking, in this sense, about both Jasmine and Hannah I saw both of them as pioneers. Both characters are a little ahead of their time, they are pushing back the frontier. Now, I've always felt that there is a lot of hardness and greed in pioneers, an aspect that American literature has usually forgotten or romanticized. Traditionally writers have put a little sheen of civility for all those white pioneers who have dispossessed the Indian nations, and who have also withstood a lot of physical obstacles. They had a kind of iron will, they were capable of hardness and cruelty and so I also wanted to show in my characters that element that to be a pioneer also requires: some selfishness, the self-centredness that appears in a survivalist mentality. And what to say about the males? I grew up in a culture where women didn't see men as the enemy, not necessarily. However, women had to find alternate ways of dominating, of controlling, of clearing the obstacles so, in a sense, my female characters are also part of a debate with doctrinaire American feminists who did a lot of talking, especially in the mid 1970s, who were excellent at discourse but who got very little done compared to the Third World feminists. This is also my private battle; I had a long-running feud in the mid 1970s with these people—and that includes a famous magazine—because of my novel *Wife* [1975, New York: Fawcett Crest], in which I was asking—ahead of my time in USA—white American women not to dictate to us, minority women, how to be free: all that looking at our bodies in the mirror to bring about consciousness raising . . . such things may be fine for middle-class white suburbanized women who do not need to get water from the well but they would not work for us.

Q. In a sense related to your words, the reader may sometimes notice that some of your female characters—who have frequently been abused or even attacked by men—are also able to react using sex as a weapon against male dominance. Is sex really an effective female tool for liberation.
A. Sex as empowerment, yes. You see, I was brought up in a society that had taken in all the prudery of Victorian and Edwardian England and so we always had to read, for instance, expurgated editions of Shakespeare's; or I could never say the word "sex." I would blush if I had to read the word "love" in a poem, and I really didn't know—even though a host of population in urban places like Calcutta are naked street people!—, we women didn't know what a male body looked like. I never knew until I got married, I am talking here about a cultural willful ignorance of sex. In that patriarchal society an enormous emphasis was put on women's chastity; and so for my characters liberation is sometimes expressed in being able to take pleasure in sex, sexuality as pleasure rather than as dutiful procreation. This often leads my female characters into trouble; for these women sex is a way of taking charge of their own bodies and of being accounted for, which leads them into trouble with religious fundamentalists precisely because my women use their sexuality or enjoyment of sex as a metaphor for liberation.

Q. Let us move now to more scientific grounds. Yesterday in your lecture—as well as in your words now—you insisted on the necessity to build what you denominate as a "we-community." However, in your narratives you abundantly use the metaphor of chaos theory to refer to the human condition; fractals, duality, bifurcation points where one must select one of the possible choices . . . ultimately, in your books your readers may have to face that other metaphoric duality where chaos theory also has to stop: fate vs. freedom. Even if we try to reproduce and anticipate the workings of the system by means of virtual reality, is there really any way out of this ultimate dilemma?

A. All right. Let me very briefly give you some of my notions about the metaphorization of chaos theory in my books. I think that I'm coming to this opposite structuring of things from different platforms that are, however, central to my own experiences. One is that as a Hindu I see salvation as the fusion of opposites; there is no good and devil, they are only seen different when you are under illusions and then they become the same thing. There is no differentiation between snake, human, and god, they are just appearance. So for me it is the fusion of opposites that constitutes the answer. There is no sin but there is the natural venom in the snake: there is the Christian idea of the serpent as evil, but the real job of the god or hero, of the agent of goodness is to neutralize the venom; not to kill the snake but simply to put it where it cannot harm the rest. Now, about the duality fate vs. freedom I have to say that it was something that I had to work through in every single thing I have Jasmine say, and what I have Jasmine say is very much what I think every day: I don't know what the answer is, which means that I must treat every moment with reverence. Then, about my use of chaos theory I must say that I have come to it after the Hindu notion; suddenly I found that these scientific theories are saying what I've always believed. In this way, these theories became very useful metaphors for ordering my own beliefs: with them I can claim scientific validity to what I have done; they also make me see Hindu philosophy in a new way, not as religion but as geophysical explication.

Q. Is this new scientific enterprise then a holy quest, as one of your characters in *The Middleman* suggests when commenting on fractal geometry?

A. Yes, the quest is one of explaining things, and to do that science is not an enemy but an alternate way that, in this case, seems to coincide to a large extent with philosophy or religion.

Q. What is your position in this metaphoric understanding of life? Behind all the cultural variety and multiplicity of life, behind all the random events and options that you represent in your books is there really an underpinning pattern— as chaos theorists assume—or is it simply wishful thinking and human necessity to produce a totalizing understanding of life?

A. No, I believe there is an underpinning structure but not in a stable sense: my key phrase here—also related to chaos theory—would be *dynamic destiny*. You are given choices but you have to cope with the choice. The same as happens with the Christian parables, in India we also have Ramic teachings, thousands of examples explaining, for instance, how two people may come across a pot of gold; one of them will kick the pot and follow his path, the other will pick it up and make himself a decent home. The pot of gold being at your feet is part of your destiny, but your decision about it is dynamic destiny, it is not determinism.

Q. I think that my last question might also be related to your apparent poststructuralist and scientific understanding of life: it concerns the power of names to build up or to be built up in society. Your female characters, especially Jasmine and Hannah, always have to or are forced to change their names, something that usually happens on account of the males they are living with. However Bharati Mukherjee the writer has not changed her name despite her married condition, something rather surprising for an Indian-American woman. Where is the power of naming for you? Does naming produce social reality?

A. This is something related, once again, to my upbringing. In Bengal every male or female has one nonsense name called *hoshmi* which is the name for daily use among your family members and intimates; I also have a *hoshmi* name and it doesn't mean anything, it's just silly nonsense syllables. And then we also have a formal name; in my case, for instance, Bharati means "goddess of learning." So I am both people: I can relax when I am called by my familiar name, but I have to be dignified when I am Bharati. This explains why I have always been aware of how a name can give you a certain sense of freedom or restriction. I am using the names as reincarnations; to name yourself is to say, "I'm going to be this person for the time being." Then, how people react to you is something, of course, outside your own control.

Now, is all this also related to poststructuralist theory in my case? Well, here I am thinking more about reinvention, refashioning of the self. However, the distribution of power is also to be found, for me, in the facility of language: all my novels are really about language and about how you control the world through linguistic fluency. Take my second novel [*Wife*], for instance, there you have a character who the more English she learns, the more at home she feels, the more self-empowered she comes to be in the new and frightening Manhattan society. Is this poststructuralism? . . .

An Interview with Bharati Mukherjee

Fred Bonnie / 1995

From *AWP Chronicle*, 28:2 (October/November 1995), 1, 7–8. © 1995 by Fred Bonnie. Reprinted by permission of the estate of Fred Bonnie.

Fred Bonnie: Why do you think there is, at this time, so much animosity toward immigrants and such a strong push in the U.S. Congress to stiffen the laws governing entry into this country?

Bharati Mukherjee: One problem is the economic recession, which has hit California particularly hard. Whenever things are bad economically, we look for scapegoats, and Asian-Americans in California, no matter how many generations they've lived there, are suddenly seen as "the other." My colleague at Berkeley, Ronald Takaki, has written a book about the history of immigration in this country—it's entitled *Strangers from a Different Shore*. He points out that Asians, the Chinese being the first of them to have come here in the mid-nineteenth century, have nonetheless always been thought of as *sojourners* versus Europeans, no matter when they came, as *settlers*. This is a tactic of continually other-izing the Asian, even though there's no reason to think of them as transients and guest workers.

Some poor Caucasians, African-Americans, and Latinos, unfortunately, are seeing Asian-Americans as a rival group. They will often complain that Asians are taking their jobs. This is sometimes coming from people who have never held a job in their lives. So, economic recession and the need to scapegoat is a major reason, although not necessarily an accurate one, for much of the hostility toward immigrants.

Bonnie: You mentioned in your talk that you think the hyphenation of ethnic groups as African-American or Asian-American is doing those groups a disservice.

Mukherjee: I personally avoid the hyphenation of ethnic groups, and the reason for that is to avoid the other-ization, the self-imposed marginalization that comes with hyphenation. I have no problem with writers and others who choose hyphenation as a means of attaining a comfortable mode of self-presentation. I'm talking more about my own discomfort with that practice, or the practice of forcing that category on someone who is unwilling to be typed in that way. If you're going to call me an Indian-American writer, then you've got to consistently refer to John Updike or Joyce Carol Oates as European-American writers. And I object to that simply because the whole idea of America is different. In every country besides the U.S. and Canada, there is a fixed notion of national identity and culture—that you have to be born into that race, complexion, and religious axis in order to claim it as your own. Only in the U.S. and Canada do we still work the romantic myth that everyone who comes here eventually melts down to become a new thing. For Americans, personal identity, national identity, are constantly in flux. That's what I find liberating. I was born into such a rigid society, where it didn't matter what my ambitions or feelings were. I was who I was because I was so-and-so's daughter from such-and-such caste.

Bonnie: Are you saying that the term "melting pot" still applies to the United States?
Mukherjee: I think it was on the Bill Moyers show where I recommended that the term "melting pot" ought to be replaced by something more accurate—perhaps the "fusion vat." (*Laughing*) In America, everyone is being constantly changed. I dislike the term "tossed salad" as an image of American salad because that implies that each radish or wedge of lettuce maintains its individual identity, when, in fact, that's not what happens to immigrants in this country. The idea of "stew pot" is appealing because the flavors become blended in a stew, and even though you can still recognize the piece of carrot as a piece of carrot, the flavor has changed and the end product is different from the sum of its components.

Bonnie: What is it about America that seems to turn people into criminals? They're perfectly law-abiding citizens in their native lands, but when they get to the United States, some become gang members or drug dealers or gun runners. Why?
Mukherjee: Well, it's democracy, and crime is democracy's downside. In a democracy, everyone gets to do his thing, even if it's a wrong thing to do. I have to believe that many of the Asian gangs I hear of or have tried to study did, indeed, exist back home. In some cases they're drug or extortion operations. One of the reasons the criminally inclined feel free to be criminals in this country is the American penal system. I don't want to see a Singapore style of public flogging become a standard form of justice here, but I am convinced that many people who would be too afraid of punishment in their own countries are not afraid of the consequences here; there's a very good chance that you can commit a crime

and never be caught. And if you are caught, the punishment won't be very severe. Also, they're not as afraid of the social consequences here; the idea of not shaming their families seems less important here.

I don't think we're seeing a sudden appearance of ethnic gangs being formed just to protect their own communities. A lot of crime among ethnic groups, I've discovered, is intracommunal—black on black, Vietnamese on Vietnamese, that sort of thing. Another disturbing thing I'm seeing is inter-minority violence. Incidents like the beating death of a dentist in Jersey City—an American of Indian origin, Dr. Navroz Mody—by a group of teenaged Latinos is really a race crime and not about taking jobs. It's simple racial hostility at its worst. I'd hate to see anyone try to justify that kind of crime by offering some cultural rationalization because there is no rationalization for brutal murder.

Bonnie: You made an interesting distinction earlier today between voluntary immigration and the immigration of political and/or economic refugees. Do you think Americans realize this distinction and treat legal immigrants more hospitably than illegals?

Mukherjee: Absolutely not. I see no differences in treatment between documented and undocumented aliens. Everyone is lumped together as having broken the rules. I'm afraid that in this country, as it has long happened in other traditionally Caucasian countries and regions—Europe, Canada—people are going to see all non-whites as smelly, dark, cunning breakers of laws and rules. We have to be careful not to take one of two extreme courses: become paranoid about new groups and traditions entering our country, or pretend that the hostility is temporary, or that it either doesn't really exist or will simply go away.

Bonnie: What, if anything, can be done to alter Americans' feelings about newcomers? Or should we just wait until the economy improves and assume the hostilities will abate on their own when Americans once again begin to ignore immigrants?

Mukherjee: I think the media must take a large share of the blame for not presenting images of the non-European in ordinary situations. I don't want to see an Indian only in an ad that targets a South Asian audience; let's see an Indian in ads for toothpaste or dish detergent—ads that will be seen by everyone. Let's see immigrants and minorities as bank tellers and office workers. As ordinary citizens, just like anyone else.

Bonnie: With our tradition of immigration, why is the notion of multiculturalism suddenly so disturbing to the Caucasian majority in the United States?

Mukherjee: The easy answer is that immigrants used to come mainly from Europe. Now there's much more diversity among the cultural traditions of immigrants. People instinctively fear the unfamiliar, especially when they sense that the new arrivals could pose a threat to the established European, Caucasian heritage. But I don't blame white people as being the only ones responsible for the current panic over multiculturalism. Part of the problem in this matter is that, yes, liberal whites are looking for some sort of absolution from guilt over the injustices that have often surrounded immigration issues in the past and, of course, in the present. So now we have government funding for language classes, heritage classes, food fairs; this is a very easy way of trying to get off the hook of guilt. But this is not multiculturalism; it's ultimately a way of patronizing these groups who are supposed to be served in some way by the funding of such activities. Do your exotic thing, hang onto your exotic costume.

I also blame the leaders of ethnic communities who have so much money and political power invested in multiculturalism as politics. They're anxious to deliver bloc votes, to speak on behalf of their entire communities rather than see people as individuals. They don't want to distribute power to the separate members of their groups. And it's so much easier for a white political leader to see dealing with one person rather than the entire group as more efficient.

Bonnie: Have we gone too far in trying to accommodate the demands of multiculturists in the U.S? Is it really in everyone's best interest to try to keep every immigrant culture intact?

Mukherjee: Absolutely not. I think it's a fallacy sustained by ethnic-studies types or politicians that there has ever been a culture that remains intact, even in its native environment. It is the nature of culture to evolve. I'm aware from just the research I've done about the last three hundred years of U.S. history and several thousand years of Indian history of how much fusion, absorption, osmosis, have occurred among various cultures just within India. To pretend that there is an intact culture anywhere is self-serving. Any culture that is, indeed, static is no culture at all. I feel very strongly that if you've made the decision to come to a new country, then you cannot hang on, intact, to what worked in the old country. It does the children a great disservice because they are forced not to fit in, psychologically, with either culture.

One of the difficult issues that arises for proponents of multiculturalism is that of female circumcision. Should Somali or Nigerian or Ethiopian immigrants be allowed to continue that practice once they've arrived in the United States or Canada? Young African-Canadian girls are resisting that tradition from the old country, and suddenly all these white, liberal, pro-multiculturalism types are having to come to terms with the question that if multiculturalism means changing U.S. or Canadian law to allow [female circumcision], would they support multiculturalism quite so enthusiastically? I, for one, certainly don't want to see practices such as clitoridectomy allowed to be continued in this country.

Bonnie: What do you say to the suggestion that newcomers who insist on maintaining their native cultures intact in this country should perhaps go back to the places they came from?

Mukherjee: If they want to hold fast to the old ways, why are they crossing borders and leaving their native lands? I think it's wrong to make accommodations for one culture when it's a transgression of our own rules. You can't say it's all right to beat your wife here just because it's your culture to beat your wife back in your native land. I get in trouble on a campus like Berkeley, where they want to say that not beating your wife is a white hegemonic idea imposed by white males.

Bonnie: Whether it comes from white males or not, isn't it a good idea not to beat your wife?

Mukherjee: I think it's a bad idea to beat up anybody.

Bonnie: You talked earlier about the empowerment of immigrants and minorities; is art a vehicle by which ethnic and minority groups in this country can become empowered?

Mukherjee: Very much so, just the way boxing was for earlier generations of African-Americans and European immigrants who were trying to break out of the ghetto. In a novel, for instance, it's possible to make the ordinary reader realize how much moral and emotional resonance there is behind the faces we see at a shopping mall or selling newspapers or cleaning offices. The greatest praise I receive is from the letter writer who says, I never realized that these people who flip through the edges of my consciousness are 100 percent human beings.

Bonnie: I've heard you draw a parallel between seventeenth-century Indian miniature paintings and your own storytelling methods. How does that work for you in practice?

Mukherjee: What I'm aiming for, as did the anonymous painters of the Moghul miniatures or medieval tapestries, is to have many points of focus so that the stories are competing with each other to create a different sense of perspective. This is what the Muslim artists of the seventeenth century intended. When European art critics discovered this art, they dismissed it as primitive, lacking a sense of perspective. Understanding this art is really a matter of learning to see it in a different way. This is what I'm trying to do in my novels and stories. I want many stories going on simultaneously to distract, to crowd the reader's consciousness; and together the whole makes up the full authorial vision. The novel *Jasmine*, for instance, isn't just the story of the main character Jasmine; it's also the story of every other character and detail, no matter how small. People want to simplify what I've done as being one immigrant woman's story. They want to reduce it to just the character Jasmine, whereas I'm saying that if you read it correctly, the novel is a story of America changing, as well as Jasmine changing.

Bonnie: Are you an Indian-American writer? A South Asian writer? Or simply an American writer?
Mukherjee: I'm an American writer who happens to be from South Asia. I hope no one sees me or my fiction as representing the entire Indian community. I hope people see *Jasmine* as one person's story and one author's take on a given character in a given situation. I think minority writers are particularly prone to turning characters of fiction into representations in a political agenda. The result is that you may produce novels that are useful as texts in social studies or women's studies courses, but they will never be fine literature.

Holders of the Word: An Interview with Bharati Mukherjee

Tina Chen and S. X. Goudie / 1996

From *Jouvert: A Journal of Postcolonial Studies*, 1:1, (1997), http://social.chass. ncsu.edu/jouvert/v1i1/bharat.htm [see for introduction and section titles]. © 1996 by Tina Chen and S. X. Goudie. Reprinted by permission of the authors.

M: Postcolonial studies seems an inappropriate category in which to place my works. I don't think of myself as a postcolonial person stranded on the outer shores of the collapsed British Empire. I haven't thought of myself as a post-colonial since I finished co-authoring, with my husband Clark Blaise, *Days and Nights in Calcutta.* Writing my half of that book was my way of thinking through who I was, where I was, where I'd rather be. If I had chosen to return to India after writing that book in 1977, or if, like Salman Rushdie, I'd spent my entire adult life in Britain instead of in North America, I might have evolved as a post-colonial whose creative imagination is fueled primarily by the desire to create a new mythology of Indian nationhood after the Raj's brutalization of Indian culture. But I didn't. I came to the U.S., initially as a student, because in 1961 the University of Iowa was the only place in the world offering a degree in the area I wanted to study, and because American universities had scholarships to offer me. When I first arrived on campus, I thought of myself as a Bengali rather than as an Indian. You were who you were because of the language and dialect you spoke, the location of the village of your male ancestors, the family and religion you were born into. I was a Bengali and proud of it, which meant that I claimed as heritage a culture distinct from that of a Bihari or a Punjabi or a Gujarati or a Tamil. That's the way we were brought up in Calcutta in the fifties. We were en-couraged to set ourselves apart from people of other Indian states. In Iowa, where I didn't run into too many Bengalis, I began to see and feel affinities with rather than hostilities towards non-Bengali Indian students on campus.

If you insist, on this beautiful May afternoon in 1996, that I describe myself in terms of ethno-nationality, I'd say I'm an American writer of Bengali-Indian origin. In other words, the writer/political activist in me is more obsessed with addressing the issues of minority discourse in the U.S. and Canada, the two coun-

tries I have lived and worked in over the last thirty odd years. The national mythology that my imagination is driven to create, through fiction, is that of the
post-Vietnam United States. I experience, simultaneously, the pioneer's capacity
to be shocked and surprised by the new culture, and the immigrant's willingness
to de-form and re-form that culture. At this moment, my Calcutta childhood and
adolescence offer me intriguing, incompletely comprehended revelations about
my hometown, my family, my place in that community: the kind of revelations
that fuel the desire to write an autobiography rather than to mythologize an Indian national identity.

J: In "A Four-Hundred-Year-Old Woman," you state that your "image of artistic structure and excellence is the Mughal miniature painting with its crazy fore-
shortening of vanishing point, its insistence that everything happens simultaneously, bound only by shape and color" (38). Would you give an example of how
the Mughal miniature translates into your writing?
M: The best example probably is "Courtly Vision," the last story in the collection
Darkness. I have an obsessive love of Mughal miniature painting. The miniatures
that speak to me most eloquently were painted during the reign of Emperor Akbar. I suppose that's because mine is a *writerly* love. Each of the Akbari paintings
that I'm mesmerized by is so crowded with narrative, sub-narratives, sometimes
meta-narratives, so taut with passion and at the same time so crisp with irony.
Every separate "story" in the miniature matters, every "minor character" has a
dramatic function. But all the strands and details manage to cohere, that's what's
amazing! And each is "framed" by an elaborately painted border. The border
shouldn't be dismissed as the artists' excessive love of adumbration. The border
forces you to view the work not primarily as a source of "raw" sociological data,
but as sociology *metaphorized*; that is, as a master-artist's observation on life/
history/national psyche cast in the aesthetic traditions of the community and
transmuted into art.

The story, "Courtly Vision," was inspired by a number of Akbari paintings,
particularly one that shows the Emperor in battle dress, leading his massive,
battle-ready army out of his fortressed capital. The painting anticipates victory,
and evokes a celebratory mood. The mood is historically tenable: Akbar, wise,
tolerant, brave, won his wars. But what drew the writer in me to the painting was
the *contextual* irony of such victory on the battlefield. Akbar built an exquisite
capital city in Fatehpur Sikri, but he had to abandon it because he'd sited it in a
drought zone. He was affably curious about "the other," which meant he allowed
in European peddlers, freebooters, Christian missionaries, and so unintentionally

facilitated the power grab by the many European East India Companies, and the eventual debilitation of the Mughals. When I started "Courtly Vision," I was aiming to close with that epiphanic contextual irony. But before I finished the first draft, the "frame"—converting verisimilitude into meta-narrative—had worked itself in. The "frame" made the reader witness to a painter's (via author's) representation of history as evidenced in a slick Sotheby's catalogue, and, through the inclusion of the cheap estimated price, upped the final irony into Europe's devaluation of Mughal art.

Until recent decades, Eurocentric art criticism dismissed Mughal miniatures as unsophisticated, as lacking mastery of perspective. The point is that Mughal artists had developed a Mughal aesthetic. They preferred to work with many points of focus. I had some idea, while I was writing the stories for *Darkness* and *The Middleman*, how much about form and principle I had absorbed from the sixteenth- and seventeenth-century paintings I so loved. But it was as I drafted the essay, "A Four-Hundred-Year-Old-Woman," that I thought through, and articulated, my Mughal-inspired narrative aesthetic. I like to move narrative by indirection, to create apparent "lumps" and "spills" along the through-line. This applies to novels like *Jasmine* and *The Holder of the World* as well as to the short stories. "The zigzag route," one of my characters confesses, "is the shortest." The indirect narratives are, of course, designed to parallel or to undermine the main character's story. The parts, when added up and "framed," should reveal authorial vision. The "frame" and "voice"—the term that we writers communally use to indicate aesthetic strategy—are what make the sum of the parts, 2+2+3, not 7 but 10.

J: So you work like a *bricoleur*, parts are used and reused and shaped and reshaped, much like the character Jasmine's identity. As with time and space in the novel, things do seem to recur though with a difference, even as Jasmine suggests she's given up one identity and moved on to another. There are a series of transformations . . .

M: Yeah, Jasmine goes through several transformations, and I like to think that she is still open to many more self-inventions. She lives on, very fully, inside my head. But when I was talking about *indirection*, I was trying to insist that the novel, *Jasmine*, be read as more than the story of Jasmine's change. That's why the novel provided so many different points of focus: the experience of dislocation and relocation is handled by each of the immigrant characters. As in Akbari miniatures, my novel compresses the immigration histories of many minor characters. Professorji, his wife, his elderly parents, the Caribbean housekeepers in

Manhattan, the Guatemalans in Florida, Du and his Asian American friend in
Iowa: even within an ethnic group, each minor character has a distinct response.
And white Americans, including the volunteer for the Sanctuary Movement, treat
these various minor characters variously. The "opposed parallel" that moved me
most as I was writing was the one between Jasmine and Du. Jasmine's very open
to new experience and optimistic about outcome. Her attitude is: *Hey, you can't
rape me and get away with it! You can't push me around! I'm here, I'm gonna stay
if I want to, **and** I'm gonna conquer the territory!* Du, who has to attend school in
the U.S., probably outwardly dresses more like U.S.-born Americans than does
Jasmine, and certainly is more familiar with American colloquialisms and pop
culture, but he's cynical of post-Vietnam America; he's aware of the limits of the
American Dream and makes his guerrilla attacks on that Dream. The total picture: that's the heady part of writing, the creating of all these . . .

J: . . . little miniature universes within the frame.
M: Right. In a way, I suppose that's being a Hindu, I mean, this being constantly
aware of the existence of many universes, this undermining of biography and individual ego. The cosmology that my characters and I inhabit derives very much
from the Puranic tales. The *Puranas* are cycles of tales (think of them as morality
tales, religious fables, there are thousands of them) that every Hindu child is told
the way that kids in the U.S. are exposed to fairytales and bedtime stories. As
"story," they really work, too! Conflict, heroes, villains, obstacles, action, surprise
revelation! But the stories *metaphorize* the Hindu concepts of cosmology, time,
and space. Current discoveries in astronomy are certainly pointing up the existence of universes other than ours. I believe in reincarnation, which, too, may be
a metaphor for some geo-biological phenomenon, why not?

J: Has your background as a Hindu enabled you to create an intimacy with the
reader, from a New World perspective, that is distinct from other stylistic and
narrative techniques you've encountered in American writing?
M: I don't know if all Hindu American writers see the world in the way that I do
and the way that I mix Islam with Hindu art, because I've been exposed to both
of these, really results in a very syncretic narrative strategy. As such, my incorporation of Hinduism might be quite opposed to how some other Hindu writer living in New York may think of Hinduism or exercise it. I don't want to lump all
Hindus together.

J: You've identified "voice" as the "prime aesthetic" of your writing. In this context, it seems particularly interesting that *Jasmine* has been critiqued for the

inauthenticity of the protagonist's voice; as Liew-Geok Leong writes, "[t]he voice of Jasmine, surprisingly articulate and assured, is not always believable, given her background and circumstances; it is her creator's voice that takes over and speaks for her, the result perhaps of too close an identification with the subject" (494). Upon reflection, do you see any validity in this evaluation?

M: Leong would appear to be ignorant of the craft-related lexicon of contemporary American writers. Just as terms such as "essentialism," "subaltern," "agency," and "signifier" are accepted by academics as shorthand for certain conceptual constructs, so "voice" is our shorthand for the process of decision-making regarding tone, diction, pacing, texture, withholding, etc. in a given work.

J: In other words, you're suggesting that your notion of voice is more expansive, that you're not striving after some sort of realistic, mimetic voice.

M: I am saying that being a scholar as well as a writer, I expect myself to do my homework very, very thoroughly, before I make public pronouncements. "Voice" should not have been confused with tone, diction, etc. Of course I am not striving after some sort of realistic, mimetic voice. I leave that to tape recorders. Art is about selection, stylization, and metaphoric revelation.

J: Other writers have been subject to the same sort of criticism in terms of voice, right? For example, the African American writer Charles Johnson has been criticized severely by some because the protagonist of his award-winning novel *Middle Passage*, a freed slave, speaks in highly philosophical language, and his narrative voice tends to be anachronistic.

M: James Alan McPherson gets the same flak for not using "inner city" American-English exclusively or predominantly. It's absurd. It's as absurd as saying that because Gayatri Spivak was born into a Bengali family and grew up in Calcutta, she has no right to public expression in non-Bengali languages, especially not in the languages of former colonialist nations such as England or France, nor to derive any theoretical model from Marx or other European white males. I believe that if you are literate, all literature that you expose yourself to is your heritage to claim or reject.

J: Again, it seems that your major concern with such critics is that, in the interests of "authenticity," they restrict you from using the assembly of creative tools in your bag, that there's a prescribed way in which "voice" is supposed to be rendered.

M: It's patronizing, elitist, and classist of such critics to presume that the poor and the de-privileged do not have sophisticated thoughts and poetic articulation.

They need to acquaint themselves with scholarship regarding oral literature. In addition, I am very bothered by their reduction of art to sociological statement. Fiction transmits its message (by which I mean its author's vision) very differently from essays.

J: Given your criticism of V. S. Naipaul along those lines during an interview some years ago ("A Conversation"), it must be particularly painful to be criticized for a certain failure in voice. In that interview, you attacked Naipaul's notion that the dispossessed are incapable of articulating, in sophisticated ways, their pain, desires, etc. He suggested to you that he feels they're incapable of speaking in any complex or redemptive way due to their psychological, social, and cultural fragmentation as a result of colonialism. You are now subject to an attack that is the flip side of the same coin. The suggestion is that you're still not allowing them to think and speak for themselves. Critics argue that you're just . . .
M: They have taken a Naipaulian position about me and my writing, from a high moral ground, and I resent that, and I'm saying that . . .

J: . . . they're the ones who want to speak. That *they* want to speak for these people and have you renounce your right to speak in the ways you wish?
M: Right. That's where my ire is located. The writer claims only to speak for her unique, *eccentric* characters. These critics, on the other hand, though they locate themselves in North America and participate in the North American competitive, materialist economy, invent or appropriate the positions of populous, Asia-based communities, and worse, they reduce the diversity of those communities' positions into one that fits most neatly into their favored theory. The Indian graduate students and junior faculty members I have talked to on western Indian campuses in the last two years have expressed growing resentment of such usurpation. The theorist they most often named was Spivak, perhaps because she is the best known of the Indo-American group.

Some recent publications by serious Indian literary critics based in India, for instance by Professors Aijaz Ahmad and Harish Trivedi of the University of Delhi, indicate an emerging resentment of the appropriation of *Indianality* and *postcoloniality* by scholars of Indian origin (or of non-European origin) who have opted for U.S. citizenship and/or permanent residence in North America. The *Jouvert* community is no doubt well aware of Ahmad's direct attack on Edward Said—and by extension, it would seem, his indirect attack on Spivak—for "internationalizing the periphery." (That's Ahmad's phrase, not mine. I myself prefer to reject the center/periphery template, and so, resist Eurocentric vocabulary.) Professor Trivedi, who lectured here at Berkeley a few months ago on the Eurocentric implications of the term "postcolonial," was more direct in his attack on the right of Spivak, a U.S. citizen and long-term U.S. resident, to speak for the "periphery."

J: Spivak has cautioned against reading her as someone who claims to "give voice" to those she represents; she has said in *The Postcolonial Critic*—and I'm paraphrasing—that to read her as speaking for "the periphery" is to read her, wrongly, as a "Third World informant."

M: But then she goes on to, at the same time, trounce others for providing versions, portraits that don't coincide with hers so that she, I'm not going to say that she's lying, but there's this problematic position . . .

J: You don't get the same reception?

M: Oh, I get severely attacked by many Indian critics, but for a very different reason! Whereas I have heard Spivak being attacked for appropriation of the so-called "periphery," I have been virulently attacked for defining myself as an American writer of Indian origin writing of the diasporic and immigrant experience. It started with a response to a journalist's question during a press conference in Delhi in 1990. I was asked, "Wouldn't you, if you had your rathers, come back to live in India?" and, thinking of my husband and children settled in the States, answered, "Frankly, no." That "no" was misinterpreted as a betrayal of my Indian heritage. But, now that so many Indian families have relatives settled in the U.S., my "immigrant" material is being read or reread in fresh ways.

J: In this discussion about who gets to speak and who doesn't, there seems to be an implicit criticism that your characters are not authentic.

M: Right, and I'm saying that this Leong should be listening to rap, doing some more "hanging out" in inner cities to see how much poetry there is in ordinary lives. How can any critic have the audacity to assume that all members of a group think, feel, react, and verbalize identically? How do you explain one brother from a dysfunctional family becoming a writer—I'm thinking obviously of John Edgar Wideman, author of *Philadelphia Fire*—and his brother becoming a murderer? So, to assume that you are identical with everyone else in your class is to not understand human beings.

J: And when she accuses you of perhaps identifying too closely with your subject and writing an "inauthentic" character as a result of that identification, would your charge be "no, you're also identifying with the subject but your identification forecloses the possibility of the life which I choose to explore"?

M: Well, not only that. I hear Leong saying that someone from Jasmine's background and circumstances cannot speak the way that she does. You see, that's very different from the way you're verbalizing it. I am saying that to think all people who are born poor are therefore incapable of thought, imagination, and speech, is a very elitist and classist kind of assumption; I need to see them as individuals rather than types.

J: It seems that you are responding to this question on at least two different levels. **M:** My response to this question is structured on three different levels. One is that the critic doesn't understand voice; she simply is ignorant about how writers use this term. My second point is that no fine fiction, no good literature, is anchored in verisimilitude. Fiction must be metaphor. It is not transcription of real life but it's a distillation and pitching at higher intensification of life. It's always a distortion. And then the third point is that just because Jasmine happens to be poor doesn't mean she is incapable of imagination, intelligence, and articulate speech.

J: Are there Indian writers writing in English whose work you admire? **M:** Do you mean Anglophone writers who are Indian citizens and are residing in India? R. K. Narayan. I keep nominating him for the Nobel Prize. I'm also very interested in younger fiction writers and poets like R. Raj Rao and Ranjit Hoskhote.

J: In addition to Naipaul, we're wondering what other Caribbean writers have influenced you in any way: Wilson Harris and his AmerIndian aesthetics, Michele Cliff, Edouard Glissant, or Maryse Condé and their notions of cross-cultural poetics, etc.
M: None of them have influenced me, though, of course, I have enjoyed reading each of them. About Naipaul, I can't say that he *influenced* me, but I can say that *A House for Mr. Biswas inspired* me when I read it as a student in the early sixties. I hadn't read any fiction about Trinidad Indians before that. That novel gave me the self-confidence to claim my own fictional world.

J: If, as with Joseph Conrad's *Heart of Darkness*, "canonical" texts exercise an influence, however disturbing, on the formerly colonized—and in some instances, newly immigrated—what colonialist texts have left their mark on you?
M: None, really. By the way, I didn't read *Heart of Darkness* until I came to the States. Of all English literature I was exposed to, Shakespeare's tragedies moved most. I could recite soliloquies by Macbeth, Hamlet, Portia, Shylock, King Lear, Cordelia with great feeling. I think it was the music of the lines, the sound of the words, that excited me. Elocution was my most favorite subject in school. I loved to read poetry out loud. Tagore and Keats, oh, they were so heady when I was a schoolgirl in Calcutta. I responded to the euphony first; then to the ideas. I didn't know any Buddhists and came from a staunch Hindu family, but Tagore made

me weep over the persecution of Buddhist converts in ancient India. Same with Keats; I'd never been to Greece, not even seen pictures of the country, but I sure could visualize the friezescapes in the "Ode on a Grecian Urn." There was something fresh about Keats because he was rebelling against the narrowness of British conventions. Though India was a sovereign nation when I first encountered Keats, my convent-school campus remained a very "English" spot. You know, we had to sing Gilbert and Sullivan comic operas, that sort of thing, and we were expected to admire the logic and orderliness of the British mind. Keats was resisting those values in his poems. I suppose loving Keats' poems for me was a quiet form of guerrilla warfare against my teachers.

J: Before deciding to use it for *The Holder of the World*, did Keats or "Ode on a Grecian Urn" ever take on a different aura for you? You have said elsewhere that your life and work should be divided into three distinct phases—as a colonial, then national, subject in India, as a postcolonial Indian in Canada, and as an immigrant, later a citizen, of the United States. Did Keats and his ode accompany you through those transformations?

M: I'm not sure I even thought about Keats for twenty years after leaving India. When I sat down to write *The Holder*, I was a very different person from the girl who had recited the odes out loud for pleasure, and the "Ode on a Grecian Urn" was very much on my mind because, like Keats, I was playing with history and imagination. That's the marvelous thing about the writing process: you don't know when and how a memory, a scrap of conversation overheard, an allusion or image, is suddenly going to surface and work itself into your story. That ode came to me; I didn't seek it out. That's the way the creative process works for me. I knew right away that I would use the Keats references to control and ironize what my characters had to say about time, and to make authorial meta-statements about writing.

J: Is there a distinction between the way that Keats sees the Grecian urn and the way you see a Mughal painting?

M: That's not the contrast that I would make. I would make it between virtual reality and the urn. The urn is still, the action is frozen, and one can only observe. I'm not so much concerned with what Keats is saying about these people as I am with how action has been stuck in time and can't be redone. The people are always going to have their hands and feet in one particular posture, whereas with interactive technology, you're changing the narrative by inputting new information according to your new mood. The ways virtual technology will be used for therapy, to help autistic children or to enable people to overcome their fears, is very close to what I'm talking about. The individual experiencing the image, not simply the image itself—both are going to be transformed by interaction.

J: We've asked you to discuss your literary influences but we also wonder what "critics" [literary and otherwise] you consider important to the development of your own critical project in delineating the future of American writing?
M: None.

J: Do you find the "writer-critic" a more effective, perhaps even more productive, type of critic than the scholar?
M: For writers and readers, yes. Writers writing about fiction see the text as *process* whereas scholars reduce it to *product*. Writer-critics explore the work from inside out; they divine the aesthetic decisions that the text's writer has made to best get across the authorial vision, and then they assess the effect of those decisions. They let the work set up the criteria by which it should be judged instead of imposing their arbitrary grid on the work; they aim to "open up" the work instead of reducing it to a dutifully followed or sloppily followed set of narrative rules thought up by a scholar. I think the best essays on the "art of fiction," on beginnings, endings, etc., to date have been written by writers. A book of essays on writing I'd recommend is *How Stories Mean*, edited by John Metcalf and J. R. Struthers. Contemporary scholars seem to have deliberately removed themselves from primary texts, so that not only do they sometimes get their data wrong (and I mean titles of works, names of characters), but they often discard those complexities in the text that don't fit their theories, and they devalue those aesthetic innovations that challenge their particular sociopolitical agendas. Scholars seem to just talk to scholars, using a language of the initiated. The "subaltern" critics might wish to speak *for* the de-privileged, but they certainly don't speak *to* them.

J: You have remarked that no longer do you find exilic writers as provocative as they once were. Yet they're still quite popular. Why do you think expatriate writers like Naipaul continue to enjoy such popularity, specifically with Western audiences?
M: I don't know how popular they are or what you mean by popularity. I think an awful lot of minority writers and expatriate writers complain that their books don't get into bookstores, that they may get reviews, or the same few will get reviews, but that there really isn't any kind of cross-fertilization of readers. I think there are two kinds of writers and I'm not saying that it's only about exilic writers or immigrant writers but all writers: those who reinforce what the public thinks, the conventional values, and those who constantly interrogate the conventional

values. An awful lot of the exilic writers, the expatriate writers, are providing the kinds of portraits, moods, positions, and problems with which the readership, the publishing industry, and the scholars—or critics anyway—are familiar and comfortable. The few who are obliterating that particular kind of discourse between Third World and First World, margin and center, or minority and mainstream, have a much harder time being understood or being recognized. I've been writing and publishing since 1971 but it's taken me an awfully long time to get any attention, largely because I was, for a while, an Indian citizen living in Canada as a landed immigrant and writing about people outside of India. Then I became a Canadian citizen but writing, let us say, about immigrants in New York. They didn't know how to classify me, whether by my passport or by my material, which was about immigrants at a time when there was no such category as "immigrant fiction" that wasn't about Europeans coming to North America during the nineteenth century. So I don't know about "popularity." Very recently there was an article I read in the *Times* on Spanish-speaking writers in New York objecting vociferously to the ways in which they are shut out when they write middle-class fiction about middle-class characters who speak in perfectly educated, sensitive English, even though they're second or third generation. The stereotype is that if you're going to write about Hispanics, you'd better make them lettuce pickers and have a spiritualist. The kind of criticism from literary critics and theorists who have encountered my own work stems from their belief that if you're India-born, you must write about India and you must write about an Indian woman or peasants being victimized.

J: They want it primitivized in some way.

M: Yes, stereotyped. It's absurd, when you think that I'm writing about the post-1965 immigration-transformed America, and that the majority of South Asians granted visas are urban, educated professionals and their families. The aim of fiction is to break down stereotypes. Unfortunately, the publishing and academic industries seem to profit more from reinforcing stereotypes. This is what African American intellectuals have to deal with too. That's why I feel I'm on the same wavelength with Henry Louis Gates, Jr., Cornel West, James Alan McPherson. Why should a minority person be made to feel guilty because she believes education leads to both self-improvement and national enlightenment? To me, class is as divisive as race.

J: Just as there is a risk of becoming locked into one's own exilic condition to the point of pathetic self-absorption, isn't there a danger of being too celebratory about the enabling aspects of an immigrant's "multicultural" point of view?

M: I'm going to object to the word "multicultural" here because I've spoken so vociferously against this whole official multiculturalism in Canada. I'm going to limit it to an immigrant's point of view, all right? Yes, my work has sometimes been cited for celebrating too enthusiastically the swagger of immigration, the energies released in the process of transformation. It is as though certain readers cannot see beyond the color of my characters' skin, or their gender, or their pre-determined view of America, without linking them, automatically, to the long sad history of New World exploitation. Yes, they are victims but they are resilient victims, unviolated in their core of need and imagination. Rocky, being white, can pick himself off the canvas, land a few blows, and be a hero; Rakesh, however, a laid-off engineer with three kids and no American certification, opens a dingy spice store and Hindi video outlet and somehow is perceived as pathetic. This is the stereotyping that has to end. My Professorji, who used to be a doctor in his home country and is now having to sell human hair for making wigs or electronic equipment in some basement video store in Queens, is somehow seen, necessarily, as a pathetic character rather than as a resilient hero, who says "all right, this didn't work, but something else will work."

J: By identifying yourself as an immigrant writer, you resist being classified by postcolonial scholars as an exilic or expatriate writer. You also don't seem to stake out an intellectual position as a writer/scholar akin to what Abdul R. JanMohamed has termed the "specular border intellectual," a category for writers from formerly colonized or enslaved places who engage in a critique of multiple locations from a position of "homelessness-as-home."
M: Just the fact you bring up JanMohamed is troubling to me. We're very, very different kinds of Indians. Simply because of skin color and South Asian ancestry, the non-South Asian is likely to lump us together just as they have long lumped the Samuel Selvons and the V. S. Naipauls together as part of the Indian diaspora. JanMohamed, having been brought up in Africa according to a different religion, a different language, a different cultural and revolutionary experience, has surely more to say about minority discourse in Africa and about how to apply his particular African training and African experience to being a minority in a white-dominated world in the U.S. and less about mainstream India and Indian writing. The mission of postcolonial studies as a discipline is to level all of us to our skin color and ethnic origin whereas as a writer, my job is to open up, to discover and say "we are all individuals." In fiction we are writing about individuals; none of them is meant to be a crude spokesperson for whole groups, whether those groups are based on gender or race or class. If the story of one

individual reveals something about the way in which human nature works, great, if it doesn't, then it has failed as art.

J: How would you characterize, then, the relationship that exists between post-colonialism and your creative project?
M: The mission of postcolonial studies seems to be to deliberately equate art and journalism, to reduce novels to specimens for the confirming of their theories. If an imaginative work doesn't fit the cultural theories they approve of, it's dismissed as defective. The relationship between the artist and the postcolonial scholar has become adversarial. It doesn't have to be, that's what's so sad. I'm not denigrating all scholarship, but only that particular school of postcolonial criticism that is hostile to art and aesthetics. All that, as a writer, I value—power of word choice and placement of punctuation, imagery, texture, pacing—all the strategies that I employ to articulate my vision as precisely as I can to the reader, these scholars treat as debris to be cleared for the exposing of camouflaged "hegemonic" agendas in the narrative.

J: You make some very clear distinctions between writers and scholars. In the field of Caribbean postcolonial studies, such distinctions are not so clear. People like Edouard Glissant, Wilson Harris, and Maryse Condé would all be considered both important postcolonial scholars and writers. Isn't there an opportunity for solidarity between scholar/writers or haven't you reached out to those voices?
M: Oh, I'm friends with Maryse Condé, and am familiar with the work of Harris and Glissant. I'm glad to hear that scholars of Caribbean studies are not as anti-imaginative literature as are the Spivak-influenced Indo-American post-colonial graduate students who write papers or dissertation chapters on my work. I find so many glaring errors in their so-called scholarship; I mean getting really basic data wrong, like titles or genre of a text, names of significant characters. I don't know how such shoddy work gets past a dissertation supervisor in any respectable university! I recently came across a paper by an Indo-American woman scholar that accused me, not my character(s), of being anti-America, and recommended that I should try to feel more comfortable living in the United States, all on the basis of having read one single story, the title of which she got wrong. It sometimes appears that all I value as a writer are being deliberately denigrated or disregarded by the scholars. What is important to me is Isaac Babel saying, "A comma placed just right will stab the heart," whereas for a lot of these scholars, judging from the papers that I've read, to worry about artistic or meter-effective placement of punctuation is to be sort of right wing.

J: In his book *In Theory*, Aijaz Ahmad critiques the notion of "adversarial inter-nationalization" by arguing that while "Said speaks, inexplicably, of 'intellectual and scholarly work from the peripheries, done either by immigrants or by visitors, both of whom are generally anti-imperialist' . . . [t]he vast majority of immigrants and visitors who go from 'the peripheries' to the 'Western center' in the United States either take no part in politics and scholarly endeavor or turn out to be right-wing people" (207–8). He characterizes you as the ultimate representative of this second type of person. Have you had a chance to respond to this assertion in any formal way?

M: Yes, yes I have. I did it for an Indian publication that is the equivalent, sort of, of the *New York Times Sunday Magazine*. They'd invited writers to write about the notion of "internationalizing the periphery," if you like. First of all, I want to know where Aijaz Ahmad gets his statistics for making this kind of generalization? I didn't find it in his footnotes and I certainly didn't find it in the text. And then, has he ever done research on my voting records? Does he know that I was a very active member of the NDP in Canada? The choice I was faced with in the late seventies just prior to leaving for the United States in 1980 was to either give up writing and run for public office as an NDP candidate, or say to myself, "Politics, someone else will carry on. I live my most real life through writing."

J: These are highly provocative rejoinders to level at Ahmad, especially considering how he criticizes Said for not checking his facts or statistics. Ahmad even goes so far to suggest that Said hasn't really read your writing, or the writings of your immigrant peers, and that Said's classification of you as "anti-imperialist" is gleaned from what other critics have said about immigrant texts rather than a firsthand reading of them.

M: Yeah, well, I don't think that Ahmad has checked his facts about me or read any of my essays either, let alone my fiction. And then I want to know, what does "right wing" mean in the context of his quotation? Does it mean simply that anyone who is not a Marxist is "right wing"? If "right wing," for Ahmad, applies to anyone who agrees with the spirit behind the American Constitution and the idea of democracy, then I suppose I am. I do not wish to trivialize democratic ideals by equating America with blue jeans and Coca-Cola, which is a very cheap, easy shot that Europeans as well as many South Asian intellectuals take. As such, I'm placing my faith in fighting for civil rights and this is where I talk about my political aesthetics in this essay. The cause that I have now put a great deal of my energy into is fighting for gay rights; for gay rights to be treated as an extension of civil rights. When I lived in Canada, it was the gay groups who worked hardest for us South Asians, in fighting discrimination. South Asians were at the bottom of Canada's race-based totem pole. The feminists let us [people of color] down as they obtained their goals regarding women's rights. If the Constitution gives me a way of forcing Newt Gingrich's feet to the fire, a way of forcing American politicians to live up to the letter of the law, then I'm going to do that. And if that means being "right wing" by Ahmad's standard then too bad. I find these categories totally, totally useless. In India, among the intellectuals that I see once or twice a year while traveling, there is no agreement about what constitutes right wing and left wing. In my hometown, Calcutta, there are four distinct communist political parties. For instance Calcutta's Maoists call the city's Moscow-Marxists "right wing," so I don't know where Ahmad is coming from, and he ought to know better.

J: Yet in terms of the "American" scene, Ahmad seems to argue that immigrant writers such as yourself have re-adopted the notion of America as "melting pot." He's suggesting that ironically, by using the melting-pot mode of writing, you're allowing yourself to be coopted yet again by the mainstream: to hybridicize in a syncretized fashion can be a very conservative position to adopt. While your writing can be seen as progressive and action-oriented, scholars such as Kristin Carter-Sanborn argue that many of your heroines are passive, women who are changed by, rather than changing, the American landscape. Despite their seeming adaptability, the argument is that you are romanticizing their domestication. These critics would like to see, ostensibly, more resistance to the assimilation and cooptation of these nontraditional immigrants.

M: Jasmine or Hannah Easton aren't passive women, by anyone's measure. They quite literally cross oceans, transform their worlds, and in the process leave behind a heap of bruised hearts and bleeding bodies! I don't think Ahmad has read my works. If he had read them, he would have known that I don't use European or Euro-American models for my narratives. I'm having to invent a whole new structure for American fiction, a whole new kind of sentence to express nontraditional immigrant emotions and psychic texture. It's very hard for critics in the U.S. and in India to understand who Jasmine is, or where she's coming from, because she's not a familiar American or Indian character. To resist and remain the way you were in India is to perpetuate, and more disturbingly, is to valorize, an awful lot of cultural vices such as sexism, patriarchy, castism, classism. Would Ahmad consider it cooptation when an American woman writer who has emigrated from a clitoridectomy-valorizing Muslim community, let's say from Togo, chooses to adopt for herself and to support—through her fiction—the U.S. social/ cultural/legal response to ritualized female mutilation? The immigrant writer decides what to let go and what to retain. It's always a two-way transformation. To resist cultural and ideological mutation simply because one wants to retain racial/ cultural/religious/caste "purity" is, in my opinion, evil. I'm against that kind of Hitlerian racial and ethnic pride; I'm against the retention of "pure culture" for the sake of purity.

I think a very significant, though probably unanticipated consequence of the controversy generated by *In Theory* has been the legitimation of "immigrant fiction" by writers of Indian origin as a genre quite distinct from "post-Independence fiction" by Indian writers residing in India, and from "exilic fiction" by India-born writers residing outside India. The works of Indian Caribbean writers like Rooplal Monar, Indian Caribbean Canadian writers like Sam Selvon, Sonny Ladoo, Cyril Dabydeen, Neil Bissoondath, Indian African Canadian writers like Moyez Vassanji, Goan African writers like Violet Dias Lannoy, Indian British writers like Hanif Kureishi, are more intelligently explored in the context of exile. For works like *Midnight's Children, The Trotter-Nama, The Great Indian Novel,* however, the most appropriate context is exilic mythologization (of personal and national histories). On my more recent annual trips to India, especially when I've taken part in panels with Indian academics on the literature of the Indian diaspora or conducted Fiction Workshops on the University of Baroda campus, I've noted my Indian colleagues' increased awareness of the discrete aims of these two genres.

J: In "Immigrant Writing," you discuss how America has "lost the power to transform the world's imagination." You suggest that no one as yet has spoken for "New Americans from nontraditional immigrant countries." Why is it the burden, or privilege—depending on how one looks at it—of new American immigrant writers to "reinvigorate" not only American writing, but also "the world's imagination"?

M: First of all, I don't think that the writer starts to work on her novel by saying, "I'm going to invigorate all of American writing." Any writer who does so will end up producing a sterile, agenda-ridden text and not literature. What I, as immigrant writer, hope for is *to transform* as well as *be transformed* by the world I'm re-imagining and re-creating through words. I'd like to think that ideas and feelings generated by my fiction will trickle into other cultures and literatures through translation, and provoke rethinking of what citizenship entails. *Jasmine* has been translated into eighteen languages. I'm very touched and humbled by the letters I get from immigrant readers who have read the book in their own language and have integrated Jasmine's adventures into their own personal/cultural experience.

J: That's an intriguing dialectic, this idea of immigrant writers and their characters simultaneously transforming and being transformed. Maurice Merleau-Ponty defines "intersubjectivity" in a related way as the trespassing of one's self on the other and of the other on one's self . . . for him, contact with "the other" is not all about assimilation.
M: Yeah, and I've written at great length on that idea, as early as 1990.

J: To move beyond Ahmad and his concerns with your writing, what relationship do you see in the future between what we've called "immigrationism"—not a term you used but one that seems to capture the spirit of the project you outline in "Immigrant Writing"—and postcolonialism? What do you think keeps the South Asian postcolonialists with whom you've expressed dissatisfaction from listening to you in the way you feel you should be listened to?
M: Arrogance. And a lack of sensitivity to literature. I think that they come to works of fiction with closed-off, ready-made, perfectly sealed theories and that they're not willing to discover any new ground. Just as in travelogues, some travelers, like a V. S. Naipaul, quite often go with preconceived notions about the country and find only what they expect to find: reinforcement and confirmation of their preconceived notions. There are other travelers, and I hope I'm one of these, who come with a fluid, open mind, and let the locals speak for themselves; they experience the place on its own terms. There are those who confirm social, political stereotypes and other writers who interrogate the stereotypes. William Gass will have a respected small audience, but he's never going to have a wide, popular audience because he isn't entertaining and comforting the average reader by expressing the ideas and articulating the philosophies that make you feel good about yourself.

In terms of seeing connections between the South Asian postcolonialists and immigrationism, I see "diasporality" as a kind of continuum with immigrants and immigrationists at one end of the scale and expatriate or exilic figures and postcolonialists at the other. Those who decide, "all right, I'm going to go on with my life, the past is going to color my present and the present is going to color my future, but here and now, I'm a different person," these people reflect the spirit of immigrant writing by keeping themselves open to new experiences and responding second by second. They're changing and being changed: you are a new person

every second of your life depending on how you act and whether you are open
to bruisings and dentings. This energy is completely opposed to the postcolonial
who, if he or she is not within the immediate postcolonial context, is simply talking about the past and ignoring or obliterating the present because it's so much
safer to talk about a dead debate.

J: Has the marketplace proven itself open to "new experiences" and how has that
dynamic affected the reception of your work?
M: In 1985 no U.S. publisher was willing to publish the manuscript of *Darkness* because at that time there was no marketing category for "ethnic immigrant
American fiction." The issues facing the South Asian community of naturalized
citizens were perceived as irrelevant to "real" Americans, meaning whites, African
Americans, and dispossessed American Indians. Editors would say, "This collection is incredibly powerful, even though it's so dark in its outlook, but we can't
imagine any American reader wanting to read about these people." The book was
eventually bought for $3,500 Canadian dollars by Penguin Canada, and came out
as a paperback original that was meant to get lost. In the introduction to the collection, I talked about seeing myself as "a series of fluid identities." Since then,
I've found corroboration in the fascinating published material of psychologists
and academics—Alan Roland's work on *the contextual self* and in Robert Jay
Lifton's work on *the protean self.* I would have had an easier time getting published, and being paid more decent advances, if I had written in the exilic tradition of nostalgia and loss.

J: What about someone whose fluidity is forestalled, who is unable to move beyond the past despite a willingness to engage in the present? Dimple, in *Wife*,
seems to be just such a character.
M: Several of my characters fail to move from expatriate to immigrant in the
"diasporality" spectrum. Some of the characters don't try, don't want to. In my
narratives, I want to represent a varied set of responses to the experience of unhousement. And these characters help to piece together an unsentimental portrait
of the United States. I certainly know what I love about the spirit of America,
but I've also written at great length about the underside of the American Dream.
Hannah, in *The Holder*, is an embodiment of the guts, imagination, and asser-
tiveness of that American spirit, and its underside—the will to imperialize.

J: As you've outlined above, much of the "energy" which marks good writing
stems from its willingness to engage in the "bruisings and dentings" of life. Are

writing programs doing enough to impress upon young writers the benefits of engaging the "real world" political, ethnic, and racial struggles in American society?

M: The answer is "No." All fiction is political and moral, but very few works of fiction in this country are *about* politics or morality. Novelists humanize "the other," and reveal a just, generous, ideal world, but they don't hector nor dictate as do demagogues and pamphleteers. I think that minority American writers are more likely to *want* to—and *attempt* to—create national mythologies through their fiction than are white Americans, because history and memory are of powerful consequence to them. The original white settlers' dream of "rugged individualism" is anti-history.

J: You've commented before that a lot of your stories are about transfiguration or psychic transformation, not economic transformation, and that you consequently are interested in psychic violence and its effect on the individual, often female Asian Americans, rather than group violence and its effect on the masses. Why do you think you've concentrated more on psychic violence inflicted upon the individual and less on political unrest and labor agitation in your work, especially as you were subject to the threats of such violence during your childhood in Calcutta?

M: Good fiction concentrates on the emotional, intellectual, and physical responses of a small cast of characters when they are thrust into a situation that is not routine for them. Politics and history, or rather political and historical events, provide the *context* for the characters' varying reactions. And, by forcing the reader to live through the particular characters in their particularized situations, the author hopes that readers will make an epiphanic connection to the world of real politics and issues around them. Remember Cynthia Ozick's story, "The Shawl"? In that extraordinarily moving story, Ozick doesn't once mention the word, Holocaust; she focuses on the conflicts of a mother and her two daughters trying to survive the horrors of death-camp internment. That's what good fiction does, and should do. When I want to directly address the evil of racism, the denying of civil rights to gay men and women, etc., I prefer to do so in essays.

As for providing the larger *context* of politics, class, and race, I've done that from my first novel on. In *The Tiger's Daughter*, individual actions are shaped by, and/or reactions to, the Naxalite revolution in Calcutta, and the imminence of the establishment of a Marxist government in West Bengal state. In *Wife*, Dimple experiences racist discrimination in a Queens shop, genderist discrimination at home, and classist discrimination at meetings with white feminists. I just wish that scholars would go back to reading the primary texts before presuming to make [mis]pronouncements on them!

In terms of psychic violence and female sexuality, I grew up at a time and in a class in Calcutta when you couldn't say the word "sex." I'd never said the word "sex" and we certainly were not allowed to think of it; I didn't even know how the male anatomy was constructed. So for me or for my characters who are coming not from villages but upper-class, urban Indian settings, sexuality becomes the mode of resistance or a way to rebel. After all, if you're coming out of a society where sex is the unspeakable, the unutterable, then doing it or acknowledging your sexuality results not only in individual rebellion but actually constitutes an attack on a whole patriarchal, Victorian, hypocritical society. And why psychic violence? Ultimately, physical injuries are less affecting than the wounds inside. You lose a leg, you get a prosthetic. But what do you do about the scarred psyche?

J: You've written elsewhere about the need to "make the familiar exotic and the exotic familiar."
M: Yes, to bring out the luminosity in the most banal moment, and to elicit sympathy for the least familiar character.

J: By privileging psychic as opposed to physical violence, does your work implicitly cultivate an "aestheticization" of violence? For example, violence appears to be somewhat "benign" in its after-effects on Jasmine—she doesn't seem to bear too many psychic or physical scars from her traumatic experiences with Suki and Half-Face. Similarly, in *The Holder*, violence seems to be surprisingly positive in its effects on Hannah, transforming her in its crucible from an "unfinished, unformed" woman into "a goddess-in-the-making." To borrow the structural trope of *The Holder*, is the violence you write about somehow like the "virtual reality" Beigh experiences, transformative and enlightening to be sure, but somehow less than "real"?
M: First of all, before I get to the idea of virtual reality and violence, I want you to come to the kitchen with me. This is Goddess Kali, the image of the Godhead as Destroyer. The Godhead as Kali is what I worship. Most Hindu Bengalis in Calcutta do. Most Hindu Bengali families have an altar to Her in their homes. I do; in my bedroom. You can see for yourself that Kali isn't one bit passive. She has strung Herself a garland of severed heads, and She's hefting Her blood-stained weapons to decapitate more evil men. Kali is what Jasmine was mythologizing herself into when she killed her rapist, Half-Face. In Christianity, humans are made in the image of God. But in Hinduism, all creatures *are* manifestations of the Godhead. Why doesn't Jasmine agonize more over having killed the man who

brutalized her? Why is her reaction "benign"? Her goal is the Hindu ideal of non-attachment. To allow oneself to be utterly destroyed by the violence done to her and done by her would be to fall victim to *maya*. You've read R. K. Narayan's *The Guide*; you're familiar with the Hindu concept of non-attachment. The difficult feat for the Hindu American writer is to dramatize the benignity of non-attachment without making characters appear uncaring or grimly stoic.

J: Considering the potential violence of representation, do you see writing—or virtual technology, in the case of Beigh becoming Bhagmati in *The Holder*—as a violent medium?

M: I don't know if I think of the medium as violence. It's certainly a medium that forces the author and the reader to take enormous risks, to expose oneself to emotions one would rather avoid.

J: Well, you have talked about the physical and psychic violence that necessarily accompanies transformation for the immigrant. Given the transformative capability of technological developments in writing, has your own evolution as a writer been marked by epistemological violence?

M: I have no idea. I started with orality. I come from a culture where grandmothers and mothers tell endless stories. There wasn't a single night that I didn't fall asleep to my mother telling stories at dinnertime. We sat on raffia mats on the floor and ate off brass plates. She mashed rice and fish into little balls and fed me, quite literally, with her fingers while she told me stories from the historical novels or biographies that she'd read. Stories about Marie Antoinette, Napoleon, Mary Queen of Scots. Bigger than life characters and adventures. I marvel at it now: my mother putting food into my mouth and, simultaneously, putting the wonder of narrative into my head.

It was by listening that I visualized and was mesmerized by conflict, by character, by romance, whatever. I started to read and write very early—I was in regular school by the age of three—and at that time, we used pens that you dip into an inkwell. I don't know if that was violence, but you did immediately start thinking in wholly different ways and the scratching—I can still see the blots of ink, the scratching on the paper—slows you down, but also gives you time to think. Then my relationship to story again became very different when we graduated by age nine to fountain pens. Also, the paper was so different over there; you could see bugs worked into the fabric, or big seams . . . the paper was rough and pocked with shiny bits. Seeing whether the pen nib would go over the shiny impurities or not resulted in a wholly different way of dealing with orthography and a different mental process which accompanies the writing of stories. There wasn't ever a time that I can remember when I wasn't writing stories and I remember what a big breakthrough it was when my father brought back ballpoint pens from Paris. They all melted in the heat but you could write so much faster! That was very empowering, and I went straight from that in the States to typewriter and when I started thinking on electric typewriter, again, suddenly my relationship with the word, and therefore with narrative, became very, very different, more conscious.

If by "technological developments in writing" you mean the availability of computers, software, data storage and retrieval facilities, information-design programs, virtual reality, etc., then I have to confess that technology has been for me a means of exploring and expanding knowledge without losing the writerly sense of wonder. Clark and I were among the very first batch of American writers to get into computers.

J: Oh, really?

M: Yes. In fact, Clark was on a program on NPR to discuss the ways in which the form and the process of writing has changed as a result of his switch to the word processor. Technology has broken down linear thought as well as linear plot movement. I don't think of technology as an enemy of Art. Technology serves the artist.

J: That sentiment is consistent with your writing in *The Holder*, where technology is employed throughout as a literary and thematic device. Nevertheless, the novel implies that such media are only actualized through data-gathering by sensitive and careful human beings like Beigh, people who have a personal investment in such projects. For example, Venn, who tries to experience the past using the interactive computer program, ends up with nothing more than a "postcard view of modern Madras"; he can't access the experience Beigh can, in large part because he hasn't cultivated the kind of sensitivity that she has from tracing Hannah's life. The technology acts as a "gatekeeper" of sorts, which we find very interesting, especially when considering how technology structures First and Third World relationships of power and hierarchy.

M: To me, creative imagination is the "gatekeeper." The technician downloads a statistics-rich experience; the artist, using the same program, wrests a vision. And each time you use that program, you learn or dis-learn some element because "you" are made up of a series of fluid identities. Similarly, each time you read *The Holder*, I hope you come up with new insights.

I'm not sure I agree with you that technology privileges "First" World over "Third." Much of the information transfer and accounting for U.S. corporations and mega-multinationals with European headquarters is done offshore, meaning in areas that you are designating as "Third." I've done homework on this. It's *class*, not geography, that's providing the hierarchy grid. Urban, upper-middle classes and professionals in Bombay, Singapore, Hong Kong, Manila, etc. have all the latest electronics and communications instruments. But the poor and the homeless in all areas of the world, including North America, are increasingly disempowered by technological advances. Your question seems to arise from the need of postcolonial studies scholars to impose politics as the dominant grid for measuring art. But for the writer of serious fiction, politics or race or gender is only one element of many hundred elements that go into the making of a character. Novelists aim for fullness of catharsis, not a political pamphlet.

J: Yet, isn't it difficult to separate the aesthetic from the political? For example, two reviews suggest that while the use of virtual reality is a clever device in *The Holder*, the representation of seventeenth-century India—with its "excessive" emphasis on violence and ornamentation—ironically reduplicates exoticized representations of India found in colonialist texts and period pieces (see Koshy and Parameswaran). These reviewers argue that any attempt to alter or deconstruct such representations through the use of virtual reality is undermined by your perhaps unconscious kinship with Orientalists of the past. How do you respond to such charges, and upon reflection, do you wish you'd used "virtual reality" any differently?

M: Absolutely not. One, this is not a book about India, but about the making of America and American national mythology. That's why I used the two women characters, Hannah the pre-America American, and Beigh, the post–de-Europeanized American, to dramatize the need to redefine what it means to be an "American" in the 1990s. Two, I'm sure the two reviewers you are referring to haven't done eleven years of research into mercantilism in seventeenth-century India as I have. Crucial new material on seventeenth-century trade, especially on intra-Asian trade, has been published in the early 1990s by Indian and Sri Lankan scholars. So it's simply ignorance of Indian mercantile and military histories on the part of these two reviewers. That's what I find most frustrating about being a scholar/writer: that academics and journalists with insufficient knowledge of the contextual material have the audacity to make such public pronouncements! I don't know where this animus comes from. Why is it so hard for them to deal with impassioned, well-researched, provocative fiction by a woman author?

J: Part of these critics' suggestions, though, is that despite careful research, your revisions of colonialist or orientalist accounts of the seventeenth century are not substantive enough.

M: My suggestion to them is that they bring greater intelligence and sensitivity to bear on the act of reading literature, including *The Holder*.

J: This is a book about the process of history making, specifically about the "American" way of making and remaking history. Yet, one might argue that the representations of Native Americans in the early sections of the novel set in Puritan New England perhaps unwittingly repeat the imperialist tendencies of many colonial and nineteenth-century American texts. Specifically, the miscegenetic encounter between Rebecca and her Nipmuc lover recalls similar encounters depicted in novels by nineteenth-century New England women, including Lydia Child's *Hobomok* and Maria Sedgwick's *Hope Leslie*. In those works, such encounters are subversive to the extent that they allow for a female voice to emerge and suggest possible "new" alliances between women and Native Americans. Yet the Native American never really "speaks" in these novels . . . a romanticized version does, and thus these amorous encounters serve, one could argue, merely to empower and exoticize colonial and nineteenth-century Anglo-American women at the expense of Native Americans.

M: Well, in my novel, I have Rebecca's biracial children very much alive and present to recount their own tales when they are ready to. Rebecca's Nipmuc lover has several prototypes in history, of course. I'll leave it to other authors to write the lover's story. Actually I'm very interested in writing King Philip's story from his point of view some day. An author focuses on a few individual characters, and hopes that a larger *frisson* of emotion and revelation comes across to the reader. I would be guilty of bad writing if I insisted on making Rebecca's lover stand for all Nipmucs let alone for all original Americans, or Bhagmati all Hindu women. Margaret Atwood has written: "You tell the story you have to tell; let others tell the story that they have to tell." My message to these academics: Read the story that I have told in *The Holder*; don't fabricate a story that I didn't tell, but that you need to pretend I did so that you can distort the text into a convenient target of hate. I've been quoted in an article in *Harper's* as saying these postcolonial scholars are "assassins of the imagination."

J: While we certainly do not intend to "assassinate the imagination," we would argue that by relegating Rebecca's biracial children to the margins of the text as unspeaking subjects, their narratives, as is the case in much colonial American writing, are endlessly deferred. Nonetheless, we feel that much of the richness and strength of the novel derives from the interventions you make in the captivity narrative tradition and the "canon" of nineteenth-century American literature.

M: Well, perhaps next time you read *The Holder* you'll have new "takes" on the significance of my meta-fictional use of Sita's, Bhagmati's, and Hannah's "captivity narratives."

J: In conclusion, we'd like to go back to the idea of Mughal painting you articulated earlier as a governing aesthetic in your writing. You've said that "I will be writing, in the Mughal style, till I get it right" ("Four-Hundred-Year-Old Woman" 38). *The Holder* seems to be very much predicated upon "Mughal aesthetics." It seems to be an excellent example of the "complication" and "elaboration" of Mughal miniature painting and reflects the "sense of the interpenetration of all things" which you have identified as a compelling aspect of such an aesthetic. Having said all that, *have* you finally "gotten it right"? And if so, where are you going from here?

M: Who knows? The characters surprised me draft by draft; the structure of the novel evolved almost in spite of myself. I should add that my structures are also inspired by my obsession with chaos theory and fractals. In fact, a couple of European scholars have published essays on the operation of chaos theory in *Jasmine*. Where am I going? I don't want to know too far ahead.

A Usable Past: An Interview with Bharati Mukherjee

Shefali Desai and Tony Barnstone / 1996

From *Manoa: A Pacific Journal of International Writing*, 10:2 (1998), 130–47. © 1996 by Shefali Desai and Tony Barnstone. Reprinted by permission of the authors.

SD: Just yesterday I read the op-ed piece you wrote for the *New York Times*. I hadn't planned to discuss it here, but some of the questions that you raise really interest me. You say that your sister probably pities you because of the "erasure of your Indianness." I was wondering if you really feel that Indianness has been erased from your life, and if so, to what extent has that occurred?

BM: Let me just preface whatever my answer might be by saying that the op-ed piece resulted from the *New York Times* asking me about my reaction to the current curtailment of rights of legal immigrants to the United States. My older sister, who is a child psychologist of some renown in Detroit and has been here for the last thirty-five years, has chosen to remain an Indian citizen but a green-card holder; whereas I became a U.S. citizen as soon as I was eligible.

Erasure of Indianness: I think that what my sister meant by that was not to accuse me so much as to say she felt sorry for me, because I no longer automatically wear—choose to wear—Indian saris. I find that Meera—we're wonderful friends; it's a very affectionate family and we call each other twice a week—that her accent has grown more and more Indian over the years because, I think, that gives her a kind of rootedness. She, who was one of the cool, stylish convent girls with short hair in Calcutta, now wears long sleeves and her hair in a bun. So she has that outward appearance of Indianness.

I don't think of myself in terms of being a Mukherjee daughter from such and such a family or such and such a caste—that's not my primary way of identifying myself. But certainly Indianness is a habit of mine now, which means that it's a cultural conditioning to certain things . . . the way that some Catholics—even if they've given up their religion—remain Catholics in habit. But I don't need, I guess, Indian clothes to feel Indian.

SD: So it's more of a surface Indianness that you are referring to, not—

BM: Well, no, I think it's much deeper than that. But if being Indian meant that you were typed, you were who you were because of where you had been born—soil, family, caste, religion, gender—then all of that has crumbled.

SD: You also wrote in the article that your sister's life in America sounds like "the description of a long-enduring, comfortable yet loveless marriage"—I really like that analogy—"without risk or recklessness." But you, on the other hand, have risked and have undergone what you refer to as "the trauma of self-transformation." What was it that led you to choose that path? Was it a conscious decision?

BM: Absolutely not. I'm afraid it was hormones! Coming to Iowa to coeducational classrooms was the first time, really, that I was in a coeducational situation. My father had made sure that we would never be in anything but girls' schools if he could help it. And so mine was a kind of whirlwind two-week courtship and a lunchtime wedding. I didn't have time to think, which is just as well.

That's the easy answer. The more honest answer, I think, is that somewhere at the gut level I must have wanted to turn my life around, or there was something that was freeing about being—and I'm talking about being in the heartland, you know, the heartland of Iowa City—a student in the States that wasn't possible for me in the very restricted, upper-class, patriarchal family that Calcutta provided me.

SD: When comparing your autobiography to your literature, especially the novel *The Tiger's Daughter* and "A Wife's Story," one of your short stories, I couldn't help but notice that there are parallels between your real-life stories and the fictional stories. I was wondering what role autobiography plays in your writing process.

BM: I wasn't aware until I came to write *The Holder of the World* that there was any autobiographical impulse—let alone element—in my work. I thought I was writing about people who were totally outside of me. I realize now that each of the novels is sort of a way station in my personal Americanization. And so, even the sentence structures seem to have changed. I think that most writers, like actors, have to dig inside themselves for the passions of their characters. And that's for the good guys as well as the bad guys in any novel. So I feel that I am invested, metaphorically, in every single character in each of the books.

SD: In a 1991 interview you talked about the frustration you had with the joint-family structure in Calcutta, and later about the "very traditional, hierarchical, caste society with overt oppression against women" in which you were raised. How has being a woman who lived in that society shaped your outlook on gender and gender issues?

BM: Well, I didn't realize how traumatized I was by the sexism being practiced all around me. I didn't know while I was growing up that there was an alternate way of conducting life. Through age twenty, I was very much within solid, solidly rooted, comfortably financed, upper-middle-class family. And I saw all around me incredible physical as well as verbal abuse of women. My own mother—I owe everything that I may be today to my mother, who was not allowed to get an education—put her body quite literally on the line, so that her three daughters could be educated. I remember, to this day, my mother being told constantly, "You should kill yourself, you should die, you are unlucky because you don't have a son." And so that has fueled, I think, all three of us sisters' desire for an education. I'm sure I got a double Ph.D. only because of my mother's image in the back of my head. There are good sides to joint families—I'm not putting it down totally—but I was amazed at how much of the oppression of women is done by women themselves within these joint families. And how the women seemed to me to have only one way of exercising power and consolidating their own position, their own safety within the joint system: to be cruel to whoever is farther down the line.

SD: In one of the articles, you mentioned your mother and how she had undergone physical and verbal abuse so that you could live alone once you returned from England. Yet you hesitated to call her a Gloria Steinem and a feminist. What are the differences you see between the kind of feminist your mother was and Western feminists? Was hers a type of Eastern feminism?

BM: I don't even have a concept of something as big as "Eastern," and I don't think my mother ever thought of herself as feminist; yet she was fighting for the best life possible for her daughters. She would say continually—this was the refrain that my sisters and I grew up with—"I will not let my daughters be the chattel that I had been." She was furious. I don't know that my quarrel is with Western feminism as such, but with the mouthy American feminists of the early and mid-seventies. Particularly Gloria Steinem and the *Ms.* magazine group, who were doctrinaire and, we now know, often conducting intergender relationships and maneuvering for power when they had an overt but totally unacknowledged racist, colonialist attitude towards women of color. Particularly women of color who were not African American. And so the Kate Millets and the Gloria Steinems insisted on telling minority women, telling me, how I should conduct my life in order to be a feminist. It was all about talk, rhetoric, and self-examination—these were the times of consciousness-raising groups and examining yourself with mirrors—whereas my mother would have died if anyone had mentioned such things. But she was able to get things done without talking about it.

I don't see myself or my mother as anti-male, anti-men, but I do see myself as a champion of civil rights. Extending civil rights to all disadvantaged groups.

SD: I see some of this expressed in the tension between your characters Ina Mullick and Dimple—and also Maya and her friend Fran. Were you thinking about these sorts of things . . .

BM: Absolutely, yes. And even in *Jasmine*, Wylie is a version of those sorts of things, but by that time I had enough sympathy for the flaws of that particular kind of feminist, so I didn't have to hit as hard as I might have in the earlier novels. I'd taken a lot of flack in the seventies from exactly those doctrinaire feminists who resented me because I had actually gone ahead and gotten my Ph.D., gotten a job at McGill University while they were still finding themselves by throwing pots or drawing up domestic contracts for who would do the dishes on what day.

SD: Maya, in "The Tenant," talks about this in her feminist class at Duke. She was criticized for being this feminine woman, but she couldn't make the others understand that this was how she was raised.

BM: You know, when I was growing up, how you sat, how you talked to males older than you—all this was so ritualized that my big battle, personal battle as an American, has been to not be so polite.

SD: In speaking about writing *The Middleman and Other Stories*, you said that you "can enter any gender and any culture, if the character and story excite" you. I was wondering if you feel that it is easier to work with your female characters than your male characters.

BM: I don't know. Who knows down the line if the male will impact? I think the novel that I'm researching now, that I've been thinking about for a long time, will have a male protagonist. But I can never predict what minor character is going to take over and what major character is going to wind up on the cutting-room floor. I want to think that every character is a little—I guess like Flaubert saying, "Emma Bovary, c'est moi"—that I am the characters but the characters aren't me. So I can see myself being just as much at home if that male character is a metaphor for whatever is engaging my passions or my curiosity.

SD: And you would probably say the same for the Indian immigrant, as opposed to the Asian immigrant?

BM: Yes. It's having to know exactly how in culture-specific ways the character is going to show his or her emotion. The Indian community I know best, so a number of my major characters have been of Indian background. But when I was doing *The Holder of the World*, I knew what that particular Massachusetts family or young woman of a certain class and Anglo origin, graduate of Yale, how this one character would react. I have to know the thinking—all the details must surface on their own without my saying, Oh, let me look at my note cards and see.

SD: Do you see a danger in putting the experiences of all Asian immigrants together, lumping them into one?

BM: Absolutely. I've worked some with the Asia Society in Los Angeles to make sure that the dominant culture—the whites or the African Americans—doesn't lump all Asian groups together, because the histories, intra-Asian country histories, the immigration histories are so different. Every time I teach a contemporary Asian American literature course, the tensions that arise from the Chinese American students reacting to Japanese American novels or Japanese literature are so volatile still.

I want to see class introduced into the discourse to acknowledge that the young Vietnamese kid in the San Jose inner-city area experiencing the problems of inner-city kids has very little in common with, say, the Silicon Valley Asian family. That's where, I think, the intra-minority fights are very depressing to me. Race should be made a little less relevant in the 1990s and into the new century, and the disadvantaged-versus-advantaged situation emphasized.

SD: Do you think that the immigrant experience of the Indian woman is fundamentally different from the Indian man's experience in North America?

BM: I'm convinced it is, but I haven't seen enough research, academic research on this. With a Canadian government grant, I've done some of this research myself in Toronto's South Asian community. But perhaps because the women are trained to be adaptable, to accommodate themselves to the husbands' families, the husbands' lifestyles, etc., etc., the Indian immigrant women are so much more able to be bridges between the cultures. They can wear pants, drive a car, do their PTA meetings, bake cookies, do Halloween costumes, and then come back to the home and be the more conventional Indian wife, who serves the right kind of Indian curried food and is nonbelligerent, nonthreatening to the Indian immigrant husband. Whereas the males—and I've seen some research on the males—seem with diaspora, with expatriation to . . . regress isn't the right verb . . . to become more and more reactionary, more and more so-called Indian because they feel threatened in terms of their status in the American work force.

You know, I feel that the Indian male who is very successful financially and who has his Mercedes-Benz and his BMW and kids in expensive private schools, etc., quite often has frozen the sense of his India and his Indianness in the year in which he left India and came as an immigrant to this country. So that it's an artificial homeland, artificial India that these guys have created.

SD: So while the actual experience in India might have progressed twenty years . . .
BM: Yes. I go to India every year, and urban Indians of that same class don't have a problem with westernization or consumerism. Even the rhetoric, the way English is used in newspapers like *The Statesman* or *Hindustan Times*, has become a weird mixture of Indian-English, British-English, and a lot of American-English. Whereas the group that immigrated from 1965 on . . . that first batch has, for self-protection—and I understand that totally—become very Indian in that sort of nervous way.

TB: A lot of Asian American writers, particularly your colleague at Berkeley, Maxine Hong Kingston, as well as Amy Tan, Chitra Divakaruni, and others, have tried to find in folk tales, or the history of their ancestral country what Van Wyck Brooks called a "usable past." Particularly a usable past with woman warriors, strong women, which could somehow be distinguished from an unusable past of patriarchy—in the case of Kingston and Tan, of patriarchal Confucianism. Paradoxically, this unusable past is quite useful for providing conflict in their prose. What's your usable past? What aspects of your history can and can't you use in your fiction, and in your life?
BM: What an interesting, complicated question. I think that the reason that wonderful writers like Maxine Hong Kingston and Amy Tan use so much mythology, Chinese mythology, is that they are second-generation Americans. It's a kind of roots retrieval: "Who were my people?" Whereas I, being fresh off the jet, want to get away from a lot of the mythologies that were so genderist, that were created to reinforce patriarchy or the class system—not just caste system, but class system. When I grew up, I didn't have the bedtime tales of Hans Christian Andersen, but the Puranic tales, thousands of years B.C., and the Hindu epics. Which means that some of the stories, like that of Sita, the perfect wife who is self-sacrificing and self-effacing, are the ones that I want to attack, critique. Or I have rereadings

of such legends in which I suddenly realize that the conventional interpretations were convenient to the male explicators, commentators. I would like to make up my own myths. As an immigrant I don't have models here in America.

TB: Have you come into criticism for that—in the way, for example, Frank Chin has criticized Kingston and Tan for changing Chinese mythology? Of course, Chin himself adapts the classic Chinese epic *Water Margin* to his own purposes in his novel *Donald Duk.*
BM: And Frank Chin is on record saying that Tan, Kingston, and so on are a kind of Christian women's whitening-of-myth conspiracy. Those are not his exact words.

TB: But that's essentially what he's saying.
BM: That they are appeasing, or satisfying—appeasing white guilt and satisfying white need for exoticism.

   The kind of criticism that I've gotten is from a very different source. It's the postcolonial theorists from South Asia—in fact, people I went to school with as a nursery-age student, who came from the same kind of upper-class background that I did, when our financial status was exactly equal—who despise fiction, or art, as being reactionary. I'm obviously thinking of Gayatri Spivak as one such critic. They want real life, meaning sociology, journalism; but a writer has to think of each character as an individual instead of representative of all South Asian immigrants. The theorists, in contrast, have to find a general principle. So I'm attacked because I married outside the community, because I'm fluent in English, because I'm—their word is "privileged"—and therefore have no right to write. Because if I'm writing about people exactly like me—women from a certain background and with a certain status—then I'm immediately elitist and have nothing worthwhile to say.

TB: Does the writing of novels with didactic purpose invite this kind of criticism, the reduction of all the complexities of fiction to sociology, social policy? How can we separate the politics and the fiction?
BM: I think that all fiction, all speech, all act, in real life or fiction, is political—meaning that it is about power. Either being empowered or allowing someone to disempower you. Having said that, I'll add that the theoreticians right now—this is the Subaltern school of critics of South Asian origin who all have these fancy chairs that come with high salaries on U.S. or European campuses—need to see literature only in a Marxist context. So fiction is judged only by the biological, ethnic, and class status of the author and what they call the "field of production,"

which means that if your book is being published by an American mainstream press—even though it might be as small as Grove Press—rather than a basement press in Minneapolis, then you have "sold out." So the reasons for looking at work become nonliterary. And I think it is also arrogance on their part that they need to see their criticism as more important than literature—they don't need the texts. Apparently, in Sri Lanka recently, for one of these commonwealth literature association meetings, someone did a statistical study that showed more papers had been done on "poor Mukherjee" than on anyone else. But so often the details, like the names of main characters, are wrong, or they think *Darkness* is a novel, which means that they're reading each other, not the texts.

SD: Do you think that since your novels and short stories put the women characters in the center, they offer a usable past for other Indian women?

BM: I don't know; I don't think of these things, and it would scare me if from now on I thought of any of this. And in fact I cringe when young Indo-Americans say, You're our role model; how come your characters have sex? I don't want to be anyone's role model. But one hopes that something will trigger in the reader the desire to question assumptions.

SD: What were your feelings on religion when you left India, and how have they since changed?

BM: I was a practicing, very observant Hindu—which doesn't mean that much because you don't really have to go to the temple once a week, as practicing Christians may have to. I had my little grotto of icons, and I still have them. I'm a very secular person, but I guess I still think of myself as Hindu. I'm a little hesitant to say this because nowadays if you say you're a Hindu, it immediately becomes identified with fundamentalism and particular political parties. I want to disassociate myself totally from that, but I do believe in the geophysical principle that Hinduism metaphorizes, that cosmic energy.

SD: And the idea of reincarnation?

BM: All of Indian religion, I've always felt, is a metaphor for physics and astrophysics, and that's why I'm so attracted to chaos theory or fractals. There are all these Puranic tales about millions of galaxies, millions of universes: there isn't just one god in this one little galaxy, and the moment you start thinking too much of yourself, Brahma is going to come from another galaxy and put you in your place.

TB: Can I read you a poem by Rabindranath Tagore that I happen to have in my backpack? This is a poem I always relate to a poem by William Carlos Williams in

Spring and All called "The Rose." I was thinking about it when you were talking about physics and Hinduism. It's translated by William Radice.

THE SICK-BED

When I woke up this morning
There was a rose in my flower-vase:
The question came to me—
The power that brought you through cyclic time
To final beauty,
Dodging at every turn
The torment of ugly incompleteness,
Is it blind, is it abstracted,
Does it, like a world-denying sannyasi,
Make no distinction between beauty and the opposite of beauty?
Is it merely rational,
Merely physical,
Lacking in sensibility?
There are some who argue
That grace and ugliness take equal seats
At the court of Creation,
That neither is refused entry
By the guards.
As a poet I cannot enter such arguments—
I can only gaze at the universe
In its full, true form,
At the millions of stars in the sky
Carrying their huge harmonious beauty—
Never breaking their rhythm
Or losing their tune,
Never deranged
And never stumbling—
I can only gaze and see, in the sky,
The spreading layers
Of a vast, radiant, petalled rose.

BM: That's beautiful.

TB: Very much what you're saying about physics, I think, and traditional Indian ways of seeing the complexity of the universe.

BM: And for a poet or fiction writer, if you're saying the goal is acquiring the perspective that makes you see you're really a speck in a giant design, then it affects the way you think of character: you dramatize character in a way that's the opposite of the way that protagonists or tragic heroes in European literature behave or should behave. It poses all sorts of narrative-strategy questions.

SD: In *Jasmine* the novel, "Jasmine" your short story, "The Tenant," "A Wife's Story," "The Management of Grief," and *Wife*, the female protagonists undergo transformations that touch on issues of Hindu reincarnation, immigration, and the American Dream coupled with some sort of feminist realization. Would you describe your literature as being an intersection of these?
BM: I don't know. When I'm sitting in front of my computer screen, I'm not really thinking in those analytical ways. Things are happening in spite of me, and there's really a kind of physical change when the writing is going well: there's just so much adrenaline pumping that there's a physiological change, and I know I'm into the characters and they're doing things in spite of me. But in the sense of reincarnation, I'm saying reincarnation is right here on this earth for Jasmine. I believe in change and resilience, adaptability, that if you can't adapt to the situation, you're going to be totally broken. What were some of the other intersections?

SD: American Dream . . .
BM: Because I haven't worked through this myself, that's why Jasmine and so many of my other characters are really trying to find a comfort zone between belief and effort, and reward of effort, and destiny—which things are planned. And so it's always that tension that keeps the Jasmines going, and whatever morality they have is not the conventional morality. Instead they say, Let me treat every moment with reverence because I don't know the function, the purpose of my being here. The two of you coming into my life this afternoon, for example; how does this fit into the larger design?

So not American Dream in the sense of "Can I have a bigger car"—I don't even drive, never quite got the hang of it, and I've certainly gone through an incredible economic and social demotion by choosing to live as an American—but that sense of discovering for yourself what you believe and who you want to be.

SD: Would you say that Hinduism and feminism intersect? I'm thinking here of when your character Dimple envisions herself as Sita the ideal wife and—
BM: Which Dimple rejects. I think this is why I'm trying to be very careful about not being identified as a Hindu writer because this is not in the religion itself; but all the midrash, all the commentary surrounding it, is so sexist, is so patriarchal,

that the legends are told and retold in such a way as to buttress patriarchy. My characters either reject Sita or reevaluate why Sita did what she did. And therefore, in *The Holder of the World*, I had an Indian woman character say that Sita is tempting the fates; she wants to step out of the safe chalk circle and see what the world out there is like. It's a misreading to see her as docile, passive.

SD: And we also see this when Jasmine is Kali?

BM: I needed that moment—it wrote itself—and then I realized that what had happened was that she had mythologized herself. I'll tell you an interesting story about the British reaction to that scene. Kali is the form that Bengali Hindus believe in: she's our patron; everyone has her icon in his or her bedroom. She is visualized as having a red tongue, a triangle hanging out, as she's doing a dance of destruction of evil. In this dance she's got all these bleeding weapons—scimitars and scythes—in her hand, and she's wearing a garland of bleeding, severed, mangled heads. So I needed for Jasmine to have a red tongue, right? Jasmine's got only one weapon at hand, so she cuts her tongue—a moment that's meant to be traumatic, motivating, and mythologizing: she turns into this goddess of destruction. In England, there was a year-long furor because *Jasmine* had been read week by week on a BBC women's program during the summer and one mother had written in saying, "This is mutilation, self-mutilation. It's like Oprah Winfrey!" [*Laughs*] I never even thought of it as self-mutilation!

TB: In one of his poems William Carlos Williams writes that "destruction and creation are simultaneous." Picasso said a very similar thing. For Williams, that's a way of mythologizing the avant-garde, the cutting edge: you have to destroy. Matisse once said, "In order to paint a rose you have to forget every painting of a rose that's ever been painted in order to paint it anew." It seems to me that Jasmine and other characters who go through the process of immigration— particularly to the United States, but also to Europe and elsewhere—have a capacity for destroying their past, for abandoning, for ceasing to be who they were, for living on the edge, for living on the frontier, kind of riding chaos perpetually. Is this for you in your personal symbol system also something about the process of creativity, or is it more about the process of movement from continent to continent?

BM: I think mainly a process of movement from continent to continent. I have a placid exterior, and a thrilling, crazy interior, so that I shouldn't have to leave a room in order to go through the chaos myself. I just try to hide it from people as much as I can. But I am convinced now that you can't straddle the fence—that if you're going to not remain an expatriate, then there has to be a traumatic, painful kind of break with the past. After that you might reclaim little bits and pieces of it and fit them into your new life in a different way, but there is no easy, painless way to make the change; otherwise, you're burrowing in nostalgia.

TB: I would assume then that it's also necessary for the culture to change, to acclimate itself to the new people who are making their home here.

BM: Yes, it is a two-way transformation. And whatever heritage I have come with is now collective, American heritage. Just as I have incorporated and absorbed so much American history—or trivia—so quickly. If I hadn't left India, or if I had married an Indian Silicon Valley tycoon, I would be a very different kind of writer because I wouldn't have been tested in what energized my material. I would have had safe, non-risk projects about conflictless, perfect, model immigrant families.

SD: Picking up on what Tony said about two-way transformations: you commented once in an interview that in America "diversity is accepted; the melting pot helps the newcomers to feel more welcome." So I was wondering if you see a melting pot where all cultures are dissolved into the dominant culture, or a melting pot in which each new ingredient changes and is changed by the others? And how does that play in your literature?

BM: I wish, at the time that I said this, there had been a phrase or I had been able to come up with a phrase more precise than *melting pot*—something like *stew pot*. The American mythology about the melting pot certainly helps others to come and say, Yes, I have a place here. The unfortunate part of the practice has been the nineteenth-century notion that you make yourself over following an Anglo or Puritan model. What I'm saying is that it's not like a salad, in which every bit of lettuce or radish or tomato or cucumber retains its original shape and taste and there's only the salad dressing as a kind of mild flavor that makes all these bits acceptable, but a stew in the sense that the stewing process has changed everything; the broth has become what it is because every bit has given some of its juices, some of its taste. I'm looking for every side to break down in some way and constantly create a new whole.

SD: Would you say that in this broth, some degree of gain and loss is inevitable?

BM: Yes, absolutely, and for everyone. That's what the whites have to understand and come to grips with if they are going to survive the new century, survive *into* the new century, for that matter. That's a very hard message to get across.

TB: Your analogy reminded me of a moment in *Huckleberry Finn* when Finn is talking about the problem of "sivilized" eating, in which you keep everything separate on the plate and how he likes it better when everything swaps around in a big pot and all the flavors mix.

BM That's right. I hadn't made the connection; that's wonderful.

SD: Why is it that the Vietnamese American character Du (in *Jasmine*) remains in the hyphen but Jasmine doesn't?

BM: Because he chooses to. I wanted, through all of these minor characters—for me as a writer, the minor characters are really pivotal in the book—to build in many different kinds of immigrants, having many different reactions to the fact that they are suddenly in this culture. And so Du, because he's gone through such unspeakable horrors as a result of the Vietnam War, may in junior high school, or high school, be able to act more American, get A's in U.S. history, but he chooses not to give up some private part of himself. There's a resentment, and he goes off to Los Angeles to find his sister.

SD: Is hyphenization insufficient? Does it make a person not whole?

BM: For me, hyphenization is a very discomforting situation for two reasons. It makes you want a way out, a net. You say, All right, so this doesn't work: I am an Indian for the whites and I am an American for the Indians—a kind of fence straddling that is almost immoral. I am trying to get white Americans and African Americans to see how deliberately and cruelly or maliciously marginalizing it is to apply the hyphen only to Asian Americans, Chicanos, and so on—and to not routinely make European-Americans of the Updikes and the Joyce Carol Oateses. It's as though they're saying there is one kind of America, and the rest of you because you're hyphenated—whether you want to be or not, we are insisting that you be hyphenated—are not really like us. So that's why, in order to emphasize the two-way transformation, I'm saying either call everyone American or make everyone hyphenated. But I'm against the hyphen.

SD: And, instead, for this fluid notion of "American"?

BM: Which to me is about believing in certain social and civic ideals rather than blood and soil.

SD: Several of your Indian heroines have entered into what we call mixed marriages, which you refer to in the op-ed piece by saying that you were "prepared for (and even welcomed) the emotional strain that came with marrying outside my ethnic community." Do you have any comments to make on this point besides what you have already written?

BM: Yes, I believe that the answer to any problem in multicultural, multiethnic societies is—and I'm using this word very deliberately—mongrelization. I come from a society of "pure" culture, where any kind of hanky-panky with blood-line, caste line, is to be despised. That means you lose your caste altogether. And so to me there's an enormous amount of danger in the false retention of pride in bloodlines, purity of bloodlines. And I think that the babysitters, the caregivers like Jasmine, who then, like a Jane Eyre, marry their Mr. Rochesters, are in the vanguard of the new transformation of America.

SD: You infuse some Hindu notions of non-dualism in your literature, and I'm thinking specifically of Jasmine. When she's still called by her village name, Jyoti, she remarks about her father's death, "but that pitcher is not broken. It is the same air this side as that." I was wondering if the theme of non-dualism shapes your heroines in any way?

BM: Fusion, yes. Seeing that what seems opposite really is simply part of the same whole. Or it's the usual mythic journey where creatures who had seemed like enemies or monsters testing you turn out to be gatekeepers on your way to getting the golden fleece or the golden chalice, or whatever. Yes, I'm afraid that there I am reflecting the Hindu belief that it all boils down to God: *God is God, God is a man, God is an inanimate object, God is a snake.* There is no clear-cut, permanent division between good and evil but just different ways of looking at things.

SD: How would you explain, then, why some of the Indian women in your stories—they're minor characters—avoid transformation or avoid the struggle against transformation? I'm thinking of Meena Sen in *Wife,* or Nirmala, the Professorji's wife who lives in Flushing, and probably that entire community in Flushing, or Santana, Dr. Chatterji's wife in "The Tenant."

BM: I'm looking for people who test their fates and then either discard or reclaim them, as opposed to those women, like the Meena Sens, who never test the fates and who live according to rites and rituals. That's a very different kind of faith from saying, I really do believe or I no longer believe.

SD: Would you hazard to comment on that lifestyle, on their chosen path?
BM: No. Who am I to make judgments other than in fiction?

SD: Do you know of any Indian males reacting to your literature in the same way that Amy Tan, Kingston, Toni Morrison, and Alice Walker have been accused of "betraying their culture"?
BM: By male reactions, do you mean from the Frank Chins? Writers themselves, or the community?

SD: Either.

BM: I don't think people in India really read my novels or any other literary novels; they all read Shobha Day, who describes herself as the Jackie Collins of India. They loved me when I wrote my first novel and was in *Newsweek*: "Calcutta daughter makes good," you know. There was nothing I could do wrong. But years later, in 1990, I made a statement in some interview that "well actually I'm an American writer of Indian origin now because I'm writing about immigrant themes," and they saw that as betrayal. If you are Indian, then you can't ever want to lose any part of that.

I don't think our community in the States really is into reading. They're so busy doing other things, so they'll read nonfiction. They couldn't care less.

SD: You illustrate women's oppression in Indian society quite often. Are your female characters—and if they are, to what extent—mouthpieces for Indian women who are experiencing oppression at the hands of an Indian patriarchy?

BM: I want to make it absolutely clear that I don't envision my characters as mouthpieces and I don't want them to be mouthpieces for anyone but themselves. Once you, as a writer, lose the eccentricity of character portrayal, then you're merely writing texts to be taught in college classrooms. That's a real, real danger to art. But I hope that my books make people think.

TB: Do you find that there are ways in which Indian women—and this goes against the tenor of what we've said so far—are more liberated than their Western counterparts? Are there any particular sources of strength for women in India that aren't really present in Western culture?

BM: Are we talking about Indian women still in India?

TB: Well, yes, I think so.

BM: In that case, the strengths are that you have a community of support. Especially in the 1990s, if the husband is beating up his wife, then the community will take a stand and give him a hard time. Whereas in a lot of the wife abuse, wife battering—which I'm afraid is not uncommon in the Indian immigrant community in the States—the battered wife doesn't have the same recourse to community support or community censure. That's the word I'm looking for: *censure*. I think that it's all about class in India, which means that the educated woman from the upper-middle class or upper class has such a support system of servants and a network; you're so well plugged in that it's far more liberated about jobs, careers. But the glass ceiling in the corporate world is even lower than it is here.

I'm trying to do more and more research into the Indian wives here—the most interesting group as far as I'm concerned, because suddenly they have been able to avoid the oppression, the ritualistic, traditional oppression by their mother-in-laws. They wait long enough for the wedding so that they can come right away, on green cards, and now they're the bosses in the household. There are more incidents now of abuse of aged in-laws by these young, hip wives. [*Laughs*] And they, even more than white American women, are able to use day-care facilities and have jobs set up, small businesses, and they're all reasonably well educated, you know. Many of them are coming with graduate degrees in biochemistry or are lab technicians, and so on. They're all economically independent in ways that the Indian wives in India are not.

TB: Do you think that there's been less of a—because of colonialism in India—decline in the status of Indian immigrants to the United States? Simply because of the language skills?
BM: Yes, yes. That's what distinguishes the U.S. Indo-American relationship from the Indo-Canadian relationship and certainly from the British and German situations, and separates the Indian immigrants from the other groups—the Filipinos and other Asians. We've been very lucky, but our luck has run out. And now with the new furor about scapegoating legal immigrants of color, especially in places like New York and California, you're going to see a new kind of discrimination.

TB: Let me ask you a few writing questions. Who are your American masters? I mean, writers who have influenced you, but even more, what passages from the novels you have read shine in your memory as passages you would like to be able to live up to or exceed, emulate?
BM: There are a number of American writers that I like. I can't say that any of them are masters. I mean, even though I admire the luminosity of, say, Updike's prose sentence by sentence, he's not someone that I want to emulate. So discarding the word master then, some of the writers whose sentences I just love are—this may seem totally amazing to you—Richard Ford, then Tom McGuane because of that energy in some of his earlier novels, like *Panama*. I like Lee Abbot, you know, who is small press but writes wonderful short stories. And I admire Joyce Carol Oates, because she takes on so many forms. I like Flannery O'Connor very much, but she's not living. When I grow up, can I be Flannery O'Connor? [*Laughs*] Some of Ann Beattie's passages are very moving to me, and I can still learn about structure from Hemingway.

TB: And a follow-up question to that. How about the early great Indian fiction writers: Saratchandra Chatterji, Premchand, others. Have they been influences?

BM: They haven't been influences simply because when I was growing up in Calcutta, even though India was independent at the time, my school was still a very Britishy spot in Calcutta and so we followed the syllabi for Cambridge University exams. As a very small child, I discovered Saratchandra and then again as a grown-up here in the United States. And he *speaks* to me.

Bengali language doesn't translate well into English, I think, because it is such an emotional language. It's a very euphonic language—even Tagore in English translation sometimes sounds sentimental or flaky, so you have to recite poems or recite sentences in Bengali. I like Saratchandra very much, but I see how much he also has been influenced by the alienation, marginalization of the individual from community, the desire to break away.

TB: So, in some ways, it's less useful.

BM: Ah, I love his work, but I can't say that it has had any influence.

SD: You've talked about transformation throughout this interview, and one thing that you said was that your characters, like yourself, have an intensity of spirit and especially of desire. Is there anything further that you can say to describe or illustrate what you mean by this phrase?

BM: Obsession. All good writing comes from obsessive passion and ambition to change the world. I'm afraid my characters and I suffer from those flaws.

Outsider Looking In, Insider Looking Beyond

Ron Hogan / 1997

From *Beatrice* (1997), http://www.beatrice.com/interviews/mukherjee/ [accessed on January 31, 2006]. © 1997 by Ron Hogan. Reprinted by permission of the author.

RH: What's it like to spend so much time writing about a protagonist who's basically unlikable, even reprehensible?

BM: I kind of like her, actually.

RH: There are *things* that I like about her, but she's not what I'd call endearing or sympathetic.

BM: I hope she's sympathetic. She's tough and vulnerable. I don't have any control over my characters. At any given time, there are scores of characters yelling at each other, yelling at me, inside my head. Some of them sort of take over, and I become totally intrigued or mesmerized by them. Devi came to me as the opposite of a character I'd written earlier, Jasmine from the novel *Jasmine*. Draft by draft, I came to understand Devi better, and the most important idea that wrote itself in the second or third draft was that she prizes clarity over everything else.

What she understands, in retrospect, is that there's a huge difference between vengeance and justice. Once that idea was articulated by my character, I realized that in order to make my concept of divine justice, which sometimes involves great violence, understandable to the reader, I'd have to dig into and share the Hindu mythology of the goddess Devi worshipped in Bengal, who was created by the Cosmic Spirit to do battle with the baddest bad ass of all the demons, the Buffalo Demon, and is therefore quite violent.

I never saw my character Devi's tale as optimistic. Here's a street smart, savvy, manipulative young woman, enraged about the fact that she was thrown out like a garbage sack on the hippie trail, who's part of a larger design in which some higher power uses her to restore some kind of balance and purge evil out of our

California. I never saw her as a mean person, more as a person capable of redemption after she's gone through some of the violence within herself.

RH: So as you were writing the novel, it wasn't necessarily that much of a surprise when she burns down her ex-lover's house at the end of Part One? That's the point for me where I stopped seeing her as a sarcastic but sweet character and started seeing her as being capable of just about anything.

BM: I knew she was going to burn down the house in the early drafts, but I didn't know what would happen as a result, other than that there was no turning back for her. The final ending of the book was what came as a total surprise to me.

RH: Earlier drafts didn't lead to that final confrontation?

BM: I don't look at my early drafts in hard copy. I just open another file in my word processor and start from scratch. Each draft helps me know my characters better; draft by draft, their voices get louder and they tell me their adventures more fully each time through. The characters thicken, becoming more dense and complex. I hear the sentences better. I do a lot of drafts. In order to get these very dense, high-energy sentences, I've thought through much bulkier paragraphs.

RH: One of the things this novel is about is coming to grips with the legacy of the sixties. The former hippies have put aside the consequences of their actions; Devi, as the instrument we've discussed, represents those consequences coming back to them and forcing the issue.

BM: As a professor and workshop leader, I'm constantly working with young people for whom Vietnam, the Kennedy assassination, and so on mean nothing. They're simply statistics. But Devi's generation is still a victim of those events, they're formed by post-Vietnam America. I've come to realize that one of the themes throughout my fiction is the changes in the way America thinks of itself and is seen by the rest of the world as a result of Vietnam. My sympathies are very much with people like the character "Loco Larry," people I see around my neighborhood who were damaged by the war. The peace protestors were noble—and both I and my husband were involved with rallies and vigils at the time—but the peace movement also masked a certain excessive narcissism. People were doing good, but at the same time they were self-indulgently satisfying their sensual and sexual appetites, and many of them never acknowledged the fallout from that kind of narcissism, how it affected the people around them. Many of the people who went to India looking to escape Western civilization misunderstood and misapplied Indian traditions, and succumbed to the imperializing impulse. They thought that their version of India was the way India really was, without understanding Indian culture.

RH: What separates you from other Indian fiction writers?
BM: I think my work from *Darkness* onward, so from about 1985 to the present, is hard for some readers to understand because I don't fit into any easy slots. I'm a woman who was born in Calcutta, but I've lived in America my entire adult life and consider myself an American. My literary soul was formed by literature from around the world, but especially American literature. I'm an American writer of Indian origin. I'm not doing an exotic ghetto, National Geographic Indian number, and I'm not making readers feel good about those locales—aren't we quaint, aren't we sweet, aren't we sentimental and emotionally expressive. I'm showing white Americans their world in a different way, so they'll never be able to walk down their own streets quite the same way after reading my books.

RH: Who do you read for pleasure?
BM: I read many different kinds of authors. I love James Ellroy's books. He has qualities that I strive for in my work, particularly an edgy humor combined with a dark vision of society, as well as incredible energy in every one of his sentences. It must seem very strange that a very demure Indian lady sees James Ellroy as a kindred literary spirit, but there you are.

RH: How much do you keep up with modern Indian literature?
BM: With Indian literature in English and Bengali, as much as possible. I go to India every year to see my family and during those trips, I empty out bookstores getting the latest books. But there are so many languages in India, so many regional literatures with prolific writers that I can't claim to know all of Indian literature, or even all of that from the languages I know.

RH: But you know enough of it to know that American readers are only getting the tip of the iceberg, as it were.
BM: Absolutely. The only writers of Indian origin that American writers know are the ones who happen to be credentialized by magazines like the *New Yorker* and, of course, published in America. Very often, the writers who are picked up and given that attention by the American publishing industry are minority writers who are expatriates. They've lived outside India for much of their lives, and Indian writers in India don't necessarily see any affinity with them. It's sad to me that Americans aren't as interested in reading translations of some of these Indian writers. We don't see many translations from non-Western languages being made available to us.

RH: Do you usually spend a lot of time on the research and draft phases of your work?

BM: It depends on the book. Once the character comes to me, I know what kind of material will be essential, what I'll need to know. My last novel, *The Holder of the World*, made much use of virtual reality. And as with Devi's job as a media escort, the narrator of that novel had a very nineties profession; she was an asset hunter, tracking down people's financial holdings. But the novel was also about seventeenth-century Massachusetts and various trading companies that established themselves in seventeenth-century India, which meant eleven years of uncontrolled and immensely pleasurable research. I love history as story, and the details of customs, manners, and social structures, the way that people thought and behaved.

RH: Media escorts and asset hunters are both facets of contemporary culture that perhaps only an outsider perspective would notice, although you don't necessarily have to be a foreign-born author to do it.

BM: A writer, in order to be at her or his sensitive and most receptive, has to be both an insider and an outsider. My quarrel with certain writers who see themselves only as expatriate Indians writing about India from outside is that they're too far out. To write about something, I need to both know it well and look at it from an odd angle. I don't want to sneer at or satirize my characters, just to look at them differently.

RH: That gives you the insight to see them behaving not as examples of a satirical point, but out of sincerely felt motivations and interests.

BM: Exactly. That's where I feel I'm very different from, say, V. S. Naipaul, who all too often in my opinion sets himself above the cultures he depicts, adopting a patronizing or snide tone. Coming back to your initial question, that's why I don't see Devi as an unlikable or unsympathetic character. I can't write unless I've come to love a character for all his or her wickedness or flaws.

An Interview with Bharati Mukherjee

Michael Krasny / 2002

Interview courtesy of FORUM, a production of KQED Public Radio, San Francisco, CA, Michael Krasny, Host. © Northern California Public Broadcasting, Inc., 2002. All rights reserved.

Michael Krasny: From KQED in San Francisco, I'm Michael Krasny. Good morning and welcome to this morning's *Forum* program, second hour. Berkeley English professor and National Book Critics Circle award-winning writer Bharati Mukherjee's newest novel, *Desirable Daughters*, is full of suspense, intrigue, and the cultural tensions of traditional India in contemporary America. Much of the novel is set here in the Bay Area, but we move too to the Tri-City, Jersey City, Newark area, and ultimately back to India. And we discover that even a highly Americanized woman like Tara, the novel's protagonist and the youngest of the novel's three sisters, is not really far from her Indian roots in terms of consciousness despite her life as a single mother cohabiting here in San Francisco's Cole Valley with a Zen-retrofitting American biker. A novel all about Hinduism, Bollywood, Silicon Valley, entrepreneurship, a teen coming out of the closet, and good guys and bad guys including a Sikh San Francisco police department officer with a Ph.D., *Desirable Daughters* is as much a story of India as it is of America, and Bharati Mukherjee joins us for this hour. Good to see you, welcome.
Bharati Mukherjee: Hello, Michael.

MK: This is a different novel for you, isn't it? You've taken a lot of chances with this in many ways.
BM: Yes, I think I have taken chances with each of my novels, but this one is very, very different in that suddenly I am coming to terms, as is Tara the narrator, who though is much younger than I am, with what my Indian heritage has left me as residue and what America I have discovered, and discovered as empowerment, and knitting the two together so that I know who I am in ways that I didn't want to know when I was writing my earlier novels.

MK: In other words, this is repression coming up from the unconscious, and all that, or the collective unconscious.

BM: I think so. It is as my narrator says, as she starts out writing this book, that she is interested in discovering the making of her consciousness as well as her sisters', and I, after the first draft, realized suddenly that that's what I was doing and wanted to do finally.

MK: Well, it's fascinating from the perspective of the East is East, West is West because you have a woman who is divorced and to a great extent that in itself is something to contend with, I mean in terms of her traditional Indian background, but who also has been or played the role of a mall siren, reading everything, I suppose, of the *Cosmo* variety of magazines and yet drawn back more and more, drawn back in spite of herself to what really is her traditional Indian background. So that in itself is just a kind of wonderful conflict.

BM: Well, I think, yes, Tara, the thirty-six-year-old narrator, is living in a world where East is East, West is West is no longer possible because of globalization, art, culture, trade. So, the India and the old stories from the epics that she had taken for granted, and maybe because of her convent school education sort of pooh-poohed in some ways, undervalued in some ways. She is now—

MK: The convent school education was a kind of Western thing. I mean, you make allusions in the novel to Radio Ceylon and rock and roll. There's stuff that comes in fairly early from the West, and convent schools is one of those things.

BM: Yes, and you take what you need or what you can from early exposure to foreign songs, foreign materials just as I did when I was growing up in Calcutta and went to a convent school run by Irish nuns from Galway. But when she is an adult, in the Upper Haight area of San Francisco, which, by the way, is where I live and I'm using my own apartment as the setting for Tara's trying out a *Cosmo* lifestyle for a while. You learn to reassess, reinterpret what you had taken for granted about your own heritage and what you thought you knew about western culture and art and music. And so, I, like Tara, grew up sort of chasing ghosts away at dusk following my grandmother as she held a holy lamp, and I and my sisters and cousins sort of clashed symbols or tinkled temple bells. It was something we were indirectly taught to repress during our school days with the Irish nuns.

MK: But lest anybody think this is autobiographical, you, for example, were supposed to have an arranged marriage like Tara did.

BM: Yes, and—

MK: —And wound up marrying a Canadian.

BM: Life kind of sabotaged all those good intentions, but I have been married to the same man for now nearly thirty-nine years even though our courtship was two weeks and the wedding took five minutes during a lunch break in a lawyer's office. I've just been lucky.

MK: This starts with a wedding, this novel. In fact, have you seen *Monsoon Wedding?*
BM: Yes I have, and I loved it.

MK: It's a delightful picture.
BM: Yes, and it's very Bollywoody and over the top, and I loved every moment of it.

MK: I really enjoyed it, also. It begins with a wedding, actually, from another century. And, it begins with a character, a tree bride, kind of a folkloric character, who becomes very important again to the consciousness of going back to India and the whole central motif that you are talking about.
BM: I wish I could agree 100 percent with you that the tree bride is a folkloric character, but in fact, in the nineteenth century, especially the last quarter of the nineteenth century, you had in my Kulin Brahmin sect of East Bengal women from that particular upper, upper, upper subcaste being married off to trees, stones, crocodiles, etcetera because a woman had to be married and worship husband as god in order to go to heaven. But there were more women than men in that particular community.

MK: But this was a real story about the snake bite and everything then?
BM: There were many stories like that.

MK: Many stories like this, but this is an aggregate kind of story.
BM: Yes, but I am not pulling my tree bride invention totally out of the hat. There were examples of people married, young girls married off to trees and stones. In this case, what I was using the tree bride ceremony for—and she is married to, a five-year-old bride is married off to a tree because her betrothed dies of a snake bite on his way to the wedding pavilion—is to show how the nineteenth-century, westernized lawyer, father of the bride suddenly realizes that there are ways of resisting colonial pressure by going back and learning to cope with and understand the purpose of Hindu traditions. So, following Hindu traditions and marrying your daughter off to a tree becomes for him a way not only of fighting off greedy fellow Bengalis like the betrothed's father—

MK: —who feel they are deserving of the dowry because somehow she was responsible for his dying by the snakebite.
BM: Right. Right.

MK: Just trying to get that all laid out there. In effect, this whole notion that you write about, and there is one moment for example when Tara, who has the name of course of "the Tree Bride," goes and touches the feet of an uncle who has Parkinson's and has to give a kind of obeisance to him that is again deserving of the men being the god. There's a sense, in fact of—
BM: —and elders.

MK: And elders, yeah, but—
BM: Respect for elders.

MK: But it's really because it's her husband's uncle, and there's somebody changing his bedpan. She's got a master's, you happen to drop, in economics, but she is still being servile because that's what a wife is supposed to be to her husband. Her husband is a god.
BM: Servile is a contested word. For some people, that kind of service will be servile. For others, the word in Bengali is "seva"—

MK: Shiva like the God?
BM: "Seva," which means total service in god's honor to someone else, and it's usually the husband, of course, a proxy god.

MK: Well, you also talk about Bengali customs to a great extent in this novel, maternal possessiveness of Bengali mothers. There doesn't seem to be quite anything like it as you see things, East or West. What you describe as a Hindu virgin protection device that mothers—
BM: Radar.

MK: Radar is stronger than anything in the world. This comes out of your own obviously deep memories and connectedness, and I did not realize this until I read your novel, but even the kind of, not only the caste system, but the hierarchical . . . the way Sindhis are viewed and the way Marwaris are viewed by Bengalis. They are all very hierarchical.
BM: Yes. I am always amazed when reviewers or some literary critics lump all Asian American writers together as being a homogenous group. Whereas within the subcontinental group of immigrants and naturalized American citizens here, we retain our old world ethnic differences. It's the narcissism of the slightest differences, as Freud might say.

MK: When, for example, Tara goes back and starts talking in her native language, she becomes a different person. She feels like a different person, because she's been using English for so long, when she is using the Bengali tongue.

BM: As I do. I find that I am totally thinking differently, and the cadences are different. I'm different, my whole facial muscles are different. My body moves differently when I'm speaking English versus Bengali.

MK: Do you like yourself more like she does when she's speaking Bengali?
BM: No, I'm two different persons, equally. I'm okay with each of the two. With my American English as opposed to British English, which I try not to slip into unconsciously, I feel I'm walking faster and that I have hope about relief for the masses. As opposed to in other languages, including British English, I feel less control over trying to help myself and society.

MK: Talking with Bharati Mukerjee, her new book is *Desirable Daughters*. Really the story of three sisters and their relationship to the past as well as, particularly two of the sisters who live in the United States, one of them lives in Bombay, but their ongoing relationships to the present as being Americans. It's also a book about gangs, Dawood gang. I mean, you've obviously done some research here, and these are real, these criminals who come and play Mr. Ripley and use secret—.
BM: They're very real.

MK: And very violent.
BM: Very violent, and I think for a long time sleeper terrorists and sleeper agents of terrorists' cells in ethnic communities in America and Canada had been dismissed by journalists as well as by police as not being important enough to merit mainstream attention, but they'll do in their own communities whatever they have to do, and they dismiss them as sort of the "ethnics do their thing." My husband and I wrote an investigative book on what until the World Trade Center bombing was the single bloodiest, by body count, terrorist incident to date, and that was the bombing of an Air India jet in June 1985, which took off from Canada on its way to India but was blown out of the skies by Canadian perpetrators of Indian origin with Khalistani secessionist politics in mind. And it was blown up off the coast of Ireland, and when we investigated that, we discovered as early as 1985, '86, how your mild-mannered school janitor or your gas station attendant—

MK: Careful, or you're going to arouse all kinds of suspicions.
BM: —or your cardiologist might have some role, direct or indirect, in these kinds of large, violent conspiracies.

MK: Which is just what has been said about Al Qaeda, in terms of their being—.
BM: Yes, yes. The gangsters that I'm writing about in this novel are, you know, smaller in their vision, narrower in their vision, and they go for not the World

Trade Center but the house that the ex-husband of the narrator, Tara, is visiting, because he's the Bill Gates—

MK: —He's a major entrepreneur.
BM: —He's the Bill Gates of the South Asian-American community.

MK: A very, very successful man in terms of technology and all. Modeled after anybody?
BM: No, he's my imagined, chosen bridegroom or bridegroom that my parents would have chosen, so late in life I invented him.

MK: Well, the thing about him as well as Tara and about so many of the Indian characters in this novel is that they operate under two sets of time, I mean, which again is something fascinating to me in terms of identity and culture clash and so forth. That is, you talk about the time on the wrist when you are working in Silicon Valley or when Tara's working in a school or whatever, and then there's Hindu time. There's kalpas and pralayas, I guess, or what we've studied as the cyclical as opposed to the linear nature of time, and you feel that that's really embedded in the consciousness.
BM: Yes, very much so. And, even in real time, wrist-watch time, I've always grown up with the English calendar and the Hindu Bengali calendar, so my novel opens on the wettest, darkest, monsoon night in 1879 by the British calendar, but it's 1285 by the Hindu calendar, and every now and then in my very American life in Upper Haight San Francisco, I'm pulled out of my American time into the Hindu time when my sister calls from India and says, "Do you know that this is Saraswati Puja Day?" or "This is Durga Puja Day."

MK: And you're back there.
BM: I'm back there, yes.

MK: Instantly, right back there. There's also, in this novel, a real—first of all, can you explain "masala" to me?
BM: Masala is a mixture of spices, and it therefore makes the ordinary vegetables that you would put into a cooking pot or meat into something far more exotic, tasty.

MK: So, we could say that when you talk about it, it's panache maybe or some-thing like that in personality; or it's color; it's vitality, liveliness, spirit.
BM: Energy, spirit, brio.

MK: Yes, okay. And, all of these three sisters seem to have it, and they also seem to have beauty. They also are very bright and have success, and yet, there is somehow the sense that they are supposed to be kind of interwoven together though they're so distinctly different from each other.

BM: Right. They're brought up to be identical because according to the patriarchal father, they should have no opinion not given to them by him, and they're supposed to wear identical clothes, speak in the identical accent.

MK: What is the line about the blossoms?

BM: Three like as flowers, three flowers, on a single twig, and that is very much a translation of a popular Bengali rhyme. And, it was said to us constantly when we were growing up as three sisters. But, the culture or sentimental education of these sisters was geared to repressing their individual personalities because if you make your own decision, that means the patriarch has lost control. And of course he has; only the family members pretend that everything is fine, and they hide the consequences of rebellion by the sisters.

MK: Which is of course what drives the plot here, is this hidden secret or this buried secret, as it were.

BM: The cost of cultural innocence.

MK: And it all seems to be not only tied to patriarchy but it all seems to be tied to a curious kind of fate or almost determinism that is operating here.

BM: I personally think of fate as providing destiny, providing scenarios, and then the individual, with his or her personality, decides what to do given that scenario. So for me, fate is quite dynamic. We create our fate given certain pieces, certain cards.

MK: Well certainly the older sister creates her fate. She is, in fact at one point your Didi, you describe her as passionate and reckless and the true American among the three sisters, therefore.

BM: Because she reinvents herself constantly, and she survives by canceling history. Okay, I didn't like what I did yesterday, delete yesterday.

MK: It's gone.

BM: And so she has had an affair. Tara the narrator discovers in her American life that Didi has had a little fling with a Christian, from a good family but Christian means there is no marriage possible between the two of them, and that there may or may not have been a son born of that little fling. And a young man appears at Tara's door one fine day in San Francisco. And, knock, knock, the past is going to assault one, as it always does, in unexpected and disproportionate ways.

MK: You've just given a nice titillation of the plot. I didn't know if I wanted to do that because I didn't want to give away too much, but that's really the fulcrum of the novel. Because this young man appears and says, "I am that illegitimate son," and it becomes a real propulsion for the plot in terms of finding out who he is and what he really represents.

BM: Yes, yes, very much so. But what I wanted is that we have our private mysteries and our personal battles to fight, and we're so self-absorbed, "Does my ex-husband love me? Can I re-seduce him? Why did my sister not tell me that she may or may not have a son from her teenage days of misbehavior?" And then there are larger schemes at work, larger melodramas happening, as we all know now, post–World Trade Center bombing. That we can lead our innocent lives of self-absorption when suddenly a larger plot is going to enmesh us in its nightmarish vision.

MK: You're okay with the characterization of this as taking on melodrama?

BM: No, because I think that people who call it melodrama simply have not lived the immigrant life of messy intensity, messy agony. And that it's an unfortunate superior way of dismissing what more and more Californians and New Yorkers, for example, are experiencing every day. Ethnic lives are full of great heights and great lows.

The True Heirs: An Interview with Bharati Mukherjee

Angela Elam / 2005

Angela Elam's interview with Bharati Mukherjee, first published in *New Letters* vol. 71, no. 4 (summer 2005.) It is reprinted here with permission of *New Letters* and the Curators of the University of Missouri-Kansas City.

New Letters: Your husband, Clark Blaise, is also a writer and professor. How did you meet?

Bharati Mukherjee: We met in 1963 as fellow students at the Iowa Writers' Workshop. He's an American of Canadian origin, and we had a two-week courtship and a five-minute wedding in a lawyer's office during a lunch break.

NL: Two-week courtship?

Mukherjee: My father was in Calcutta when I was growing up in the 1950s. He was an old-fashioned kind of patriarch when it came to management of his daughters' lives, but progressive in his thinking about the country and economics. He refused to send any of us three sisters to a coeducational classroom. So when I came to Iowa, it was my first experience of coeducation. Something happened. And happened fast.

NL: It's amazing that your father didn't already have a husband picked out for you.

Mukherjee: He was choosing. He said, all right, you're going to be learning how to scribble stories, which seems like a safe kind of accomplishment for a young woman. It'll make you more desirable as a bridal candidate, and while you're getting your M.F.A. degree in Iowa for two years, I will have found the most perfect Bengali Brahmin bridegroom. He did, but destiny, or I, seemed to have other ideas. As a result, I had to send a cable to my father saying, "By the time you get this, Dad, I'll already be married."

NL: I heard a story about how you ended up going to the University of Iowa, because at the time, it was the only writing workshop that offered a creative-writing M.F.A.

Mukherjee: No one in my family had been to the United States for graduate studies. We all looked to England or Germany or France for the graduate degree. America was not on our radar at all. A group of UCLA students and a drama professor came into India and passed through our town in 1960 as part of an experiment in international living; that group came to our house for dinner, and my father, in a small-talk and expansive way said, "This daughter wants to be a writer. Where should I send her for the two years?" One guy pulled the Iowa University program out of the hat. If he had said, "Send her to Arkansas," I probably would be speaking with an Arkansas accent and would have been married to a Southerner and would have had a different life, with a totally different kind of fiction. Or, if that man hadn't come through, I would have married the decent and accomplished nuclear physicist whom my father had picked for me. If I'd have married that man in an arranged way, I probably would have had just as happy a life, but totally, totally different. My fiction, again, would have been more Jane Austen-ey and in an Indian setting.

NL: Would you have been writing in English, even?
Mukherjee: Yes, I would have been writing in English. This is part of the colonial legacy, and I found myself introspecting through that as I was writing *The Tree Bride*. What if there hadn't been the English, not only coming over but imposing educational policy through people such as Thomas Macaulay, saying we want English-speaking little clerks among the natives? Let the education system be sure that they are proficient in English and that they have the desire to buy consumer goods from Lancashire or Yorkshire, but we don't want them to think like Englishmen and have Gladstonian ideas. That language and educational policy meant that large sections of middle-class urban people are English speaking. The fancy girls' school run by Irish nuns that I was sent to because I was so-and-so's daughter and I couldn't go to a less fancy school, had accent inspectors come from London every year to check the British Broadcasting Corporationness of our accents, so that we wouldn't be accused of a Peter Sellers sing-song kind of parody of Indian English. In my girls' school in Calcutta, run by these Irish nuns, elocution was the most important subject. Forget science and math and all that. Elocution. Next was table manners. I realize now, I mean, thinking back on it as a mature adult, that those were colonial hangovers. If you spoke English with an Indian accent, that meant you were not quite right. Or if you didn't hold your knife and fork the way you were supposed to in London society, then again, you were not quite right. That's a colonial legacy.

My high school certificate does not say Calcutta University but Overseas

Cambridge University, and the curriculum, therefore, was geared to Cambridge University demands. I had to take, as my mother tongue, Alternate English, Extra English, and not my real biological, inherited mother tongue, Bengali.

NL: All I can think about is the character Bish, in *The Tree Bride*, saying, "There are no coincidences." In some ways, *The Tree Bride* goes off on this metaphysical search about that and the relations of things.

Mukherjee: *The Tree Bride* has turned out to be the prequel in what I now think of as a projected trilogy. *Desirable Daughters* was the first book I wrote in this trilogy when I didn't know that there'd be anything more than one book. The narrator for both *Desirable Daughters* and *The Tree Bride* is a thirty-six-year-old woman called Tara; she is educated and from a self-confident reasonably affluent family and is one of three sisters, the only sister who submits to having her marriage arranged by her patriarchal father. She becomes the bride of an immigrant Bengali engineer, who goes to Stanford University and becomes the Indian Bill Gates of the Indo-American community in the Silicon Valley.

NL: In the book, he gets all these names people put on him. The Guru, the Mogul. Mogul was so wrong for him, but Americans group these Asian titles in one area.

Mukherjee: Tara is caught between ideas she has inherited about how time operates or how destiny operates, and her gradual Americanization and her exercising of free will. But, for her, the world is full of magical coincidences. She thinks, "All right, if I'm to find the clue to mysteries in my life when I'm psychologically, emotionally, psychically ready, the clue will come and I'll be able to recognize it." But Bish, her husband—whom she in one of her misadventures and self-searches decides to divorce and then try to get back together with—is an engineer, is logical, is rational, and that's the other aspect of Hinduism and thinking about destiny: There are no coincidences but convergences that are mathematically provable if you can figure out the right equation. All events are computations and permutations, and so if you're mathematically correct, you'll be able to figure out all you're given, Bish would say. Facts. As an information designer, he wants to put together all this messy pile of facts until it makes sense. So, information design is a way of explaining what appears to us as chaos.

NL: So my sixth-grade math teacher was right: Math will bring you closer to God.

Mukherjee: Yes, and you know, Hindu thought and religion are really a process of metaphorizing, of making up stories or making visual, geophysical cosmic theories. We know all about the discovery of new galaxies and constellations. Chaos theory is close to the Hindu explanation of how the world works. Quantum physics is really what our creation, destruction, re-creation is all about.

NL: That's threaded throughout *The Tree Bride* and into, as you say, the prequel, *Desirable Daughters*. Even going back to your book of short stories, *The Middleman and Other Stories*. Speaking of that book, it's the first time somebody from India had won the National Book Critics Circle Award, is that right?
Mukherjee: I was the first naturalized American to have won that award.

NL: Those are stories about people straddling two worlds.
Mukherjee: Straddling two worlds, yes: These people are the traditional heirs to the American dream, but suddenly America has changed on them; and people like me, who have come from nontraditional countries to America, are having to make accommodations or reject some of the old, while they graft on some of the new. For me, *The Middleman* was a breakthrough, because I realized that my material is about the two-way transformation that America was going through in the eighties, and more so today. It's not simply the immigrant coming and saying, "All right, I've got to Americanize." Melting pot was that old theory that the newcomer will have to become an American. Whereas in real life, more and more nonwhite immigrants are coming in, documented and undocumented, and Americans— traditional Americans—also are having to adjust to that fact.

NL: What's interesting about *The Tree Bride*, though, is that this character has dealt with her assimilation into the American way of life and is now looking back and trying to figure out her roots and who she is as a person. That was a fascinating shift for you as a writer, because most of the people in your earlier works are looking forward and how to make it in that new world. This story looks back to see how those two worlds are braided together.
Mukherjee: You're absolutely right, Angela. What I realized, when I finished *Desirable Daughters*, was that for Tara, her adventures in *Desirable Daughters* were about personal pursuit of happiness. I don't like that; I want to test myself. The moment I finished that final scene in which Tara has this vision of her namesake and female ancestor from the nineteenth century—the tree bride, Taralata, who was married off to a tree in 1879 because of peculiar circumstances, and who became a freedom fighter—I realized that there had to be a roots search. I found myself embarking in an urgent way in an American-roots search, except that the Hindu vision of roots is different from the normal American roots novel, where you track an individual family, find the Italian village or the African village from

which the great-grandfather or great-great-grandfather started. For us, colonial forces—the encounter between the imperialistic white man, good and bad, and the language imposed, the sense of right and wrong, democracy or feudalism imposed—has gone into the very shaping of what language I write in. The opposite directions I feel culturally become intensified through tracking an individual family, how one encounter, let's say, with an Englishman by the tree bride in the nineteenth century and early twentieth century, has enormous and continuing repercussions in Sausalito or San Francisco for this very modern Indo-American family. Nothing is ever lost. How you deal with that perception, again, decides what your next circumstance, incident, will be.

NL: Early in your novel *Jasmine*, too, that's how Jasmine deals with the world, although she's not as self-aware as Tara in *The Tree Bride*.
Mukherjee: Yes. I think Tara grows in self-awareness even from *Desirable Daughters* to *The Tree Bride*, because she's undergone firebombing; and her ex-husband, with whom she wants to get back together, has been so badly injured, crippled, burnt, in trying to rescue her from this firebombed house that she's had to deal with much bigger issues than simply who she is and what she thinks of this personal happiness.

NL: I found it interesting that you had yet another man crippled by an accident: In the novel *Jasmine*, Bud, the husband to Jasmine, was—I don't know how much I should reveal—
Mukherjee: Go ahead.

NL: Anyway, one of the joys of reading your work is how you circle around something. We know that he's crippled, but we don't know how; we're wondering how, and you hold it off for a certain amount of time. You don't just tell the story in a linear fashion.
Mukherjee: Absolutely. I think of my aesthetics as the art of indirection, and more important, the art of compression. I want to be able to squeeze many facts into a single paragraph and then pick up a little thread and unravel it some more, thirty pages down, instead of telling a linear, direct story. I love strong character, and I love plot.

NL: How do you actually make plot work, structurally?
Mukherjee: I do a lot of research for every novel. A lot of interviews, if necessary. In *Jasmine*, I was writing at a time in Iowa when there was a farm crisis, in the mid-to-late eighties; and among my friends was a forty-two-year-old banker who was shot to death in his office, just a few miles from where I lived, because

another forty-two-year-old Iowa farmer who'd gone to school with the banker, thought he was being foreclosed upon. There was great violence out of misunderstanding and the economic circumstances. I didn't want my character to die, but I knew that there had to be sufficient violent damage in order for me to dramatize the confrontations and the miscommunications, so that's why we have Bud Ripplemeyer, the Lutheran blue-eyed blonde, much-older lover of this undocumented Jasmine, in the novel. When I had finished what I thought was my final draft, the final scene had Jasmine just go off with her Columbia University professor/love from another phase of her life, and an adopted Vietnamese orphan boy, with Jasmine pregnant with Bud's child. Then I thought, Oh, poor Bud in his wheelchair.

I then realized that there was a character hanging in the background, Bud's ex-wife, so I made sure that she didn't go off and get remarried. In *The Tree Bride*, I discuss the violence of gangs that want to destroy the economy—there's a reference to "the villains," the suspected villain, the firebomber, being part of a named gang, a real gang. I knew I liked Bish Chatterjee, the husband, and I could see that Tara toward the end of *Desirable Daughters* was saying, "Maybe I misjudged him; maybe he wasn't such a patriarch after all, such a controlling husband after all." So I needed that metaphor for people having gone through extreme trauma that brings them together and makes them reassess their relationships.

NL: It also makes them different. Bish is such a likable guy. I'm sure your readers were glad you explored this. Knowing how you write, there are tips that you give people, as I said earlier. For instance, the man whom Tara met in the village, but we don't find out about that story for a few chapters. You're such a tease as a writer.
Mukherjee: Just listening to you talk about the looping structure, I realized that the arc of this trilogy is also a similar kind of looping. The mysteries we thought were solved in *Desirable Daughters* turned out to be only the beginnings of other mysteries, providing different, deeper answers.

NL: I'm thinking you're not always aware of mysteries, as the writer.
Mukherjee: Not in the first draft. That first draft for me is about getting into my unconscious; it comes out of somewhere deep inside me.

NL: Which brings me to the mechanics of writing. When you go about your writing process, do you have a plan when you start, or do you sit down and just let it flow forth?
Mukherjee: With novels, I have a strong sense of character, and a strong sense of

setting, and the main conflict that the character is undergoing. I don't know how the conflict is going to be worked out, let alone worked through, however; so the first draft is a time for me to go with the character and see what adventures she or he places herself in. The minor characters then grow out of these adventures.

Then I don't look at the hard copy of the draft. Doing a draft is just getting to know the story, the people, the scenes and their tensions. I open a new file: *Tree Bride II*. I then will realize that some of what I had been setting up in the first draft is not at all necessary. Other things in that first draft have come through in spite of me and are far more urgent and interesting. Those other things come from somewhere other than my consciousness, other than intended. I'll go with that, and some characters may die by the wayside.

NL: So you don't return to the first draft and rework it?
Mukherjee: No, no.

NL: Wow.
Mukherjee: That's only with the penultimate draft versus the final draft, and then it's a mostly cosmetic revision. I believe in the precise picking of diction: that the verbs, for example, must do a lot of the narrative work, instead of the author explaining, explaining, explaining directly, or characters explaining directly; so that kind of choice, or cleaning up sentences, paragraphs, punctuation, all that is the final cosmetic. The earlier drafts are all about realizing what psychologically drives not just my protagonist but the whole novel, itself, the momentum of the novel. For a couple of stories in *The Middleman*, and certainly novels like *Jasmine*, I didn't know that the ending was going to be the way the final drafts turned out. The character said, "Uh, uh. I ain't doin' what you want me to do."

NL: What is your preparation to write a novel?
Mukherjee: I do a lot of research, I guess because I've been in the university for so long, and the universities that I've been associated with, such as California-Berkeley, have such good library holdings. Before I begin, I do the research I think I will need; but once I start writing, I put away all the notes. I will have so absorbed what nineteenth-century Bengal or seventeenth-century colonial Massachusetts might be like, as in *Holder of the World*, the details of clothing, culture, punishments, legal systems, that they will rise, those facts will rise to my fingertips naturally in the appropriate dramatic moments.

I don't like to have pellets of research just standing there undramatized or in a show-offy way.

NL: So do you enjoy the research part?

Mukherjee: I love it. I think if I hadn't gotten my doctorate in English and comparative literature, I would probably have done my degree work in history.

NL: That explains why you use history in such a wonderful way in your novels. Chapter Five in *The Tree Bride* gave us a vivid sense about colonial history in India. History isn't always written in such a gripping way.

Mukherjee: I want to make those historical facts sensuous to the reader. I want to put the reader inside the scene rather than have, you know, spectators.

NL: Jane Smiley not long ago told me she, too, loved the research; she loved the writing, and she loved the rewriting.

Mukherjee: I echo Jane's words.

NL: She also went to the Iowa Writers' Workshop and then taught in Ames, Iowa, for some years. It took her longer to set a novel in Iowa, though; even in *The Middleman*, you had a story set in Iowa.

Mukherjee: The reason that I was able, as a twenty-year-old, to come to the M.F.A. program at the University of Iowa was because a group of Iowa ladies funded my scholarship. It was a group called the P.E.O. Sisterhood, which appointed an International Peace Scholar, and I was that International Peace Scholar; so Iowa always has felt like home to me, an alternate home. Our older son was born in Iowa City when we were graduate students. So, the Midwest I like very much.

NL: In the novel *Jasmine*, there was a passage that you mentioned as being pivotal. Where was that?

Mukherjee: That passage occurs one third of the way through the novel, yet it was the first passage I wrote as I was starting out the first draft of *Jasmine*. When I wrote it, I realized that these are the people whose lives and whose accommodations are inspiring me as an immigrant, a naturalized American writer. When I was writing *Jasmine*, the character was an undocumented alien, and the book of stories just before that also included characters who had come *sneaki*—you know, who had snuck into the United States or were not always welcome. That was 1989. In 2002 and 2004, *Desirable Daughters* and *Tree Bride*, we have a different America, a different traditional American attitude about immigrants from non-European countries. People coming over, like Tara and her husband, Bish Chatterjee, who are making great engineering and Intel progress in places like Silicon Valley, are cosmopolitan. They have self-confidence. They might say, "I can be here, and I also can be three months in my retirement home in India, or a villa in Italy with ease." So, I'm looking at different kinds of immigrants in different books.

NL: You were never illegal.
Mukherjee: Right.

NL: There was an event in your life in which you and your husband both decided to make major life changes because of racism. Can you talk about that?
Mukherjee: Yes. My husband is an American of Canadian origin. His mother was a sturdy prairies Anglo-Canadian, and his father was from Quebec, French-Canadian, the eighteenth child, who was given away to the church, from which he ran away. So, for my husband, Canada was a place of romance where a Romeo and Juliet kind of love had happened between his parents, and he, the only child, was the proof of that. So, when we were looking for our first jobs in 1966, Montreal was the only place we looked. We were lucky—we both found wonderful jobs at universities. Montreal in the late sixties felt very European; it was a bilingual city, and at the same time, it had North American amenities, and given our biculturalism, multilingualism, what a great, what a perfect place for us to lead our lives and to bring up children. And we had two sons.

Everything was fine for the first several years. Then in about 1973, the liberal party, headed by then-Prime Minister Pierre Elliott Trudeau, out of compassion took in five thousand Uganda Asians who were Ismailis by religion. They had British citizenship, but Idi Amin expelled them from Uganda, and Britain refused to accept them in spite of their British passports. It was an act of kindness by the Canadian government led by Trudeau to accept this group of five thousand refugees. There was, however, an unexpected, immediate, and violent racist reaction against these non-Europeans, who had money and who were buying houses in good neighborhoods. Suddenly, the Canadian government at that time floated policy papers asking the question, "What kind of Canada do we want?" in purely racial terms. The government described people like me, with brown skin and still Canadian citizens, as "the visible minority." That's the government phrase. The policy papers also stated that we, the visible minority, were "straining the absorptive capacity" of Canada. Meaning that there were too many brown people and that Canada wouldn't remain the same.

This gave permission, I think, informal permission, to people on the street to take it upon themselves to indulge in physical acts of racial discrimination, not simply spitting on Canadians with brown or black faces. I've been shown to the back of the bus on intercity bus rides; I've been identified as "you must be a whore," because you don't look as though you belong here in the lobby of a fancy hotel in Toronto where my husband, my very white-looking husband and I were staying, but when my white husband was not next to me. Or physically harassed by teenage boys in subway stations in fancy areas of Toronto. It was episodes like that. The race related violence got worse through 1979. Unlike the United States in the seventies, Canada did not have a constitution of its own. It had not been repatriated, and there was no legislative agency of redress; there was no Bill of Rights, and so people like me who became victims of racial discrimination had nowhere to go. We were told, Canadians are so much more kind and tolerant than Americans down south. You can count on the goodwill of us Canadians. I realized at the time, I might have to run for political office if I stay on in Canada, and change the laws. Or, I better let lawyers or people who are better trained change the system, because I want to be a writer. I had to get out or go crazy. So, we left our wonderful jobs and home and pulled out, with the children who thought of themselves as Canadians, and went without permanent jobs to the United States.

Out of that has come a kind of seasoning in me, as a writer as well as a person. Otherwise, I could not have written the kinds of tough, compassionate stories of the lives of immigrants, of what we've all gone through in this process of landing in a city, landing in a country where we're not always made to feel welcome.

NL: In some of your stories, a larger perspective of racism can be seen, however. Not only by the immigrants.
Mukherjee: I want to see it from both sides. As a writer, I understand both sides, how threatened the traditional heirs to the American dream must feel.

NL: Human nature can be petty.
Mukherjee: I'm perfectly fine with human nature being petty as long as there are laws in place so I can fight for my rights and, if necessary, I can sue the pants off them. No, that's not correct. I can show where someone is wrong and should be taken to justice.

NL: I just have to ask you this: What's it like living with another writer? I mean, you have been so wildly successful. Is that difficult?
Mukherjee: My husband, Clark Blaise, is the author of many books of fiction, especially collections of short stories and nonfiction. He's considered a national treasure in Canada. It's this incredible gesture to me that he pulled out of Canada to live here where he is not as well known. Just a couple of months ago, McGill

University gave him an honorary doctorate in recognition of his contribution to Canadian arts and literature. So, he has his life. I wish more Americans recognized his work.

NL: Also, a lot of publishers choose not to publish some Canadian authors in America.

Mukherjee: Most. But to have a spouse who writes means that we're able to read each other's work; especially, Clark reads my work, makes suggestions, which may or may not be taken. It's like life. Because we write different kinds of fiction, we're not competitive in the ways I think a husband and wife writer team might be if they were aiming for the same market or the same readership. Marriage has been a forty-year fiction workshop.

Saying Yes to Opportunities:
An Interview with Bharati Mukherjee
Bradley C. Edwards / 2007

An original interview. © 2007 by Bradley C. Edwards. Reprinted with the permission of the author.

BCE: I wanted to ask you first if you would describe the experience of serving as chairperson of the committee that chose the National Book Award.

BM: It was *exhilarating*, and it was *exhausting!* The hardest part was having to run down three flights of steps to pick up all these heavy couriered boxes of books. But the reading—I decided that, all right, I'm going to devote myself to reading and a kind of literary community service this year—meant putting my own novel-in-progress on hold and just *savoring* the reading. I think about three hundred were submitted, and there were five of us on the jury. I laid down early on rules about whether everyone was going to read everything or whether we were going to parcel out the list. My preference was that everyone read everything and then by a certain date we each make short lists of thirty books that we wanted very much for everyone to discuss. So the process involved many conference calls, and we became a community of five who were excited by literature and by talking about literature. For me, the most exciting part was acquiring such a solid sense of the trends in American fiction in the year 2006. There are so many wonderful books, some of them dazzlingly experimental, others gimmicky. The individual judges had sometimes very eccentric tastes and each felt strongly about her or his choices. So part of the pleasure was talking through what books we really felt strongly about and persuading the rest of the jury of their magnificence. I saw one trend emerge: many of the novels published five years after 9/11 were responses to 9/11. Some novelists took it on directly as did *The Zero*, one of the novels on the short list. Others addressed it indirectly, exploring the consequences on their characters' lives, and some just used that traumatic, terrorist event as a metaphor. A few of the novelists seemed to me to have latched on to 9/11, used it in hokey, gimmicky ways in hopes of producing a best-seller on the fifth anniversary of the tragedy. We jurors met in person as a group only once, on the day of the announcement. We came into New York with our agreed-upon short list of five. Reducing from five separate long short-lists to one short list of five titles which would be published was the hardest part of negotiating. When we came to the actual picking of the winner over a fancy lunch at Aquavit, it was very easy. On secret ballot, it was a unanimous decision.

BCE: In 1990, you said that "for contemporary American writers, fiction exists only in a vacuum of personal relationships." Having just read so many American novels, would you say that is still true?

BM: No, no I wouldn't. I think when I made that statement in 1990, we were still riding the crest of minimalism, and so the kind of fiction that was popular in establishment magazines like the *New Yorker* was really about white people from a certain kind of background by white people from that same kind of background for readers who understood their codes. The fiction didn't accommodate or tolerate messier emotions and large emotional turmoil that couldn't be contained within good manners. I think that now we Americans have included those messier feelings and conflicts, we've been forced to acknowledge them because of mass migrations and hard-to-monitor borders. We have to recognize the presence of the *sin papeles*, entrants without papers, undocumented entrants, on street corners of many of our towns and cities. Now American writers and readers are having to deal with the fact that there is a world out *there* and in *here* that does not share the cozy in-group codes of pre-9/11 U.S. literature impinging on middle-class white American life. I think that minorities like African American groups and women's groups, people with a cause from way back when, women's fiction from say the 1970s on and African American literature have always had to place the individual ethnic or racial protagonist in the context of the other. Whether we welcome them or not characters from unfamiliar locations, languages, religions, backgrounds have crept into U.S. fiction, and they have brought with them their value systems. There's more political awareness in U.S. fiction, I think. Certainly the books that I read in 2006 deal very much with not just domestic bliss and confrontations, personal relationships, but with the context of the threat of violence from wherever. In brief I would say that because of 9/11, fiction writers have been forced to recognize America as part of a global scene rather than America existing in isolation.

BCE: Thinking about this issue while reading *The Tree Bride*, I wanted to ask you if Tara is representative of the American preoccupation with personal relationships before she realizes that she is the object of larger schemes.

BM: Yes, when I was writing *Desirable Daughters* I thought that it was just one novel complete in itself. I didn't have any concept of writing a sequel, let alone a trilogy. There I was interested in three sisters who find themselves for different reasons in the United States at a fairly young age breaking away from their traditional Indian communal identity and negotiating individual identity. Now the three sisters are in very different ways trying to think through what does home mean? Is it homeland that you inherit, which is a kind of imaginary ancestral village that you may never have been to? Is it just the caste that you have inherited, the class that your father has made accessible to you, or is home something that you carry inside you or that you fashion, invent on your own? The three sisters find very different ways of discovering the trauma of derailment. I had Tara who revels in the kind of individuality that gives license to act out your desires, and I thought that was going to be it—individual accommodations in the context of American race relations, social relations, changing gender relations for the immigrant Bengali wife. But as I was writing that last scene, I realized that I'm not really talking about, and I cannot *only* talk about, the individual accommodations and revolutions, transformations. Unlike perhaps the European immigrants before me, the naturalized Americans of South Asian origin, people like Tara, people like me, have been formed not just by desire, ambition to go as far as you can. We have been shaped, deformed, pummeled by political, social, colonial forces. Even the language that I write in is not simply an arbitrary choice on my part but the consequence of Macaulay's educational policies in colonial India. So suddenly I began to realize that I and my character had to do a roots search, which is a very American phenomenon. If I had married an Indian, stayed on in Kolkata, and written novels about Kolkata, I would never have really worried about who am I, what is my identity. I *am* my class, caste, mother tongue, and ancestral village; and that would have been it. That would have been enough. But having moved cities, countries, continents, like Tara, like Jasmine, and having gone through the process of discarding the communal identity that I was given and groping for an individual identity that's still evolving, I realized that now I had to relearn my family history and Bengal's history, especially the history of middle-class Bengali freedom fighters resisting the colonial British. I had to come to new terms with the roots that I had taken for granted. I had to understand my upbringing as a thinking adult. And I was rediscovering my past from the perspective of an expatriate Bengali and a naturalized U.S. citizen. So it was a very American phenomenon—a roots search—that I was going through and that my character, Tara, was going through. For *Desirable Daughters* and *The Tree Bride* I made more than one trip to the ancestral towns of my parents, to Faridpur and Dhaka, which are now in Bangladesh (formerly East Pakistan). Because of political conflicts after the subcontinent was partitioned into India and Pakistan at the time of Independence in 1947, I had not been able to visit my "homeland." The first ever trip I made to Bangladesh, to see the house (what's left of it) in which my mother was born, walk the path to the Buri Ganga river that my mother had as a child when she learned to swim, touch the one remaining original wall of my father's high school, was because I was starting *Desirable Daughters*. If I had stayed in India I would probably never have felt compelled to write *Desirable Daughters* and *The Tree Bride*.

BCE: You've said so many times that in India your name tells everything about who you are.

BM: Yes, yes, exactly. There are no secrets about caste, class, and cultural upbringing, mother tongue, etcetera.

BCE: Is it too much of a stretch to link the firebombing of Tara's house to the idea of suttee or the story of Sita and Ravana?

BM: I wasn't thinking of that at all. Having done the research with Clark on Khalistani terrorist cells operating in North America and the kind of incredible violence that was perpetrated by a terrorist cell in June, 1985—the terrorist bombing of Kanishka, the Air India jet in which 329 people were killed—I was very aware of the ways in which an individual life can be disrupted, decimated by the political machinations of groups of fanatics, let's say, or political activists. 9/11 hadn't happened yet when I was writing that scene, so I was thinking of this as a way for a political group working together with the underworld trying to destroy the economy of repatriation by getting one of the intellectually and monetarily rich Silicon Valley Indo-Americans. So that has been my inspiration. I discovered after the book came out that, indeed, there were plots to kill off the techno gurus, the leaders in information technology or computer technology in India, and attack them perhaps outside also. So that's what I was going for, nothing mythological. Because I grew up listening to those myths, and Hindu epics and moral fables, like all Bengali children of my generation, and because I was forced to do an M.A. in ancient Indian culture when I was nineteen to twenty years old, I have always been very fond of, or obsessed with, the value of mythology to a fiction writer. I've used this quite consciously in *Jasmine* and *Leave It to Me*, in which gods, goddesses, come down to earth in shape-changed form. And, unconsciously in *The Tiger's Daughter*. But in the house-burns-down episode in *Desirable Daughters*, I was really thinking of political, social attacks. By the time I came to write *The Tree Bride*, I understood that there are cosmic ways in which good and evil play themselves out. So, for me, the perpetrator of the fire-bombing was no longer just a member of a terrorist gang, but perhaps also the ghost of the original Tara Lata who wants her family to fulfill the funerary rites that she had been denied when colonial British officials secretively killed her in prison. Tara Lata's ghost demands a proper cremation so that the soul can be released.

BCE: I asked about the story of Sita because it struck me that that's a story you've used many times, and it seemed almost an inversion of the myth having Bish carry Tara across the fire.

BM: I think that's a wonderful way of looking at it. I hadn't caught on to it myself, but it may very likely have played in my head.

BCE: Whose work do you admire today? May I repeat a question you asked V. S. Naipaul? This is how you phrased it: "Are there any living writers you find exciting or wise . . . writers whose work reflects the anxiety about change and an absorption in essential questions you find bracing?"

BM: I love Alice Munro. I love Mavis Gallant. I have learned a lot from Willa Cather's dramatizing of the problems of Scandinavian immigrants into the Midwest. I've learned from Jewish American literature, especially from Malamud's fiction. I identify with a lot of his characters in *The Magic Barrel*, for example. E. L. Doctorow I am in awe of. Pynchon—in a million years I would not expect to write with his kind of vision, but I admire his writing. Also Richard Powers—I thought *The Echo Maker*, which won the National Book Award in 2006, was able to bring together large scientific problems, issues, phenomena with extremely compelling storytelling, building characters. So this was, for me, the book that I was most moved by as a judge. Philip Roth is an amazing writer and man of letters, and I hope he wins the Nobel Prize. Then I like authors like James Ellroy and Elmore Leonard for the energy of their sentences, their ability to capture a "voice," and I love Cheever's mellifluous sentence-making or his kind of snatching images out of the blue, out of nowhere, and his charmingly eccentric, justright endings. So I like different people for very different reasons. Did you want only living authors?

BCE: Actually I did say living, but any.

BM: The two that I feel I have most responded to, and probably because they have lived through, and been inspired by, times of crisis, are Chekhov and Babel. Growing up at a tilt time in India's history, during the period of India's nation-building, I was living and witnessing the struggles of Chekhovian characters. Social change—momentous, scary change—was inevitable. How adaptable was my traditional family to such mega-scale change? Chekhov's fiction really *spoke* to me. Then, much later, when I had accepted my immigrant status

in the New World, the energy and the brashness and the art of compression of
The Odessa Tales by Isaac Babel even more forcefully. Chekhov and Babel were
formative authors for me, but not models. Because in the seventies, eighties, and
even early nineties, I was writing about North American residents who hadn't yet
been written of too much in American fiction, I had to improvise a form. Babel's
art of compression appealed to me. The art of compression is not minimalism. It's
the exact opposite of minimalism. What I learned from Babel's stories is that you
can pack in thirty kinds of emotional and linguistic nuances into one clause and
thirty different historical, political conflicts and concessions into one paragraph.
I'm writing about formation, deformation, reformation of individual and communal and national identities in my novels, but I don't want to do it in a thousand
pages. I want to do it, if I can, in three hundred pages. At the same time, I'm sort
of interested in the ways in which, say Flaubert—I'm very fond of Flaubert and
Madame Bovary—how do you write about a time when the rules are changing?
As author, are you inside or outside the work? How do you write about national
identity while still keeping the dramatic momentum going and having humanity,
sympathy to whatever extent, distributed to good guys and bad guys? The writers that I love, in terms of the writing of national identity are people like Flaubert in *Madame Bovary* or Toni Morrison in *Beloved*, or Louise Erdrich, let's say,
in *Love Medicine*. How do you tell an American story in which the form is not Eurocentric in origin? How do you combine folk culture, contemporary pop culture,
and multi-mythology, multi-history, multi-politics? That's what I feel I am doing in the trilogy, and did in *The Holder of the World*, piecing together multiple
worlds and times into a new unity. What I am interested in are discovery of information and information design. How do I, as a novelist, integrate into my own
imagination and into my novel-in-progress all that I have researched, intuited,
thought through, while working on it? Of course, once I've mastered the information and made it my own, I lose myself in the emotional, intellectual, physical
conflicts of my characters. In *The Holder of The World* I reimagined historical
events, I pieced together information from many different sources, for instance,
bills of lading from East India Company ships, seventeenth-century English captains' logs, colonial American adventurers' diaries and the exotic artifacts they
brought back from India and China, samplers their wives and daughters sewed,
historic accounts of battles between white settlers and the Nipmuc, and of the recorded wheeling and dealing between East India Company employees, like Elihu
Yale, and Indian potentates on the Coromandel coast. Then I had to find a way
of using a first-person point of view—Yale graduate, Beigh Master's—that would

still contain multiple perspectives on the forging of national identity in times of crisis.

BCE: It seems to me that, in your novels especially, a key way in which you pack so much information is through numerous, often oblique references to literature, cinema, and popular culture, and I wondered if you would comment on your use of reference and allusion?

BM: It's always been natural with me. Long before I was exposed to American contemporary fiction, I responded to the world that was going on around me. As a teenager I was exposed to Bengali literature. In Bangla, formal literary language is very distinct from colloquial language. In Bangla classes in school, we students were required to write essays using the literary form of the language. But that formulaic diction, syntax, imagery bored me, even when I was thirteen. I wanted the pieces I wrote to be more than lifeless exercises. I managed to persuade the teacher that writing in colloquial Bangla gave my essays more energy, more personality. I'm curious about the world. I'm like a sponge, absorbing everything, and it all becomes part of who I am, what I can respond to. I'm not one of those writers who needs a hermit cell to shut out the world. I want to invite the world in, so I guess that's why I never turn my TV off, as you know. In some ways, I feel that TV commercials and popular media are the equivalent of the kinds of centuries-old epic tales that we were brought up on, that they had the same force of making a large community even in an atomized state.

BCE: Often your allusions are culturally specific, for example to an Indian film star or an American sports icon. Are you intentionally writing to audiences in both cultures, and what do you expect a Midwesterner to make of Amitabh Bhachchan or a Bengali reader to do with a mention of Walt Frazier or Musial, Brock and Gibson?

BM: All right, this is a two-part answer. I expect the scene to be compelling enough so that even if the specific reference is not accessible to a reader, whether it's in India or San Francisco or Lagos, Nigeria, that the intention of the reference will be clear and that if you get the actual, precise reference, then it's just more nuanced. This is why I feel that with Toni Morrison's *Beloved* you don't have to know all the history. In Louise Erdrich's novels, you don't have to know all the dates of dispersal, resettlement, and so on, but you can get from the way the characters are placed in their misadventures what the large issues, large conflicts, large troubles, and large accommodations are. You don't have to know all the Chippewa myth in detail in order to be able to appreciate Erdrich's fiction. So, in the same way, I want people to go with the character, the psychology of the character, rather than worry about getting all the references. Who do I write for? I think of myself as an American writer who is writing of a particular time in American history. So, if the book is translated and published in other countries, I'm thrilled, I'm flattered, I'm buoyed up by that. But I'm not writing in deliberately universal English, and I'm not writing for a universal audience out there.

BCE: So you're aiming more at an American audience and if the rest of the world enjoys it, then that's good.
BM: It's my primary audience.

BCE: Are your novels read much in India?
BM: Some. *Desirable Daughters* had an Indian edition and apparently it made the best-seller list. But not *The Tree Bride*, it doesn't have an Indian edition, even though it's the most Indian of my books. I feel that now that so many Indians living in India have relatives in the U.S. and Canada the immigrant adjustments are not as foreign to them, as inaccessible, or as boring to them [laughs]. They're not indifferent to the problems that the immigrant generation and first generation of South Asians are going through.

BCE: May I ask you some questions about your family?
BM: Yeah, of course.

BCE: You've mentioned often that you married Clark after a whirlwind courtship. What were the highlights of those two weeks, and what about him initially attracted you besides his blue eyes?
BM: He wore this Britishy, I guess it must have been Canadian, Britishy trench coat that made me nostalgic about my school days in England, and he had these very ruddy cheeks [laughs]. And his sense of humor, yes, totally, sense of humor and storytelling ability. I just don't mean writing fiction but story after story after story. I think he was my way into consciousness of North American popular culture and sports and so on, and I soaked it up through him. The highlights of the two weeks were he invited me out to a play at the university. Because of the rumors going around that I had all these bodyguards that my father had planted in Iowa City, Iowa, who would kneecap any young man trying to ask me on a date, he got us tickets in two different rows. We didn't sit together, and I thought I was watching *The Madwoman of Chaillot* when it was *Death of a Salesman* [laughs]. So, I was that out of it. On the way back, we held hands when he explained it was *Death of a Salesman* [laughs] not *The Madwoman of Chaillot* that we had seen, and that was that for me. It was very intense. It had to be fast because of visa re-

quirements. I was on a foreign student visa, and I had a full scholarship for Ph.D. studies for Bryn Mawr. My trunk had been sent, and so it was a matter of if I don't get married I have to go to Bryn Mawr in order to continue my student visa.

BCE: Then you were married and were able to stay on at Iowa.
BM: So I then went to my mentor in the English department and I was given, at the last minute, a teaching assistant.

BCE: Who was your mentor?
BM: The late Curt Zimansky. He was the head of *PQ, Philological Quarterly*.

BCE: *The Tree Bride* is dedicated to Quinn Xi Anand Blaise. What do you like best about being a grandmother?
BM: I wish that I was living closer. Now I have two granddaughters, both adopted from China. I love seeing the world, seeing New York since Quinn is a very Upper-West-Side child, seeing Manhattan through her eyes. Every time we visit, Quinn has picked up so many more skills and the sophistication of word-phrasing. Otherwise, the obvious is that you can enjoy their growth, their live-liness, but then you come home [laughs] and you don't have the day-to-day responsibilities anymore. I didn't take any kind of break for having my children. One was born during Christmas break and the other during summer. So juggling motherhood, wifehood, and a full-time career, getting my Ph.D. while doing teaching assistantships and then a full-time teaching career—when you are junior faculty, you have a lot of stress—all that was hard.

BCE: I know exactly what you mean [laughs]. How old are your grandchildren?
BM: The older one, to whom *The Tree Bride* is dedicated, turned four in February, and the younger one is two.

BCE: Has having grandchildren changed you?
BM: I don't think so. Having a dog has [laughs]! Faustine, my Papillon, weighs around five and a half pounds, but has a mega personality. Having her to look after and be responsible for has really lifted my spirits, made me very happy.

BCE: How long have you had Faustine?
BM: About seven years.

BCE: Only recently, seemingly around the time you became a grandmother, is when you started to write about mother-son relationships prominently in your novels, and I wonder if becoming a grandmother may have had some effect of giving you a perspective that spurred you to write about being a mother.

BM: Interesting question. Maybe at an unconscious level it freed me up. Otherwise, I would think time, you know? The mother-son relationship is very central to who I am in life, but I never thought I would be able to get enough distance to write of it in fiction. I find that writing autobiographical essays or autobiographical fiction is very, very hard. For *Desirable Daughters*, the germ of the idea was that it would be a nonfiction book with input from my older sister and younger sister, the communal biography of women from a certain class at a certain time in India's and America's history. But I couldn't do it as nonfiction, and it wasn't until I invented the characters and their misadventures that I felt free to write. Somehow, in creating myself as Tara, I've been able to get enough distance to tackle the relationship that is very, very important to me, the mother-son relationship.

BCE: May I ask about your sons?

BM: Bart, our older son who has the two little girls, is a camera man in film and TV in New York. He was passionate about TV and film from when he was two years old! The younger one, Bernard (who is named after Bernard Malamud, by the way) did economics at Reed College in Portland, Oregon, and stayed on in Portland. He loves that city, loves the Northwest. I feel very, very close to them.

BCE: This impulse toward autobiography seems to have recurred throughout your career, but you keep resisting it. For example, you called *Days and Nights in Calcutta* an "accidental autobiography." Your most recent two novels are set here, in your home, which leads me to ask, how much of your own life makes it into your fiction?

BM: I don't think my own life makes it, deliberately or substantially, into my fiction, but *place*. There are certain places that I can write about. I have to know the turf extremely well where I have set my stories. Certain cities that I have lived in or neighborhoods I've lived in speak to me and I possess them, make them my own, make myself belong, and make them belong to me, when I'm able to write about them in fiction. Saratoga Springs, in upstate New York, is one of those places that I feel I can write of again and again. The Upper West Side near where I have my apartment still on 108th Street and Broadway, that is a neighborhood full of life that I feel I'm a part of and can set endless stories in. Queens I know very well, from my teaching days there, and Montclair, New Jersey. *Desirable Daughters* uses the Indian ghetto in Queens and uses the more affluent New Jersey places where the richer Bengali immigrants have settled, like the Lucent Mahal. Home for me is not all of San Francisco but my neighborhood. More and more home is the neighborhood I have chosen to make my own, chosen to belong to. So it's about confidence, and of course the character of the neighborhood. Confidence, it's all about confidence. But for *The Holder of the World*, I imagined very exotic locales in great detail, and that's based on research. I have to have access to very good libraries. That's probably one of the reasons that I continue to teach, the access to libraries. But once I start writing a novel, I put away all the notes because I don't want it to feel as though it's heavy with detail. I want it to come to me *dramatically* at just the right moment and just the right amount as befits a character and the novel's voice.

BCE: What do you make of the current popularity of diasporic South Asian literature?

BM: I'm amazed at how fast the interest has grown in writing in English by writers of South Asian origin, whether they're living in India, living in South Asia, or they are expatriate writers living here or immigrant American writers like Jhumpa Lahiri and me. The size of the community of such writers and the body of work produced has happened so fast. When I started in 1972 with *The Tiger's Daughter*, I had to create an audience, explain what this was about, and now the *New York Times*, in the review of *Desirable Daughters*, starts out identifying me as the *grande dame*. I just don't know if this has happened with other immigrant American literary communities. How few years it's taken—just a decade, a decade and a half—for us to have such a prominent place in world literary consciousness or American literary consciousness.

BCE: Are you in contact with these writers, the members of this community?

BM: I know a lot of them, yes. Jhumpa, Amitabh Ghosh, Salman Rushdie. Clark had written the front-page review of *Midnight's Children* for the *New York Times Book Review*, and we first met him at a small dinner party in Manhattan soon after. Clark and I co-wrote an article for *Mother Jones*, "After the Fatwa."

BCE: I was wondering if you are still friends with him and if you had seen him?

BM: Not recently. The last time I saw him, since the fatwa, was at a "secret" book party hosted by Sonny Mehta and Knopf for him in San Francisco. We guests weren't told *where* in the city we were to get together until just hours before the party. [Mukherjee added the following message during the editing of this manuscript: "UPDATE: We met again on March 23, 2007, in Manhattan at the India Abroad awards night when I presented him the award for Lifetime Achievement. It was a very cordial reunion.]

BCE: A moment ago, you were talking about the importance of place in your writing and in your life. You've lived and traveled so many places. How does San Francisco rate among the great cities that you know well?

BM: Oh, I think it's the most gracious, most livable, most pleasurable city, and I am so glad that chance and luck have made it possible for me to have called this home for seventeen years now. I love being bi-coastal. I like the energy of New York, or of the Upper West Side anyway, and I like the quality of life that San Francisco's weather and city culture provide. Clark loves our house in Southampton, Long Island. He's glad not to be in Manhattan itself. But since I don't drive, I'm a city person. Having grown up in Calcutta, which is a very crowded city, I need concrete underfoot. I need real sidewalks. I love the sense of neighborhood. That's what the Upper West Side provides and Cole Valley here provides. You've got your coffee place to hang out in for hours; you've got your produce boutique; you've got your trusted butcher; you've got your fitness center (which I don't use, of course); and you've got interesting neighbors.

BCE: Why do you say "of course?"

BM: I'm the most unathletic person in the world. I'm weak and lazy [laughs].

BCE: I arrived a bit early and walked around the neighborhood, and I was struck by all of the dogs tied up outside of the cafes and all of the strollers. It seemed like such a lovely place. I thought, what lucky children to grow up in this neighborhood.

BM: When I moved in, Cole Valley was very different. It was a very mixed neighborhood in terms of income, education, profession. Then, because of the Silicon Valley boom, a lot of young people with enormous disposable incomes came in, and the old people retired, sold their houses, or died in their houses. Builders removed a lot of those little houses and put in duplexes, and they went for very, very, high prices, like a million dollars for a two-bedroom flat. The young people came in during the Silicon Valley boom, and then they stayed on after the bust. They liked the place, and then they had children [laughs].

BCE: I wanted to wish you a Happy St. Patrick's Day.

BM: Yes! Happy St. Patrick's Day! Are you Irish in any way?

BCE: I think so. Doesn't every American claim to be part Irish? You've said this was the biggest holiday at Loreto House. How was it celebrated there?

BM: All classes were suspended. All day we sang Irish songs and played games, and the nuns flew shamrocks out from Ireland or wherever, and we pinned them on our starched white blouses. We wore school uniforms—all white with pale blue ties in the summer, white and navy in the winter, but on March 17 we had to add something green. In that era, the nuns were all from Ireland, and many of them spoke brogue.

BCE: This was an exclusive Catholic school for girls run by Irish nuns in Calcutta. How has that early indoctrination in Catholicism affected you as an adult? Do you retain any aspects of the religion?

BM: Of Catholicism? No. The nuns realized that in this new era—this was soon after independence, the fifties—they needed to influence the minds and social outlook of the young women who were going to become wives of the nation's leaders, whether in business or politics. They knew that they couldn't convert us. They had a few scholarships for the Anglo-Indian community or Indian Christians. But they knew that the majority of their students, Hindu and upper-class, were not going to convert. There was no question of that. We non-Catholics studied three of the four gospels—no Gospel According to St. John, I don't know why—Acts of the Apostles, and moral science, which was also about Christian values but was presented to us as ethics, separate from religion. The nuns tried hard to counsel us against abortions while the government of the newly sovereign India campaigned hard for family planning, for population control. That education in Christian scriptures was very useful to me as a student of English literature. I could not have understood references in Milton without that background. We had to say prayers before every class, and lunchtime and, I guess, at the end of school. But at home I would make up my own Hindu prayers, keeping the format of the novenas or Hail Mary, just changing the names.

BCE: Really?
BM: Yes, yes. That lasted for a very long time.

BCE: So Hail Mary became Hail what?
BM: For me and my sisters, the general name is Bhagavan, God. In Calcutta, we Hindu Bengalis worship the godhead in a form of Goddess Kali we call Addya Ma.

BCE: To what extent are you a practicing Hindu?
BM: I think of myself as someone who has faith. My family, like most traditional Hindu families in Calcutta in the forties and fifties, was inspired by Paramahangsa Ramakrishna, and his disciple, Vivekananda (who may be better known in the U.S.). Ramakrishna taught us that you don't have to chant formal prayers, perform prescribed rituals and fasts to be a believing, practicing Hindu. I used to have an altar in my study. In the early days, the first, say, fifteen years or so

in North America, I was very careful about some of the rites, trying to put fresh flowers, and give fresh water and fruit to the icons every day. I certainly have always had my little table or shelf with a shrine, but it became harder and harder to follow those daily rituals of my childhood and girlhood. When the children were young and they brought their friends over, it was a little difficult to explain that Kali who has four arms, wields a sword, wears no clothes except for a garland of severed, bleeding heads, is a metaphor for the righteous destructive power of the "unmanifest" godhead, and so on [laughs]. Last summer, because my two toddler granddaughters were visiting, I had to dismantle my reachable shrine and put all swallowable and breakable icons high up on bookshelves.

BCE: Which gods are featured in your shrine?
BM: Oh, many, many different kinds. But the principal ones that I pray to are Addya Ma, Vishnu, Narayan, Ma Durga, who is the mother goddess, Ma Saraswati, Ma Laxshmi. I mean I chant all these names at one go. Ma Saraswati is the goddess of education and learning and Bharati is one form of Saraswati. My father always carried a sandalwood icon of Vishnu in his shirt pocket. When my family moved to Varodara, I added Ganesh to my list, because Ganesh is very popular in western India.

BCE: Ganesh?
BM: Yes. But Bengalis are not really into Ganesh. So I've learned that since the move to Bombay and Baroda.

BCE: That's the sandalwood icon Jasmine carries, Ganpati.
BM: Clearer of obstacles.

BCE: Do you believe in reincarnation, and, if so, what is your interpretation?
BM: I've worked it out for myself by thinking of it as recycling. Hindus cremate the dead. Once the body is cremated, the soot from it goes into the atmosphere. Into the air, the earth, the sky, lakes, oceans, rivers. So it's not as though I expect to be reborn as a rat or a bat, but I do expect particles of me to merge with nature. I want to think that death does not destroy intelligence—I don't mean intellect but consciousness. After death, the consciousness stays on and in some way adds to the universe. I grew up with tales of people who could remember their earlier lives. I don't want to dismiss the concept of earlier lives altogether as I did when I was a schoolgirl in Loreto House. Now I tell myself, who am I to state definitively that that kind of physical rebirth is not possible? But for my own peace of mind, I think that only the consciousness sort of hangs in there, merges. I have read, especially for the last two novels, all that the Hindu scriptures say about the actual passage of the spirit—once the body dies what happens until it is reborn—

and it is fascinating. Talking about faith, my interest in cosmology, quantum theory, and geophysics all comes from my initial interest in the Vedic descriptions of the cosmos. Scientific and mathematical concepts are delivered through accessible and entertaining stories. Hindus privilege *story*. Even the *Bhagavad Gita*, which contains the code of ideal conduct for us, comes to us in the form of *story*. In it, God Krishna comes down as a charioteer and instructs Arjuna, who doesn't want to fight his cousins, why he must fight. I'm sure this traditional respect for *story* has gone into my making as a writer.

BCE: What's your philosophy or interpretation of karma?
BM: I want to think that it's dynamic; it's not static. I am faced with a situation. How I am going to react to that situation probably depends on my free will, but I would not have the scenario presented to me if it hadn't been scripted.

BCE: By?
BM: That's a hard question because I'm always still thinking through, and ideally, if you look at Hindu religion in the Vedic context, there really is no god. There's only the energy that continually creates, then maintains for a period, with some entropic problems, then dissolves altogether, leaving nothing but a little life sap. Then the process starts all over again. The Hindu deities are metaphors for aspects of this energy. Brahma is creator, Vishnu is preserver, Shiva is destroyer. You don't have to be literate to understand *story*. Intellectually, Hinduism seems to me to be saying there is only energy and no higher intelligence doling out conduct-based reward and punishment to the living. But the form of the religion that has come down to all of us is from the medieval period is Bhakti, devotion. I'm always shuttling between the sense that there really is nothing—it's how you choose to make your life and then you'll be absorbed into nature—and the sense that there is a god out there or goddess out there who is presenting me with scenarios. *Well,* maybe now you're making me think! I wonder if destiny is really about mathematical permutations and computations? We have a whole group called Vrigumaharajas. They are not priests but they calculate your lifetimes. Past and future. It's just a mathematical game or mathematical adventure. So I don't know if destiny isn't about fractals and "the butterfly effect"; that nothing is unplanned, that every movement has consequences.

BCE: This is what you've called convergence?
BM: Yeah, yeah.

BCE: On this topic, you begin *Jasmine* with an epigraph from James Gleick's *Chaos,* and chaos theory seems to inform the aesthetic of that novel.
BM: Totally, yeah.

BCE: More recent novels feature innovations in computer software and information systems. Which science engages your imagination today?

BM: I think it's a combination of both. The novel that I'm working on right now is about information technology and call centers and the ways in which barriers, temporal barriers as well as territorial borders, are breaking down. But at my core, I guess, is my notion of chaos theory.

BCE: Your father was a noted chemist. He arranged marriage for you with a man who is now one of India's leading nuclear scientists.

BM: He must be retired by now [laughs] because he was quite a bit older [laughs].

BCE: So many of your characters are scientists. Is that a conscious choice?

BM: I think so. I find that I'm not really interested in writing about English professors [laughs] or writers, and I don't know enough about painters to feel confident about casting a character as a painter. The more interesting people, the majority of people that I grew up with and whose stories here I'm interested in are people in professions. I think that a lot of it has to do with the fact that the South Asian community so prizes professionals, doctors, engineers. They may write in secret, have manuscripts in their desk drawers, but they're also forced to, culturally encouraged to, have a profession.

BCE: You and Clark have devoted your careers to writing, which you called a useless profession. To what extent is that an ironic assessment, and can literature make a practical difference in the world?

BM: When did I say that [laughs]? Well, I don't know about practical, but I'm surprised now that I called literature a useless profession because I feel that one can change hearts and make people see problems not as problems, or issues not as issues, conflicts not as abstract conflicts but as accessible, approachable, "might-be-mine too" through fiction, that people are readier to understand the other when reading a novel or a story about the other than in a scholarly treatise. So literature can help bring about change of hearts and minds and then put pressure for political, legislative change. Didn't Abraham Lincoln say to Harriet Beecher Stowe, "So, you're the little lady who started the war"? I want to believe that.

BCE: You mentioned writing having a political effect. Are there any issues that are particularly engaging to you or any causes that you support?

BM: The issue that I obsess about is healthcare. I think it is absolutely shocking, intolerable, that we do not have free healthcare for all citizens. In a general way, what I would say is that I still believe in the idea of America and the ideals that are embedded in the U.S. Constitution and Bill of Rights, and I will work through my fiction, through my lectures, to make sure that that idea and ideal are not compromised, corrupted, or hijacked. I still have faith in the possibilities that the U.S. Bill of Rights and Constitution offer, and I think that one should exercise one's voting rights to make sure that that idealism is fulfilled, is validated.

BCE: You mentioned that you watch four TVs at a time and that they're always on.
BM: But they're in different rooms, so it's not that I'm watching four different channels at once.

BCE: What do you tend to watch?
BM: Twenty-four-hour newscasts.

BCE: Exclusively, or are there any television shows?
BM: I love Jon Stewart, *The Daily Show*, and *The Colbert Report*. And I like Keith Olbermann. He has been the conscience of our nation in recent years. He comes on after *Hardball with Chris Matthews*. It's a news show, but he's relentless in his attacks on corruption.

BCE: So even the television shows that you watch are essentially parodies of the news stations. Are there any other shows, any sitcoms or drama?
BM: *The Sopranos, American Justice.* Well, if I've got nothing to do, as I'm channel surfing I may pause on *The Real Housewives of Orange County* [laughs], and I love cooking shows, especially those *Iron Chef* contests [laughs]. What else do I watch? A lot of PBS, of course. *Real Time with Bill Maher.* I can't stay up late enough for most, and I don't have TiVo. I like the Geico commercials about the cavemen.

BCE: What about sports?
BM: I watch because Clark watches. I just turned off the basketball [laughs] when I heard you ring the doorbell. But Clark has been an absolute nut about spectator sports. He likes to explain, so I watch a lot. Sometimes it's very exciting. I have to have team loyalty to get really worked up, and I have to have popcorn.

BCE: You've used sports a lot in your writing, so I wanted to ask you about that. Who is your pick to win the NCAA basketball tournament this month?
BM: I don't know [laughs]. I'll have to check with Clark [laughs].

BCE: Do you have a favorite college basketball team? You mentioned team loyalty.
BM: Well, I'm afraid Iowa is the one that we would have wanted to win, but it's not doing well.

BCE: The West Coast Offense is a metaphor for an aesthetic that you said you've been using since *The Middleman and Other Stories*. Were you truly inspired by football, by the concept of the West Coast Offense?
BM: Yes, and I would not have had access to that, would certainly have not watched, not known who Joe Montana was if I hadn't married Clark.

BCE: One of your interviews mentioned that you had just come from a football game at the University of Mississippi. How did you end up there?
BM: The president of the university, who had been a professional kicker, invited us to the homecoming game because of that reference to the West Coast Offense. I guess the word got back to him that I was into football. He was so thrilled that he said you've got to come back for the homecoming game and be my guest. So there we were up in the president's glassed-in special area.

BCE: That seems to me to be just one more in so many interesting situations that you've been in. Beyond sports, how do you meet such a wide range of people?
BM: By being curious, saying *yes* to opportunities that come. You know, going "All right, let's see what happens." That kind of being open.

BCE: Do you have diverse circles of friends in San Francisco?
BM: You make friends in this dog-friendly neighborhood through dogs, so, because of Faustine I know a lot of dog sitters, crafts-type people, computer whizzes, the Google kind. Then I have my writer friends, of course. I have my academic circle of friends. You were asking about how I have such a wide circle.

BCE: Twenty years ago you said, "My obsessions reveal themselves in metaphor and language" and "Obsession is essential for a writer." With what are you obsessed now?
BM: How do we think of national identity in an age of mass movement, mass migration, and globalization? That's really what I am thinking through in my novel-in-progress. If my children are a quarter French, quarter Anglo-Dutch, half Bengali, and my older son is married to an Irish and German Catholic girl out of Chicago, and my grandchildren are one hundred percent Chinese, what does it say about what it means to be an American today? What does it mean to be Indian? In the many call centers outside the U.S., say in Bangalore and Hyderabad, that service American customers, hundreds of non-American employees have to learn American idiom and acquire an American accent so that they can understand, and be understood by, the customers. How does it affect your sense of identity if you are living in an Indian town, but during most of the hours that you are

awake, speaking American, dressing American, having fun head-banging style [laughs] in nightclubs that play American and European music?

BCE: Have you visited call centers?
BM: Oh, yes, yes! I've done a lot of research. I have a lot of their training manuals.

BCE: Are many of them able convincingly to create American personas for their telephone selves?
BM: Some can. Others struggle. I mean, you can tell after the first sentence that this is not happening in Moosejaw but in Bangalore. There's a social revolution going on in places like Bangalore because these kids are not academically the top students. They're not ever going to get into IIT and become world-famous engineers, doctors, or corporate types, but they have some facility in English. They have telephone voice and telephone poise, and they are now, as a result, earning more than their fathers. Now that the credit system has come in, they are buying scooters, motorbikes, even cars, and buying apartments not only for themselves but for their parents, which is disrupting the parent-child hierarchical relationship. Many of these young people come to big call-center towns from villages or smaller provincial towns. They have the opportunity for more social and sexual freedom than they would have had if they'd stayed with their families in their hometowns. India is going through an incredible social revolution.

BCE: You detail this in your current novel. Is it still titled *Bangalore by the Bay*?
BM: So far, yeah.

BCE: In another interview, you said, "I want to think that power is my central obsession." Does power still interest you?
BM: Power and survival, I guess.

BCE: How does power come into the scenario you just described, the social revolution?
BM: Well, these young people, who would have had dead-end lives, no opportunities whatsoever in the pre–call-center India, pre-age-of-globalization India, are now able to think of themselves in self-confident ways and actually financially do a lot better than their parents, who have worked very hard. A lot of them are women in these jobs, so that women are becoming empowered.

BCE: Women working, that's a recurring motif in your work, the effect on identity of women getting jobs.
BM: I also think that claiming their sexual identity, or recognizing their sexual needs, impulses, is another way of self-empowerment for my characters.

BCE: You've spoken about American feminists misunderstanding works such as the story "Jasmine" in the mid-eighties or the novel *Wife* in the 1970s. How are your more recent novels interpreted by feminists?

BM: I think my work is now being seen by some as postmodern, post-feminist, whatever that means [laughs]. Postmodern I understand, that I want to scramble the way one tells the story, and post-feminist perhaps means that the ideal is not that the woman discards the man and has the strength and resilience to go off and live in a shack by herself on some remote beach but that she can have a re-lationship with men without feeling that she is betraying her gender or yielding power. I try not to read anything about my work.

BCE: Really?
BM: Yeah. Reviews—I read reviews if I'm forced.

BCE: You don't read scholarship?
BM: No, because I don't know how to find them, either [laughs].

BCE: Surely you do, you're an English professor.
BM: No, I've avoided them.

BCE: You've used Adrienne Rich as an emblem for a 1970s-era American feminist. Did you speak with her at the National Book Awards?
BM: No, I didn't have the chance.

BCE: Had you met her before?
BM: In the seventies when she was doing a lot of these conferences. I admire her work, and I now understand historically the important part that she played in the feminist movement.

BCE: You mentioned sexuality a moment ago, and you've also said that all Calcut-tans are worshippers of Kali. Do you think that might explain the prevalence of sexuality and violence in your work?
BM: No, I don't think so. The Calcutta I grew up in was a strange mixture of Vic-torian and Edwardian prudery and Kali worship. But I didn't think of Kali as a sexual figure. We had a *thakurghar*, God's room, at home. One of the icons was of Shiva as a stone lingam resting on a stone lotus. But, I had no idea at all that that was a sexual symbol. I didn't even know what lingam meant [laughs], except that it was a religious word. Certainly, not only did the nuns have us read expur-gated editions of Shakespeare, but the Hindu mythology or iconography, temple carvings, and all that had sexual content we were kept away from. In fact, I don't

think I knew about the erotic temple carvings until I came to Iowa [laughs] and was asked about them. *Kama Sutra* I knew because of my study of ancient Indian culture, the treatise, but I didn't have to actually deal with it for my master's exam [laughs].

BCE: When did you catch on about the lingam?
BM: I guess long after I got married [laughs].

BCE: You recently tore your meniscus in the Frankfurt airport while running to catch a flight to Istanbul, which sounds like a very cosmopolitan way to be injured. What happened after that? Were you able to continue to Turkey?
BM: I had to be wheeled from the plane to the luggage carousel in the Istanbul airport. I was being met by people for whom I was lecturing. At first they didn't recognize me because they didn't expect the speaker to be in a wheelchair [laughs]. Once we got together, we went straight to the American Hospital emergency room. I must say their facilities were very impressive, the speed with which they did x-rays and all that. I did my lectures, often wheeled from hall to hall on various Istanbul campuses, but I didn't know why I was in such pain until I got back home and had a MRI done. Again, San Francisco is such a gracious and efficient place that I was able to get a surgery appointment right away, and now it's a matter of slow recovery.

BCE: How did you find Turkey?
BM: I was there only for two or three days on this trip, but, oh, Turkey, Istanbul anyway, is fabulous! I was able to meet many writers, among them Elif Shafak and Buket Uzuner, and journalists as well as academics. Orhan Pamuk had just won the Nobel Prize, and the city was abuzz with reactions. Being deposited among Istanbul's intellectuals and writers was a wonderfully intense experience. A couple of my books have been translated into Turkish, and a number of the scholars I met had follow-up questions.

BCE: Which books?
BM: *Jasmine* and *Desirable Daughters.*

BCE: You've lectured in so many countries, and your work has been translated in how many languages?
BM: Depends on which book. *Jasmine* into eighteen languages.

BCE: In which countries do you find your most appreciative audiences?
BM: I never know how or when a particular novel is going to touch hearts, and

most recently I got a whole page of questions from Basel University where a
class was reading one of my books, I think it was *Jasmine*. But it's just a continual delight and surprise to me that books find their way into different
countries.

BCE: Is there a difference in the way your fiction is perceived in Europe, India,
and America?
BM: I don't know about all of Europe, but just thinking of—I'm just speculating
now—the way it might be perceived in England is very definitely different from
the way it is perceived in the U.S. and in India. The Americans recognize that I
am writing in the immigrant American tradition. The British still look for fiction
coming out of South Asian diasporic writers in a postcolonial context. The reader
looking for a postcolonial novel by an India-born immigrant author wants to
hear about Indians in India, not Indians settling for better or worse in New York
or San Francisco. My very first novel was very much an expatriate novel about
Calcutta, and it was wildly popular with English-speaking readers in India. As
my interest moved from writing about expatriates coming back to India to writing about lives of these immigrants in Greenwich Village or the heartland, and as
my sentences became more energetic, less formally British, and as the cultural adjustments or the conflicts became more traumatic for my characters, it was hard
for a while for Indian readers to find accessible the situations that my characters
found themselves in because they had relocated voluntarily to the New World and
the language they were speaking was more broken American than perfect, fluent
British or broken British. In my second novel, *Wife*, the protagonist, the wife of
an Indian immigrant engineer in New York, reacts to television shows. She's going
crazy, and her only contact with the outside world is through television. So because my readers in India didn't know the shows, or maybe rarely watched television, it may have been hard.

BCE: Which languages do you speak?
BM: I get by in three Indian languages and English, French. I have a little bit of
German—my German reading knowledge is better than my spoken—and I'm
learning some Spanish.

BCE: For the Indian languages, I assume Bangla, Hindi—
BM: And Gujarati because my sister has lived in Baroda (now Varodara) in
Gujarat since 1959.

BCE: That's where you did your master's work.
BM: Yeah.

BCE: You've said that Iowa has always felt like home to you, which surprises me when I consider the urban, cosmopolitan life that you've led. To what about Iowa and Midwesterners do you respond?

BM: I think it's to a kindliness, you know? A non-judgmental inclusiveness. I'd never been in a cafeteria until coming to Iowa City, and I was slow in the dorm's cafeteria line, totally bewildered by the new foods and the choices. The locals explained how things work, how to handle vending machines, use washing machines and dryers. They included us international students in family rituals, like having us as houseguests for Thanksgiving and Christmas holidays and inviting us to visit the family farm during summer breaks. If I had landed in New York and gone to NYU or Columbia, just the aggressive energy of New York, the constant, sort of rough, daily interchange would have driven me back home within two weeks [laughs]. Besides, I fell in love in Iowa, got married there, our oldest son was born there. I've spent so many years on and off there.

BCE: Is the pursuit of happiness the essence of American culture?

BM: Certainly the sanctioned right to pursue happiness as opposed to the obligation to discharge duty.

BCE: You've said before that you think of America as a place of constant change. Do you still agree with that?

BM: Yeah, absolutely, and it can change for the good; it can change for the better, or change for the worse. Change is the norm here. We expect change. Every other country I've lived in values fixity, and regrets change.

BCE: In *Wife*, Milt Glasser is the consultant who knows how to apply for things, and he represents America to Dimple. In *Jasmine*, Taylor, the physics professor, represents America for Jasmine. Who or what profession represents America for you today?

BM: It's IT, the Stanford kind of communications wizards. Unlike Milt and Taylor, they may not have been born in the U.S. It's Silicon Valley, it's the coming together of information technology, spirit of free enterprise, and the availability of venture capital. I think that they are the cowboys of our era, these IT engineers. If the cowboy was the iconic American in classic Americana, then these are the cowboys in the sense that they are out there homesteading and adventuring.

BCE: One of your goals as a writer is to show how America not only changes immigrants but is changed by immigrants. What do you see as the most significant ways Indian immigrants have changed America?

BM: Oh, I think they're very much into engineering technology and computer technology. I was looking at a research study done recently at Duke University showing that the majority of new start-up companies are by immigrants, primarily by Indian and Chinese immigrants. There was a time when South Asian Americans were thought of as science geeks. But now you find them in every field; they are lawyers, corporate boardroom stars, TV and print journalists, media-savvy talking heads and medical experts (think CNN's Dr. Sanjay Gupta) [laughs]; they are actors, film directors, stand-up comics (think Aasif Mandvi on *The Daily Show with Jon Stewart*) [laughs].

BCE: You've said that the melting pot no longer works as a metaphor for American immigration. You've also spoken of "mongrelization." Do you think "mongrelization" is the most accurate metaphor for American assimilation?
BM: Yeah. "Assimilation" is no longer useful because of the politicization of that word. I don't like "hybridity" as a word because it seems to me to imply a kind of scientific, laboratory setting in which experiments are being controlled by a scientist. "Mongrelization" is a word that I want to take back from its original pejorative connotations. To me it implies a kind of accidental, spontaneous coming together—you don't know what is going to result from this coming together—and the energy that a new group or new species brings to society. So, for me "mongrelization" means that you don't care about preconceived social hierarchies, about racial or class status.

BCE: It occurs to me that "mongrelization" is essentially a metaphor about dogs, and dogs appear throughout your fiction and nonfiction over the years, often portrayed negatively. Because of that, I was surprised to know that you have a dog that you quite apparently love [Mukherjee laughs]. What breed is your dog?
BM: Papillon, which is "butterfly" in French. She was seven months old when she was given to me as a gift by a friend who could no longer look after her. Faustine's in the center of our lives [laughs].

BCE: Is she your first dog?
BM: As an adult, yes. As a child in India we had a golden cocker spaniel. He was the center of the Mukherjee household [laughs]. I have an oceanic love of animals. As a very small child in England, I belonged to the RSPCA, the Royal Society for the Prevention of Cruelty to Animals. It's a cause for me.

BCE: Movies appear in your writing from your earliest novels to your most recent publications, and you've written an essay on *Love Me or Leave Me* as a movie that changed your life. What is your favorite movie of all time?
BM: Hmmmm. Oh dear!

BCE: You can choose more than one.

BM: [Laughs] I love *Casablanca*, of course. I love all of those old MGM musicals because they speak to me not of the movies themselves but of an era in my life that I can never recapture and an era in Calcutta's social history that is long vanished. The matinee shows of MGM musicals on Thursdays, which was a midweek holiday at Loreto House. My mother, sisters, and I picking up my father, tearing him away from his downtown office, and all of us going dressed up to the movies. Going to the movies was more the occasion than the movie itself. My father loved Doris Day [laughs].

BCE: Can you think of any of the titles of these MGM musicals?

BM: Yes, *Seven Brides for Seven Brothers*, *Pillow Talk*, all of those Rock Hudson-Doris Day movies. Howard Keel and Ann Blyth musicals. I'll say *Love Me or Leave Me*, because it was so disturbing but had great songs. *Lili*! I liked Leslie Caron in *Lili*. Oh, and the other one where she's with Maurice Chevalier, *Gigi*. Okay, so I'll pick *Gigi*.

BCE: Why *Gigi*?

BM: Just the songs and the idea of watching a movie with my parents about the training of a courtesan was so marvelously reckless and licentious but sweetened by the fact that it was American made and had all these great songs.

BCE: What are some recent movies that you recommend?

BM: I liked *Babel* very much, and the structure was interesting. You know, I love *going* to the movies. I don't get the full benefit if I rent DVDs and play them at home on the TV screen. I like some fast-paced thrillers, like *Zodiac*, like *Syriana*, like the Matt Damon *Bourne Identity* films, and *The Queen*. And I like the smaller-budget art films that come to the small, cozy movie theater at the Embarcadero Center, where I saw *The Namesake* last week.

BCE: Did you know Satyajit Ray?

BM: Yes, yes, and he occupies a lot of space in our co-authored *Days and Nights in Calcutta*. He was a great man. He was a *truly* great man, and he was grand in size and scale, and his furniture, therefore, was also grand, and the apartment where we would meet him quite regularly. His apartment was one of those old colonial-day buildings, with very high ceilings and tall French windows, and he would answer—for such a famous auteur and film director—he would answer the phone himself, "*Hello, so-and so*." He really invited Clark and me into his life and world and arranged many, many special screenings of his films for us. He didn't own copies of them. He would have to arrange with a producer to give us a screening.

BCE: That must have been something in the days before VCRs, a private screening at his house.
BM: No, in the studio, like Tollygunge Studio where he made them.

BCE: Which filmmakers do you consider to be important today?
BM: I'll tell you the *kinds* of films I like. On the one hand I like high energy, fast pace. On the other I like those Eric Rohmer *Contes Moraux* films, moral tales of tangled relationships that are very quietly, very slowly, worked out in beautiful countryside. I like Martin Scorsese as a director very much. I like a lot of Jonathan Demme's films. I like Stephen Frears.

BCE: What do you think of Mira Nair?
BM: I just saw *The Namesake,* and it's a charming and deliberately slow-paced film. I think that of the Mira Nair ones that I've seen, I loved *Monsoon Wedding* and even more *Mississippi Masala.* I haven't seen all her films.

BCE: But you loved *Monsoon Wedding?*
BM: I *loved Monsoon Wedding!*

BCE: What did you love about it?
BM: The humor, the delightfully brash vulgarity, and the irony that the innocent character in that movie is the U.S.-based bridegroom and the knowing, complicated, sexually experienced character is the India-based bride-to-be, who keeps breaking her society's rules. And the largeness of scale, the color, the dances.

BCE: You end *Days and Nights in Calcutta* with a description of a Bengali wedding, and I noticed you used several of these words. What about it is "vulgar"?
BM: There's nothing solemn about it. I've seen the bridal couples' families bicker openly, complain about the quality of hospitality, criticize dowry gifts, guests show off their marriageable sons and daughters, wedding banquet servers slop course after course out of huge serving buckets. It's like soap opera: huge cast, overheated emotions. I *love* that kind of intense domestic drama.

BCE: You've described your own wedding as a civil affair that took place in an office during lunch hour, which seems the very opposite of the Indian wedding you've just described. Did you regret not having an Indian wedding?
BM: *No!* I'm very, very thankful that I was able to avoid being a participant in a Hindu Indian wedding. I love being an observer, but I wouldn't want to be any

of the principal players. It takes very long. It's many, many hours in front of a sa-
cred fire, and there are many chants and many rituals. Also, some of the Hindu
marriage rituals have ingrained gender hierarchy, so that the woman follows, the
bridegroom leads.

BCE: Violence is always apparent in your work. Where do you find the inspiration for the evil characters, characters such as Abbas Sattar Hai, Half-Face, Jeb
Marshall?

BM: Different places. Since a lot of scholars have commented on the violence in
my novels, first I want to talk about how I grew up at a politically, historically violent time in India's history. The "Quit India" movement took place in 1942, and I
don't know how much of it I ingested unconsciously, but through the early forties
funeral processions of teenage martyrs went past our house. The whole neighborhood, even toddlers and grandmothers, rushed to the sidewalk and joined in the
nationalist chants as the funeral processions made their way to the burning ghats.
Then the famine in the early forties brought hundreds and thousands of people
from the villages into big-city Kolkata, and my father organized soup lines (more
accurately, rice-gruel lines), as did a lot of upper middle-class neighbors. So I was
never too far from firsthand experience of violence or from witnessing of violence. In the mid-forties there was a lot of harassment, physical harassment, ar-
resting, detention, public flogging of young neighborhood boys who either sang
banned songs, recited banned poetry considered nationalist, or were members
of youth physical culture clubs where they worked out or learned ancient rites of
lathi play. That's a big stick. Indians were not allowed to own guns, but the *lathi*
then became the symbol for "we are prepared to fight." Before Independence,
when I was living with many uncles, aunts, cousins in one joint family household, our house was surrounded by police, led by an Anglo-Indian Sergeant. I remember him as a huge, blustering fellow in a tight uniform. He grabbed a young
uncle who was a member of a neighborhood physical culture club and took
him away. Then my father had to work hard to get him released. This kind of
Independence-related violence wasn't the only kind of violence I witnessed on
my block. There were rows of homeless people living on sidewalks and on the
grassy edges of tram tracks on our street. I couldn't help but watch the random,
casual violence of hungry, uprooted, powerless street people. And during the
Hindu-Muslim riots prior to Independence, sirens would go off at night, alerting
our neighborhood to threat of attacks, and we would all rush, carrying infants
and bedridden relatives, to the roof for safety.

In the fifties, my family had to cope with a different form of violence. I grew into girlhood at a tilt time in Indian, or at least in Bengal's, economic history. My father belonged in the first generation of nationalist entrepreneurs in Kolkata. He was a very benevolent man but very much a patriarch. He, like many in his pioneering generation of Bengali industrialists, distrusted the motives and methods of emerging labor union lawyers and leaders, who were England-educated Marxists from elite families. I suspect, he thought of these upper-class Marxists as outside agitators, causing trouble for factory owners. The fifties was a decade of threats of strikes and lockouts. My two sisters and I were Loreto House pupils in those years. The Loreto House nuns had no patience with strikers. They insisted that no strike should stop us from taking part in school productions of Gilbert and Sullivan. Several times we had to be escorted out of the factory grounds by the Lal Bazar Flying Squad, sort of the equivalent of SWAT, so that we could sing in the chorus.

So violence wasn't something I only read about in books or saw on TV—there was no TV in Kolkata when I was growing up. Violence was part of everyday life. And then, I'm convinced that there's a psychic violence that all dislocated people go through. If I had lived on in Calcutta, married a Bengali, I would know what the rules are, would know the social as well as physical terrain and what behavior is expected of me. I would know the price of acquiescence and the price of resistance. But I moved from an India of traditions I knew too well to the Judeo-Christian New World I didn't know at all, and where I felt I was being patronized or exoticized as a brown woman. For the first time, race problems affected me quite literally, physically. That was traumatic. Migration inflicted a kind of psychic violence. In fiction I want to use violence not just as realistic portrayals of historical events or dramatic events but as a way of talking about the violence that even the act of reading, in a positive way, should put a reader through.

BCE: Could you explain that? How could reading be a violent experience?
BM: Reading forces the reader out of the comfort zone of her or his familiar world and values. It *tests* the reader. When we read, we live imagined biographies, experience alien moral dilemmas, give in to unexpected emotions, thrust ourselves into unlikely adventures. That has to jolt us. I don't know how far I want to push this [laughs]. As a writer I want my fiction to offer my reader the promise of the possibility of things working out if we don't give up trying. Cathartic hope is what I get out of the novels I admire.

BCE: You lived with death threats as a result of *The Sorrow and the Terror* for at least two years. Would you describe the nature and number of those threats?
BM: We were denounced in certain Gurdwaras in Canada, put on a death list.

That was on AP news wires, and there was a lot of media attention, and frankly alarming, especially because we were doing the Canadian book tour for *The Sorrow and the Terror* at the time. Some of the language—the crude things they wanted to do us—was very frightening. As a result, our flights were booked under three or four different itineraries and under different names. This was before 9/11 so that you didn't have to show your passport and go through all the security. Our hotel reservations were made under different names and for rooms in specially secured floors.

BCE: Was there a formal lifting of the threat?
BM: I think they just got bored or moved on to other targets.

BCE: So there was no edict then, no "We no longer wish to kill them"?
BM: No [laughs], I'm not aware of it.

BCE: The enormous amount of research you and Clark did for *The Sorrow and the Terror* is apparent, and for me the interviews are the most poignant part of that book. Would you describe the experience of meeting with the surviving family members?
BM: Oh, it was absolutely heart-wrenching! I have never seen such grief, such pain, and in many cases, such forbearance. The bereaved were finding ways to cope with the enormity of having their entire families—spouses, children, siblings, cousins—wiped out [snaps her fingers] like that. There were some who resorted to Hindu faith, especially to great faith in reincarnation; others who consulted psychics in order to find out where their loved ones were going to be reborn; others who placed their hopes in their children's swimming skills to make it to shore after the plane plunged into the ocean; still others who were so numb with grief that they couldn't change anything in the children's room or wife's closet. If the Scrabble game had been played by a kid and left on the floor before getting on that flight, then it stayed on the floor exactly where it had been left. And the endless playing and replaying of home videos from when the family was happy and intact. You know, children were everything to these immigrant families that had made this big move for the sake of the children, and all the children who perished on that flight seemed to have been top students with a lot of extracurricular activities. The bereaved men, most of them engineers, were into technology, into making home movies. They had recorded every moment of family life, and after the tragedy, they would come home from work and just sit for endless hours replaying the home videos. It relieved some of them to talk about it to Clark and me because most of them didn't think of going to a psychiatrist or a

counselor. They wanted to get their stories out to the world, and not just relive vanished family life in the isolation of their game rooms. Towards the end of *The Sorrow and the Terror*, there's a line that goes something like this: "Mr. Clark, tell the world our story." That really was what kept me going. I would break down just listening to their stories.

BCE: I remember that sentence. He said, "Tell the world how 329 innocent lives were lost and how the rest of us are slowly dying."
BM: It's the most important book and, for us I think, the most life-changing book that we have researched and written.

BCE: Why do you say it's the most important?
BM: Because of what we witnessed and what we discovered through our investigative research, and the interviewing of both victims and victimizer-sympathizers. I didn't know the terms "sleeper cell" or "sleeper agents" in those days. Talking to the alleged perpetrators and accomplices of perpetrators, learning about what ideology and fanatic loyalty can make someone do gave me a new "take" on human capacity for hate, greed, hope, and yes, love.

BCE: You mentioned how some of the survivors turned to religion. It seems that there are echoes of Hindu philosophy and explanations of tragedy from that book that appear in many of your later works, *slokas*, things like that. Did writing that book make you a more spiritual person?
BM: I don't know if I can call it spiritual, but far more conscious of the cosmic play, that my individual life is intertwined with cosmic crises. If by spiritual you mean, did it make me have more faith? No. But thinking about a level beyond what can be controlled by individual free will or by trying to influence national policy through voting, that there is something else out there that is larger than any single person. I grew up in a traditional, practicing Hindu household, and my mother certainly was a religious woman. My father, who was a famous scientist, entrepreneur, and a member of the Bengal Chamber of Commerce, also consulted horoscopes or one guru that he had in Varanasi about auspicious days for making important decisions. Growing up as a Hindu I totally accepted that weddings have to take place on an auspicious date, funerals have to be done in a particular way. The great attack on my mother by my father's relatives was that because she didn't bear a son, neither my father nor she could go to heaven because, when a father dies, the body has to be lit on the funeral pyre by the oldest son. No son is bad news for the father's soul [laughs]. I aimed for—still do—the Hindu ideal of non-attachment; I believe that one should do what's right because it *is*

right, and not because of the reward or punishment that the act might result in.
I also accepted the Hindu world-view in which the invisible aspects of the cosmos are as real as the visible. That's the perspective from which I wrote my first novel, *The Tiger's Daughter*. For both me and the protagonist of that novel, the occult world had as much substance as the daily one. That's why I felt I had to use an omniscient point of view. By the time I came to write the second novel, *Wife*, a very secular novel set in Kolkata and New York, I had become more interested in this one wife's breaking away from traditional Hindu codes of wifely behavior. I was far more interested in how she was going to resolve the problems of her relationship with her husband, how she was going to adjust to the emotional trauma of being plucked from her hometown, how she was going to respond to her New York friends' obsession with gender power imbalance than in working out her salvation [laughs]. You know? It all happened naturally. I didn't sit down and think through any of this. When I'm writing, the work has its own momentum, has its own arc, its own compulsions. The characters take over, and I go with their psychology, I find dramatic situations in which they can work out desires, conflicts. But in *The Tree Bride* I really did want to think through what it means to be Hindu? What comforts one as a Hindu? To what extent do ancient rituals have a place in working out psychological problems? *The Tree Bride* is very different from my earlier novels.

BCE: You just said that it's a very different book than any others you've written. I think it's the best book you've written. What's your opinion?

BM: Thank you. It's the most complicated. *The Holder of the World* was also very complicated. As a writer, I was trying to bring all my maturity, intelligence, anxieties, and need for order, need for understanding, to bear on the formation of identity. What makes one? What shapes her? What forces, political, social, historical, gender, chance, have gone into the making of this identity. I wish more scholars would look at my body of work. I've always written my fiction and my essays through the lens of emigration/immigration, uprooting/re-rooting, India/the New World, and have asked readers to view my writings in the contexts of diaspora and transnationalism, and *not* in the context of India/Britain, Indian national/postcolonial tensions. Indo-American postcolonial scholars of the eighties and the nineties self-servingly stuck my writings in the category of postcolonial Indian literature. *Jasmine* was the story of immigration and two-way transformation in the U.S. of the late eighties, from the first-person point of view of an undocumented entrant. The eighties was a time when the "melting pot" myth was still operational here. The South Asian immigration story of the 1990s, 2000, and future, however, is about an America that no longer expects meltdown from its newcomers, no longer expects to control the borders, and has issued many different kinds of visas—H-1 for special technical, H-1B temporary technical—in order to fill slots that U.S. industry requires. That means that neither America expects them to nor are the new entrants expecting themselves to give their entire loyalty to the United States and to think of themselves as American. It's not just the nursing profession that wants to get special status visas for Filipino nurses. Every industry is trying to get cheaper technological help, specialized help, because the tech experts on H-1B visas are paid on a lower scale than U.S. citizens with the same skill. The educated immigrants coming in today have a very clear sense of self, pride in education, pride in self worth, confidence in their global mobility. Their primary loyalty is either to the corporate entity, Hewlett-Packard here, Hewlett-Packard there, or to the self—what can I get, where can I maximize my financial circumstances? So *Desirable Daughters* and *The Tree Bride* are exploring an America very different from that of *Jasmine*. The South Asian immigrant and naturalized American characters in them have a much greater range of opportunity and success in the corporate and social worlds.

BCE: You've spoken of ways some of your work is interpreted or misinterpreted, I can't remember your exact words, but—
BM: In the eighties and early nineties, India-born postcolonial scholars on U.S. campuses would take me to task for including sex and violence in my fiction. Young South Asian students would say to me, "We want you to be a role model. Why aren't your characters offering us role models? In *Jasmine*, why does she need males as sort of mediators in her self-evolution?"

BCE: Another group that you seem to have had a history with is the postcolonialists. What is that about? Your first words to me, the first time we met, were, "You're not an angry postcolonialist, are you?" [She laughs] What makes them angry?
BM: I think the critical success of *The Middleman*, *Jasmine*; the reception of them as explorations of new seams in American culture and immigration history rather than as exilic Indian literature. Definitely my manifesto, "A Four-Hundred-Year-Old Woman," which appears in *The Writer on Her Work, Volume Two*, by Janet Sternburg. In that essay I was saying to the mainstream white American: whether you like it or not, we non-white immigrants are here to stay, we are not visitors or transients. I was announcing my intention to resist conscious and unconscious marginalization of our citizenship status. I was charting the psychic terrain of the newly emergent transnational American. Postcolonial studies professionals

chose to misinterpret my statement. The current scholarly discourses—diaspora discourse, globalization discourse—hadn't yet gathered momentum.

BCE: V. S. Naipaul seems to have gone from being a model to a rival.

BM: Not rival; rival, not at all. Model—when I read *A House for Mr. Biswas*, I was blown away by his writing about people who had not been written of before, and by his ability to make them interesting, complex. His characters suffered through large, messy emotions they couldn't appease, and conflicts they could barely talk about, let alone resolve. That was the first of Naipaul's works I'd ever encountered—I hadn't heard of him growing up in India—and I was struck by *his* version of the family epic. I was also blown away by Naipaul's invention of a new kind of English, his mixing of Indo-Trinidadian patois and formal British English to capture the characters' bilingual, bicultural consciousnesses. But his politics! The more I read his nonfiction, and when I encountered him to co-conduct (with Robert Boyers) an interview for a special issue of *Salmagundi*, the more uncongenial I found his political biases. We are both authors of Indian origin, but our Indian heritages and our physical and emotional connections with India are radically different. Naipaul has written often about tragedy as geography of birthplace. In *A House for Mr. Biswas* he has Mr. Biswas mourning the fact that he was born in a nowhere speck in a country that is nothing more than a dot on the map of the world. I was born into a Hindu Bengali Brahmin family in big-city Kolkata, grew up as a member of its majority community, came of age in Independent India during a period of nationalist euphoria, and was consciously trained by the Loreto House nuns to assume leadership positions. Naipaul's ancestors moved from India to the Caribbean during the era when the Caribbean plantation economy needed the services of South Asian indentured laborers. He came of age in a hierarchically multiracial, colonized Trinidad, in which the Indian community was a minority with little power and only fragmentary memory of ancestral culture and religious rituals. He has worked out his coping strategies in terms of *where* and *when* he was born. In his books, he seems to accept London as the center of civilization. In his travel books, he seems to valorize white British ideals and practices at the expense of the local. I am discomfited by his dismissal of some postcolonial nation states in Africa as "the bush." In his second nonfiction book on India, he labels Indian civilization as "a wounded civilization." But reading that book, I felt I was touring an individual wounded psyche rather than a "wounded" subcontinent. With the exception of *An Area of Darkness*, I find that in his travel books, Naipaul starts out with preconceptions and includes only those travel experiences and interviews with locals that confirm those preconceptions. *An Area of Darkness* I thought was a very interesting book, and in the early eighties I presented a paper at the Canadian Learned Societies urging readers to read this book not as a travel book about India but as a "roots search." Searching for roots is a very New World phenomenon. Only in *An Area of Darkness* the non-white New Worlder doesn't like the roots he finds [laughs].

BCE: You've conducted many interviews. Has conducting interviews changed the way you answer questions?
BM: No, unfortunately, I should have learned by now how to give pithy [laughs] answers! I find myself taking every question very seriously and doing periphery, darting into the center, then digressing. No, I haven't learned how to [laughs]!

BCE: What do you think is the key to a good interview?
BM: I think a good interview is one in which the interviewee is thinking about the question or about an issue in a new, unexpected way, a fresh way. The question should be interesting but at the same time not familiar, so that you're really groping for an answer. At the same time, I think a good interviewer has to keep the parameters clear so that it's bringing out the vision of the interviewee even if the interviewee doesn't know what that vision is [laughs], I'll put it that way. Like your question about if researching and writing *The Sorrow and the Terror* has made me more spiritual, I thought that was a really interesting, new kind of question.

BCE: I noticed that a lot of the spiritual quotations in that book appear again and again in your later work, so it made me think that they must really have entered into your consciousness.
BM: I was also convinced, during much of the writing through *Desirable Daughters*, that my horoscope was correct and [laughs] that I would die on a certain date. A lot of stuff in my horoscope is correct, including that there will be severe damage to a leg, so I thought I would be in an automobile accident or something [laughs]. But I'm hoping to recover from a torn meniscus.

BCE: Is there anything left in your horoscope that hasn't occurred yet?
BM: I don't know because I think my horoscope is locked up in my younger sister's steel safe in India [laughs], and I don't want to look at it anymore. There was a time when I would, on trips to India, seek out fortune-tellers and horoscope readers recommended by friends. Now I've stopped that altogether. I feel that since my horoscope prediction about my death didn't come true that these are all grace years, bonus years.

BCE: So you truly believed you would die that year?
BM: Yes, absolutely.

BCE: Did you plan your life accordingly?
BM: Yes, yes, totally. My first thought was disappointment: "My God, what am I going to do with this time?" That's in the essay I wrote, "Destiny's Child."

BCE: In that essay, you have a great image of cheating fate by going to the dentist. Who would have guessed that would be the way to derail your fate?
BM: Right! And that this very cool Chinese-American young dentist with spiky hair—he says he doesn't speak Chinese, has never been to Taiwan or the mainland [laughs]— should be the unsuspecting instrument of wondrous derailment!

BCE: Are we currently in what you have called a "tilt time" in history?
BM: *Yes*, yes, and how the U.S., not just the administration, but how ordinary residents handle the debate on this mass migration is going to make or break us as a nation. What does it mean to be an American? Is it enough to have a legal document that lets us shuttle back and forth across borders? Or is there a national identity that comes from citizens sharing a belief in the civic ideals enshrined in the Constitution and the Bill of Rights?

BCE: What do you think of the U.S. military presence in Iraq?
BM: Well, I hope we'll get out as soon as possible.

BCE: You've been interested in terrorism for a lot longer than most Americans. Do you think the U.S. can win what General Abizaid called "the long war" against terrorism?
BM: I think it is possible to reduce the automatic hostility that many people, whether in Europe or the Middle East or Asia and Africa, have for America by investing in infrastructure—schools, hospitals, roads, economies—in countries that need it. But can we win a war against terrorism period? It would be very hard because there are so many freelance cells operating in so many different countries. How do you stop them? What immigration has done is brought the contributing immigrants and at the same time the connivers, convicts, terrorists. Just as we saw with 9/11, many of the suicide bombers had legitimate visas. So, is it possible to stop every suicide-bomber or suicide-bomber-wannabe obsessed with causing destruction? Probably that's not realistic [laughs].

BCE: What do you see for the future of the relationship between the United States and India?

BM: Oh, I think the Indian middle-class has always been very pro-American, and the middle-class is a speedily growing segment of the population. The business-people and the information technology industry people have always been pro-America, pro-free enterprise. They often send their children for higher education to the States rather than to Europe which still retains some colonial attitudes toward brown people. Current political and economic relations between India and the U.S. are beginning to reflect this. India has a vast domestic market, and it is recognized as an exporter of intellectual property and consumer goods. All this contributes to greater and greater cooperation. The relations weren't always this cordial. The rhetoric of many earlier Indian regimes was nonalignment neutralist during the Cold War. And because the U.S. needed to have Pakistan as an ally for its war in Afghanistan, U.S. foreign policy favored Pakistan over India, exacerbating political hostilities between the two South Asian nations.

BCE: You've often mentioned reading the great Russian and European novelists as a child. Your dissertation was on E. M. Forster and Herman Hesse. When did you come into contact with American authors?

BM: During the year that I spent in Baroda (now Varodara) getting my master's in ancient Indian culture and English. The public library there—a dusty, cavernous place—contained some American writers. I read all of Faulkner and all plays by O'Neill. They were the only Americans I'd read before arriving at the Writers' Workshop in Iowa City. Faulkner's fictional world felt familiar. I translated race relations of Faulkner's American South into class relations, caste relations. I think I devoured O'Neill because as a teenager I was interested in theater and tried to write a play. In the Form and Theory class at the Writers' Workshop I had a very eccentric, brilliant instructor named R. V. Cassill. He had us read *Giovanni's Room*, *Nightwood*, Richard Yates's *Revolutionary Road*. Suddenly it was all new, and they had big stories to tell.

BCE: I'm interested that you said Faulkner because the obsession with the past in your two most recent novels seems very Faulknerian to me. Do you think of him as an influence as you're writing *Bangalore by the Bay*?

BM: No, and I think it has to be whatever I absorbed as a very young person because after that I also read Virginia Woolf, who was very big in India, and so were people who were scrambling time, manipulating time in their novels. I had to study Dorothy Richardson, Virginia Woolf, and on my own I made Faulkner part of that interest. Clark is really a big Faulkner fan. I have loved in his novels the creating of a world in which the forces are so dark and they head-butt; the confrontations are so visceral and violent; and the consequences are so extreme. But

I wasn't consciously trying to create my Yoknapatawpha. I mean, it is an imaginary village that I have conjured up—who knows if Faulkner is even more present in my mind than I think or thought? What I was doing with Mishtigunj and with John Mist was reflecting on the early paradise-like fusion of cultures that was possible in eighteenth-century India. As Britain embarked on its colonial adventure and appropriated India as the most sparkling jewel in its imperial crown, relationships between whites and locals changed. The three white guys, John Mist, Vertie Treadwell, Nigel Coughlin, in my last two novels are guardians of, or emblems of, of different periods in Anglo-Indian relationships. John Mist lands in India in precolonial times. He is an English foundling who runs away from the inequities of his orphanage life in England, is mistreated by the white East India Company community in Calcutta, escapes deep into rural Bengal, and founds a kind of utopia, Mishtigunj, where Hindus, Muslims, and an Englishman can live peaceably together. Vertie Treadwell is a colonial administrator, who has none of John Mist's respect for India and Indians. But I wanted Vertie to come off as not an entirely unsympathetic character. Vertie has been damaged by events in his family life in England before he sails to India, is marginalized by the British colonial hierarchy, and then is shunted off by his superiors to a remote colonial outpost, where he is free to exercise power over locals. In Nigel Coughlin I wanted to create a kind of George Orwell figure, who is both inside and outside the colonial bureaucracy. Coughlin is socialist, he's gay, and he's a colonial officer. His relationship to India is more complicated than Vertie's. He thinks of himself as sympathetic to freedom movements. But in a moment of crisis, when he discovers that the Tree Bride has been providing sanctuary to local freedom-fighters, and that she has been trying to get news of colonial brutalities to a journalist in England, he champions the cause of the British Empire instead of the cause of national sovereignty. I don't know what all that was in response to [laughs]!

BCE: Faulkner. That was good. That was a Faulknerian answer. You've described your best writing as occurring when you are "in the zone." Do you use a routine to connect with the muse?
BM: [Laughs] No, I don't have the luxury. My life is so chaotic, and I have so many commitments in so many areas, and I travel so much that I don't have the luxury of telling myself that between 7 A.M. and 10 A.M. I'm going to write no matter what happens in the world. The good thing about not having any fixed routine is that I'm not tied to a certain hour, a certain mood, a certain desk, for inspiration. Whenever I have a moment, wherever I am, whether it's in a cramped Manhattan apartment with an ironing board for a desk, or in my cluttered San

Francisco study, sitting in my back-saver chair with my laptop on a cushion on my lap, or in a Red Carpet Lounge of an airport, waiting for a connecting flight, I've got to be ready to go the moment the screen comes on. I need to have TV on all the time, not just because I'm curious about "Breaking News," "This Just In," but as a way of shutting out my relational selves. While I'm writing, I'm not a Berkeley professor with a million emailed queries from students to attend to; I'm not serving on any committee; I'm not a National Book Awards judge; I'm not mother, grandmother, wife—I would love to have Faustine sit on my lap while I'm writing, but she doesn't—anyway, I have become my characters.

BCE: The research in your recent novels is impressively extensive. How do you make time for the library?
BM: I check out whole shelves and bring them home, and I read constantly. I love history. That's why I need to teach at a university with excellent library facilities. It may be for confidence. I don't consult research books while I'm writing, but I want to have absorbed everything about the time, what people wore, what they ate, what they talked about, what they worried about, furniture, décor, what was showing, what they did for pleasure, what they were drinking, eating, before I start writing, so that when I come to write I don't have to look at my notes but whatever detail I need will appear on its own.

BCE: When you are writing fiction, is voice still your primary concern?
BM: I know that I'm onto the right draft once I hear the voice, yes.

BCE: What is the right draft?
BM: I may have thirty different beginnings, but I know these are exercises because I'm not hearing a voice speak it to me. Once that happens, the narrative writes itself, very fast.

BCE: You write about your mother's belief in premonition. Have you experienced premonition?
BM: No, I don't think so. I've been visited by [laughs] ghosts, especially in this San Francisco apartment, when I first moved in. Then I did a total renovation, and the ghosts left.

BCE: Were they ghosts from your family?
BM: No, no. They were people who had lived here before [laughs]. Clark and I had a long commuting marriage, so I was here alone, and I just felt that these presences were kind of sitting on my bed or at the foot of my bed. So I changed

bedrooms. I don't know how much is just overactive imagination, but the ghosts aren't here anymore [laughs].

BCE: Could you see them?
BM: No, no. I felt them.

BCE: You write about seeing the ghost of an uncle.
BM: Yes, yes, and he breathed on me [laughs].

BCE: But with these San Francisco ghosts it was simply a feeling that you were surrounded.
BM: Yes, they were hostile. They were a little scary.

BCE: You've spoken of discarding parts of one's identity as a healthy aspect of immigration. How have you changed recently, and do you have intimations of the sort of person you will become?
BM: No, sorry [laughs].

BCE: How about recent changes? You've talked about specific reincarnations in your life, that you were an obedient daughter, then you were a graduate student and wife, a political activist.
BM: I don't know that I visualize it as my future, but my hope is that I can find a place with a comfortable study [laughs]. You know, my immediate goal is to have an efficient desk with perfect lighting and endless time to write the two or three books of fiction that are percolating in my head.

BCE: Do you plan to retire?
BM: Who knows when? Someday, yes. I like the interaction with my students and some of the classes, like this current graduate fiction workshop. These graduate students are from law faculty, math, philosophy, they're all good writers, and they're providers of good feedback. It's fun for the three hours on Tuesday afternoons; I really look forward to it. And they bring me what they're reading, or they make references to comic books or TV shows that I don't know, so it keeps me on my toes.

BCE: You have so much art in your house, and you've spoken of Indian miniatures. Do they hold the same influence over your aesthetic of fiction today, or is there another art form that you find inspirational?
BM: My narrative structures are still very much influenced by Mughal miniatures, not Hindu miniatures of the eighteenth and nineteenth centuries, but the

Mughal miniatures that have so many different foci. All the stories compete with each other. The elaborate border competes with the multiple narratives in the center, and each individual story is interesting, but the whole is more than the individual stories. I try to use minor characters to undermine or reinforce, provide different kinds of variations on whatever the protagonist is trying to work out.

BCE: In only one interview have you discussed considering suicide after you left Canada. Is that something you care to talk about, that time in your life?
BM: I think the character Dimple, for example, thinks of suicide constantly and is a depressive. Certainly when I lived in the joint family, or even when I moved out, the extended family is very important, and there are always people who are depressed. One aunt actually had to be put into an asylum periodically. I'm terribly aware of the fragility of the psyche and how the most confident-appearing among us can think seriously of ending life. What interview did I say this in? Who was I talking to?

BCE: I recall it was the opening, and you talked about it as a designer suicide, that you had chosen a cotton sari in which to be found and that you had selected a bottle of pills and Clark—
BM: It was a cotton dress, actually [laughs].

BCE: Clark was watching baseball, and then you shouted to him but he couldn't hear you because of the game.
BM: My goodness, I hadn't remembered saying that.

BCE: It struck me because I only saw it in that one interview, and I thought the part about baseball was a great touch with everything you've said about him with sports. A lighter question: What's your favorite food?
BM: Mmmmm. I guess grilled lamb. It's called lamb raan. It's an Indian dish, lamb marinated in yoghurt and Indian spices, then grilled. Oh, I have another one that's very Bengali. Malai prawn is the name of the dish. It's prawns in coconut milk, best served in scooped-out green coconut.

BCE: Your essay on your dreams is fascinating. Have you had any memorable dreams recently?
BM: I dream all the time, and some are recurring dreams or nightmares. One used to be about a house I loved that we owned in Saratoga. It was this huge Victorian mansion that had about sixty-four windows and a carriage house with a mechanical turntable for cars. Then we moved to Iowa, and so sold the house. But it was not just my perfect house, but it was me in some ways; my recurring night-

mare was I found myself living as a tenant in a tiny portion of this house that I had once owned. It was a really very crippling kind of dream. Then a couple of years ago we had the chance to re-buy that house, of course for about six times more than we had paid, and I saw it in a realistic way. I thought, oh my God, this needs so much renovation work, and now I've stopped dreaming of it. I have anxiety dreams before classes start, every semester, even now after all these decades of teaching, anxiety dreams that I'm not going to be able to find the classroom or that I'll suddenly have discovered that the semester began three months ago [laughs] and I'm only just going to my first class.

BCE: Are there any questions that you wish I had asked?
BM: I can't think of any.

BCE: Thank you so much.
BM: You're very, very welcome.

Index